MILTON, EVIL AND LITERARY HISTORY

CONTINUUM LITERARY STUDIES SERIES

Also available in the series:

Forthcoming titles:

MILTON, EVIL AND LITERARY HISTORY

CLAIRE COLEBROOK

continuum

Continuum International Publishing Group

The Tower Building, 11 York Road, London SE1 7NX

80 Maiden Lane, Suite 704, New York, NY 10038

www.continuumbooks.com

First published 2008

British Library Cataloguing-in-Publication Data
A catalogue record for this book is available from the British Library.

ISBN: 978-0-8264-8492-5 (hardback)

Library of Congress Cataloging-in-Publication Data
Colebrook, Claire.
    Milton, evil and literary history / Claire Colebrook.
        p. cm.
    Includes bibliographical references.
    ISBN 978-0-8264-8492-5
    1. Milton, John, 1608-1674 – Criticism and interpretation – History. 2. Evil in literature. 3. Life in literature. 4. Meaning (Philosophy) in literature. 5. Symbolism in literature. 6. Good and evil – Philosophy. I. Title. = 20.

PR3587.3.C66 2008
821'.4–dc22

                                                                          2007029469

Typeset by Aarontype Limited, Easton, Bristol
Printed and bound in Great Britain by Biddles Ltd, King's Lynn, Norfolk

Contents

Acknowledgements

I am grateful to the department of English at the University of Edinburgh, both for the generous research conditions provided and the academic and intellectual support I have been fortunate enough to receive. I am particularly indebted to Sarah Carpenter and Randall Stevenson, both of whom have been supportive above and beyond the call of duty. I would also like to thank the English department at the University of Melbourne for the sabbatical period I spent there as a research fellow in 2004. I also acknowledge the support of the British Academy for providing a research grant to consult materials in the New York Public Library and Huntington Library. Finally, I am once again grateful to Lee Spinks for reading and commenting upon this manuscript.

This book is dedicated to Geoffrey Carnall.

List of Abbreviations

Quotations from Milton's poetic works are taken from John Milton, *The River-side Milton*, ed. Roy Flannaghan, Boston: Houghton Mifflin, 1998.

PL   *Paradise Lost*
PR   *Paradise Regain'd*
SA   *Samson Agonistes*
COM   *A Mask presented at Ludlow Castle, 1634.*
CPW   Quotations from Milton's prose works are taken from John Milton, *Complete Prose Works of John Milton*, ed. Don M. Wolfe, 8 vols, New Haven: Yale University Press, 1953–82.

Introduction

Life, Economy, Evil

This book is about the ways in which evil is figured within Milton's poetry, and also about the ways in which the imagery and poetics of evil have dominated our reading of Milton's position within literary history. Throughout this book I will be connecting three not self-evidently related concepts: evil, life and meaning. There is much talk today about the meaning of life,[1] but such talk has a long history going back at least as far as Aristotle, for whom all life is defined through meaning. To understand what something *is* we must understand its form; each living being is defined by the form it strives to achieve. All living beings are specified by a proper potential, so that what something is essentially – its substance or true being – is neither matter nor form considered separately, but the tending of matter towards proper form, and forming as the full realization of matter's potential.[2] If we want to know what something is, then we ask what it is for: what is its highest or proper potential; what activity brings that living being to its fullest realization?[3] Even today when we talk about the 'meaning of life' we answer such questions by referring to how life comes into being and what life must do if it is to go on living. Even a contemporary scientific approach, such as Nick Lane's *Power, Sex, Suicide: Mitochondria and the Meaning of Life*, answers the question of the secret of life by explaining the processes from which complex beings, such as humans, emerged.[4] We understand what life *is* – or what life means – once we understand its genesis. Life's meaning, in its broadest sense, is determined scientifically by examining how life comes into being, but this does not answer what many people take to be the real problem of the meaning of life.

If we emerge from random and contingent material processes then our lives must be absurd, pointless or without sense. If questions of the meaning of life go beyond material processes to consider how life might be meaningful *for us*, they tend to refer to some ideal of what we ought to be. This can take a naturalist or a theological form. If there is a God who designed us and determined our proper end then the meaning of life is not a problem. *Evil* might be a problem – for how could a creative and designing God will destruction and chaos?[5] – but meaning would be given in the plan of creation and our journey towards redemption and beatitude. Perhaps, now that nature is 'disenchanted' or no longer seen as bearing an intrinsic purpose, we need to find meaning outside the natural world; today, more than ever, we require God or religion to give life meaning.[6] But this necessity for meaning to be bestowed upon nature by some transcendent being has not always been with us. Both prior to the Christian tradition and entwined within Christian theology, there have been naturalist understandings of the meaning of life. Indeed, as I will go on to argue in the chapters that follow, there is a certain concept of life – as meaningful – which underpins both theology and naturalism, and which survives in some of our seemingly modern and sceptical arguments regarding the ways in which we make sense of the world. The landmark argument for the connection between meaning and life, the argument which dominates both the Scholastic tradition and contemporary appeals to life as essentially intelligible, comes from Aristotle, who insisted that all life strives to realize its highest potential and that the highest human potential is the intuition of life's first principles. This naturalist understanding of form and meaning, which still has some resonance today,[7] inflects both the theological tradition within which Milton was writing and the tradition through which Milton has been interpreted.[8]

According to this Aristotelian understanding of life and meaning, the definitions we give of beings are not arbitrary but have to do with what living beings *ought to be.* Accordingly, human life can be said to be defined by its proper potential; we are properly human when we realize our potential to do those things that are intrinsically or definitively human.[9] For Aristotle the defining potential of human beings was reason, and reason was essentially social, political and theoretical. More importantly, such rational potentials that define us as human, or give meaning to the term 'human,' also place human beings in a privileged relation to meaning. It is because we are rational that we can intuit the essences or proper definitions of beings; we do not just see the world in its immediate presence but also see how things ought to be. In relation to our own lives – and this is the aspect of Aristotle's philosophy that has been so important for the present – a good human life gives form to itself. To be properly human is not simply to arrive at a pre-given definition, but to create one's life as an ongoing and meaningful narrative, where the past is directed towards a future. A good life is, therefore, a meaningful life. Life in its naturalist sense – physical, biological life – is not meaningless because each being goes through time in order to arrive at its proper form. For human beings this naturalist sense of life is supplemented by a metaphysical sense: in addition to physical growth and fulfilment our natural being also orients us towards narrative self-creation.[10] We use language, define ourselves socially and understand our world in relation to others. A life without meaning is, therefore, less than human. If we failed to speak, failed to intuit the world in terms of meaningful relations and ongoing narrative time, then we would be failing to reach our potential. We would be denying or negating our life. It is in this regard that life, in both its naturalist and metaphysical senses, is connected to meaning: human bodies are capable of language and interaction, allowing us to intuit the essences or proper definitions of other living beings. We are, by nature, beings capable of living meaningfully. The good life for human beings is therefore a life of meaning.[11]

By extension, evil has always been defined as the negation of life, as non-relation, inertia and, most importantly, an absence of sense. Just as the concepts we use to define goodness resonate with concepts of life as fruitful, productive, actualizing and expanding, so our understandings of evil draw upon and reinforce images of corruption, inertia, stagnation and non-realization.[12] This semantics and mythology has a naturalist grounding, so that notions of evil emerge from cultural distinctions between growth and putrefaction, between health and defilement.[13] Although the history of myth, theology and philosophy offers complex and varied ways of thinking about evil, the very possibility of any concept of evil requires a strong sense of proper life. While we can offer very different accounts for the meanings of 'good' and 'bad' – does 'good' mean what one ought to value, what we want others to value, or what enhances our pleasure? – 'evil' refers to that which destroys, corrupts or denies life. We can use good and bad as terms *within* moral debate. Evil, by contrast, is often seen as beyond morality, debate, understanding and negotiation.[14] This is what connects mythic, primitive and ritual notions of evil (as corruption and defilement) with sophisticated philosophies of evil such as Kant's account of radical evil. For Kant the less than virtuous citizen may rationalize the breaking of a promise by false moral reasoning, or he may even act well but do so primarily for reasons of expediency; such an agent is evil precisely because he has at one and the same time acknowledged the law while failing to give it the utmost priority. Kant therefore regards evil as having no true being, for the evil agent nevertheless has some relation to the law, even if the relation is one of negation or non-fulfilment. What cannot be accepted within our understanding of the human and life is *wickedness* – the refusal of all law and the negation of all considerations of oneself as a moral agent and of others as persons.[15]

Evil in its mythic, Satanic, (frequently) political and popular senses refers not to a position within morality but to a negation of morality: a position beyond ethics and discussion. Milton's Satan, unlike Adam and Eve, has not been deflected by false moral reasoning or by failing to act on what he knows ought to be done; he has decided to base values not on morality, norms or the order of the world but on nothing other than his own 'inconquerable will'. Milton captures the sense of Satanic evil by presenting Satan as a rhetorician and a self-consuming subject: he has no reference point other than his own self, and no ground for language other than the effects he strives to achieve. Evil in *Paradise Lost* is just this detachment from a world of ordered, creative, connected and expansive life. For both Milton and those readers who have aimed to defend the success of Milton's theodicy, there is a definite horror expressed at any aspect of existence which remains within itself, no longer capable of perceiving a life or order beyond its own limited and enclosed being. What we must *not* do is allow the lure of Satan as mere will to seduce us as readers; either we should read beyond the limits of Satan's rhetoric to see the deeper sense of Milton's theodicy[16] or, following William Blake, we should see the success of Satan as a hero as a sign of Milton's unavowed but inevitable affirmation of a life and energy that was fettered by religion.[17] Evil in *Paradise Lost* has an essential and curious relation with reading, meaning and literary value. For it is not simply the case that we read *Paradise Lost* and then decide on either its literary merit or its theological and ethical cogency. If we assume the poem is a successful and rational theodicy, then we find ways of identifying the self-refuting and logically inconsistent nature of Satan's rhetoric. We assume a notion of literary value as sense and coherence, and read and judge accordingly. If we assume that Milton was of the devil's party, then we more often than not find the failure of the theodicy to be the success of the poem, as though great poetry will express its true and radical spirit despite the author's manifest will. How we determine the poem's sense depends upon our notion of literary time: whether the true sense of the text – despite Romantic Satanism – is determined by placing the work back in its inaugurating context, or whether the later radical readings disclose the radical truth of the poem. In either case the relation between reading and ethics is one already staged in Milton's poetry itself, which regarded the failure to read, or the tendency to focus on the material letter, the body, noise or spectacle, as a pernicious detachment from the life and spirit which is the text's origin. The possibility of the detachment of the text, either from its context or from its authorial provenance, is the possibility of the loss of meaning. This is why 'deconstruction' was often descried as a form of relativism and lifelessness, a failure of responsibility and thinking.[18] The condition for the possibility of a text – its taking on of a material and repeatable form – is also the condition of its perversion, misreading and failure.

In this sense evil is the absence of meaningful time, an idea that has been made explicit in recent forms of moral theory which argue that one can only lead a good life if one has a sense of one's life as a whole; acting well is acting according to *who I am*.[19] If there were no ongoing recognizable self, then I could break a promise here, change my views on justice according to whom I was judging, would have no concern for the future and would therefore act on every whim. A life can be good, not because there is some external object or goodness that a self might simply know, but because the self creates and establishes an end or idea which will order the decisions it makes through time; without that temporal ordering there would not be 'a' life, and without that ordered and ongoing lived time there could be no sense of the good. A self who was capable of any action at any time whatever would be without character, without a sense of who she ought to be. Time is intrinsic to goodness and not just a sequence within which good acts take place.

Just as the opposition between good and evil draws upon notions of time and meaning, the explanation of meaning relies upon a moral binary of life. Meaning is only possible with an ongoing time that is directed towards synthesis, communication, actualization and relation. We can understand a text, action or word only if we have some order or context, and we have contexts and meaning only if we have continuous and ongoing time. Meaning requires both the existence of an established order, and the capacity of individuals to re-live and revive that order with each subsequent action or conversation. Evil, by contrast, has always been figured through a time of fragmentation, chaos, contradiction and a radical separation devoid of all growth, progression and becoming. Well before the 'ethical turn' in literary theory, we can discern an instrinsic connection between reading and the warding off of evil. As I have already suggested, evil is not only a term within moral debate; it is also a concept that functions to delimit and define just what counts as debate, and what counts as a self within debate. Jürgen Habermas's theory of communicative action, although it presents itself as post-metaphysical and pragmatically liberated from any determinate conception of the good life, nevertheless argues for the formal necessity of ethics in human language. For Habermas, in so far as I act I am already within a world of others, aims and purposes; to that extent all life is *communicative* – because we are always already within a context – and all communication is a form of action in so far as it creates and enables social relations and networks.[20] It would make no sense to speak or argue without the ideal of some notion of agreement, even if that ideal is posited as a regulating principle rather than a state that may actually be achieved.[21] Habermas is the most explicit of the contemporary theorists who claim to have liberated speech and thought from some ultimate metaphysical ground while nevertheless maintaining the inescapable ground of the meaningful self. It would make no sense, so this tradition argues, to speak without an aiming for agreement or a commitment to what one says as true.[22] For Habermas this aiming of all speech and action towards intersubjective recognition should lead us to be wary of certain claims about the status of literature that have been made in the French philosophical tradition that follows Friedrich Nietzsche and Georges Bataille.[23] Because this tradition has accepted an overly rigid conception of reason (as totalizing and instrumental), it has celebrated literature as a liberatory 'unreason' beyond the bounds of sense and communication. This collapse of the distinction between philosophy and literature, or the rational and aesthetic, is for Habermas an emasculation and fragmentation of thinking which precludes ethics and responsibility. The proper legacy of the Enlightenment, Habermas insists, lies in the notion of reason not as a set of rules but as an ongoing reflective practice. Literature should not be regarded in an avant-gardist manner as the transgression of sense and communication, but as one practice among others that will enable us to comprehend our 'lifeworld' or the horizon of meaning within which we necessarily think and operate. At the heart of Habermas's approach is a commitment to the primacy of recognition: in so far as I speak and act I do so in relation to others. It would be paradoxical or a performative contradiction to speak without an appeal to consensus. In the chapters that follow I wish to explore another sense of recognition, one that was articulated by two quite different thinkers. According to Alexander García Düttmann, the demand for recognition does (as Habermas insists) necessarily place the self in relation to others; at the same time, *precisely because one demands recognition from others*, one is also refusing the notion of selfhood that is already given and normative.[24] Far from the self being a necessarily normative horizon that would preclude contradiction, contradiction is the very structure of the self. In so far as I speak I must take my place in the constituted norms of language and social practice, but in so far as I claim recognition as a *subject* I refuse to be reduced to the recognition others bestow upon me.

From its earliest reception *Paradise Lost* has been recognized as a contradictory text, as being at odds with itself. One dominant way of thinking about that contradiction has been to see a conflict between the spirit and the letter: this would be the Blakean reading, where it is supposedly received religion that fetters Milton's otherwise liberatory imagination.[25] Against this notion that the text nevertheless expresses its true and radical spirit I wish to explore another possibility. Here, Milton's orthodoxy and commitment to a goodness from which evil is derived – giving us a fallen condition in which we now *know* goodness only through evil, even if there had been a time when goodness existed sufficient unto itself – is not an accidental Christian condition which befalls an otherwise radical poetry. On the contrary, the very possibility of a poem – its separateness from an original act or spirit – requires both that reading recognizes an animating sense and that at the same time the conditions for that recognition (the text's separateness) preclude any resolution. The necessary recognition that subtends all reading is split by the very possibility of recognition. In order to read I must posit a sense that precedes and gives order to the text – so in this respect reading is necessarily vitalist, presupposing a creative and animating origin. At the same time, that which has usually been figured as parasitic and evil – the diremption between creative life and the detached systems or technologies through which life is known and represented – is the very condition for life. One recognizes a text as possessing a life and spirit only if one regards the letter as insufficient to itself, as cut off from the life of its origin. It is precisely the text's separateness and distinction which requires the act of reading, an act that must at once recognize a sense that is not its own, even if that sense can only be effected through the labour of reading.

Another way of thinking about the necessary impossibility of recognition is through the quite different philosophy of Gilles Deleuze. For Deleuze it is the privileging of recognition which has assigned the necessary discontinuities of difference to figures of evil. We regard as accidental, negative, unreal, violent or malevolent any forces that cannot be represented, recognized and maintained through an extended and meaningful time. Accepting the conditions through which the world is represented and through which subjects understand themselves as coherent and continuous selves, we fail to consider the real conditions of experience, which for Deleuze are given in those moments of a text in which language itself operates in its own anarchic and intensive matter. It is because thought has always understood itself as primarily concerned with recognition, communication and *act* that it has dismissed as evil those features of experience which cannot be assimilated or restored to the ongoing coherence of the man of good will and good sense. For Deleuze,

> Thought 'makes' difference, but difference is monstrous. We should not be surprised that difference should appear accursed, that it should be error, sin or the figure of evil for which there must be expiation. There is no sin other than raising the ground and dissolving the form. Recall Artaud's idea: cruelty is nothing but determination *as such,* that precise point at which the

determined maintains its essential relation with the undetermined, that rigorous abstract line fed by *chiaroscuro*.[26]

It is just that evil and fracturing difference which Deleuze isolates as definitive of literature, and this because above and beyond its communicative features literature also tears language away from the relations of recognition.[27] Not only is such a notion of language presented in Milton's poetry – with Satan being presented as a dissembling, sophistical, ill-willed and inconsistent being – but Milton's poetry itself often functions in just such an 'evil' manner. Despite all the critical labours exercised in demonstrating how Satan ought to be read, including Stanley Fish's remarkable demonstration that Satan presents us with a trial of reading as moral self-knowledge,[28] literary history and popular culture have resisted good thinking and common sense and found Milton's Satan and his avatars to be all too appealing.[29] I certainly do not think that this should lead us to the William Blake conclusion – that Milton's real sense lay in his more devilish nature – for it is just this capacity of a text to work contrary to its originating sense (but not through an appeal to its proper latent sense) that I wish to explore in the conclusion of this book. This would require us to take seriously the charge of the *lifelessness* of Milton's poetry: that even though a sense can be recuperated in all those passages that appear as linguistically opaque, the text requires just such operations of working through and always remains suspended from the sense posited in any such readings. In the following chapters I want to look at the ways in which good reading, good sense, life and the resistance to evil operate as themes within Milton's poetry. This is so even though Milton's poetry – as has long been noted – harbours the potential for a disarming lack of life: a capacity for language to operate as its own proliferating system without any apparent reference or animating spirit.[30]

Jerome McGann has argued – against the image of Romanticism as a literary movement that somehow intimates an ultimate unity beyond the fragmentation of speech – for poetry as a social act.[31] If we want to read a text we need to understand what it seeks to do, the linguistic forces and conventions it draws upon, and the new language games that it makes available. Although such an approach to poetry liberates us from the idea of the poem as a sign that harbours an ineffable sense, which it would then be the task of the interpreting critic to reveal or disclose, and although such an approach allows us to consider the poem as having emerged in time, conditioned by forces beyond the words on the page,[32] the emphasis on the poem as *act* maintains a normative image of life and meaning. McGann is explicit about the pragmatic background to his arguments for meaning as act: no word or text exists in isolation but makes sense only in relation to other texts, and only in a context where agents strive to achieve certain effects.[33] What is left out of consideration is the text as a self-enclosed object, detached from conditions of production.[34] But it is just such a detached, enigmatic, self-enclosed and *inactive* object that exemplifies Milton's Satan, a figure that continues to operate in ways that are inconsistent both with the sense we have made of Milton's context, and with the sense that has been insisted upon by the history of pious criticism.

Poetry and Evil

Evil is both a figure within Milton's work that has raised interpretive problems – how do we read Milton's Satan? – and a symbolism that has inflected critical practice. To read a text is to bring that text to life, whether by discerning its status as a social act, a performance, an intention or an object of sense. Stanley Fish's exhortation that to be seduced by Satan evidences a lack of critical and poetic acumen is typical of the ways in which criticism has repeated the norms of good and evil that tie good reading to good life, and that define evil as deflection, lack, failure and unreason. Fish is right to argue that Milton's poetry stages good reading as a metonymy of good life: just as Satan's failure to read the conditions of the world leads to his own fall, so our complicity with Satanic self-enclosure evidences our fallen inattention to the true logic of the text. Fish's argument makes sense, though, precisely because there has been a long-standing theological commitment to the good life as the life that reads and creates its own proper and coherent narrative. If we can align good reading with good life we can do so because we regard life as meaningful and possessed of an order and logic that it is the task of the good citizen and reader to discern or fashion. Milton, as a rationalist vitalist, is perhaps the exemplary defender of a life that will come to its proper fulfilment in good poetry and good reading. He was committed *both* to the idea that there were transcendent norms of reason *and* that those norms expressed themselves in a dynamic, progressive and productive life. Reading, for Milton, entailed recognition of the eternal laws and forms of the world along with the ways in which those forms produced difference, change, growth and history. Milton's description of evil – as the negation of life, and as having no genuine being – not only underpinned his political theory, his poetics and his presentation of history as progression towards realization and the full actualization of potentiality, it has also governed the critical methods through which we have approached Milton.

This was evidenced most clearly in the 'Milton problem', when critics in the early twentieth century attacked Milton's work for its lack of 'life' – its excessive wordiness that precluded it from direct, sensible and vibrant relation with the world.[35] The valorization of 'life' did not begin with New Criticism's attacks on Milton's poetry, for it also inflects the Romantic reading of Milton, which accused the poet of writing in fetters, and of repressing a devilish energy that found its way into the poetry despite Milton's theology.[36] When we look back at the Romantics, and Blake in particular, we tend to repeat this vitalist ethic: if there were an energy or force to Milton's poetry it was diminished by his rigid theology, but this energy can be released if we read the revolutionary Milton presented in Blake's illustrations or his *Milton*. Literary history, on such a reading, can be seen as a 'line of vision', a prophetic resistance to the rigidity of law, stasis, convention and the 'same dull round'.[37] Annabel Patterson, with reference to Milton, refers to 'the literary as the privileged space carved out for independent thought by unspoken agreement between writers and rulers, from Augustan Rome onwards'.[38] Poetry *is* renewal, defamiliarization and a revivification of the word. This ideal of revolutionary and radical life (in the sense of not being contained by any predetermined form) also informs new historicist methods. In an explicit criticism of deconstruction, Catherine Gallagher and Stephen Greenblatt have argued for a return of the text to its context, for only such an approach opens the text from its purely literary status to its broader and more dynamic contexts of emergence.[39] In all cases one must overcome the rigidified systems that have domesticated the dynamism of poetry. The norms that underpin literary history and criticism – the norms of animation, renewal, resistance, dynamism and actualization – are tied into the vitalist axiology that ties evil to negation, non-relation, inertia, non-production and enclosure.[40]

Although the theology and philosophy of evil is complex and varied, I will be examining a persistent symbolism of evil grounded on an image of proper life. In brief, evil – before it is analysed theoretically in philosophy, theology and theory – relies upon normative images of the living body.[41] Whereas images of God, goodness, virtue, 'man' and the proper polity are grounded on organized, bounded and self-maintaining life, evil is associated *either* with the chaotic fragmentation of the body *or* with a body devoid of life (a corpse or mere thing). The poetics of evil has been dominated by a double symbolism, whereby the goodness of active and proliferating life is opposed *both* to the chaos of mere elements without unity or bound, *and* to the body detached from all relation and temporal progression. There is therefore a contradictory imperative in the image of proper life that was brought to the fore by both Henri Bergson[42] and Sigmund Freud:[43] life must maintain itself (and therefore establish a border or boundary) but it must not be so self-enclosed or detached as to cease living. Good life must (ideally) be both self-sufficient and complete, a demand which no organism can fulfil. It can only make its way in the world by being open to what is not itself, while maintaining some sameness or relative self-permanence through time. The positive symbol of this perfectly poised life is (prior to modernity) God: a complete and perfect being who also creates what is other than himself. Today that image is given in the homeostatic organism that balances its own state of equilibrium by monitoring its internal states, and by going out into the world only as required for ongoing life.[44] The negative counterpart to that well-bounded organism is evil: given both in the completely enclosed, self-absorbed and self-consuming body and in the unbordered, meaningless and fragmentary night of chaos. That double symbolism of evil pervades both the tradition of Christian poetry within which Milton was writing, and the secular and Enlightenment tendencies of rationalism. Milton presented both the evil of a Satanic individualism that turned in upon itself and recognized no being other than its own will and force, and the evil of an unbounded and arbitrary circulating system. (That second image of evil occurs throughout his poetry, in the images of language circulating without intent, of the exploitation of nature as mere matter, and as the two bodies of Sin and Death who are involved in cycles of consumption and production devoid of growth, form and purpose.)

Evil and Reading

If we think through these two motifs of evil (as both lifeless enclosure and unbounded void) then we confront some of the deepest problems of reading and criticism. For reading also has to operate between acknowledging the proper borders of a text (its self-sufficiency) and the text's capacity for future re-readings. Why must a text be read, and how does reading give life to the text? How do we judge certain readings, or failures to read, as accidental, parasitic, improper or unhistorical? Images of misreading have, I will argue, always depended upon the two figures of evil against which Western thought has defined life: evil as detached self-enclosure, and evil as chaotic unboundedness. Both of these images of evil also have historical implications.

One of the ways in which modernity is often condemned has been to contrast the nightmarish and purely quantitative system of capitalist exchange with a world once defined qualitatively, where each being is defined according to its intrinsic or specific essence.[45] It is possible to read Milton as opposed to the overwhelming quantification of modernity, where individuals become nothing more than acts of force or will, and where the world becomes nothing more than blank and neutral raw material for appropriation. In this sense Milton would be anti-modern, and would be drawing on a long history of imagery that favours the organic and self-maintaining body over the world as reduced to so much material devoid of form. If Milton's poetry offers a critique of capitalism – and we can think here of Satan's telling use of economic and appropriative language – he does so by drawing upon a theological and philosophical history that has always resisted the notion of matter which does not bear within it some proper form or essence. In looking at Milton's poetry I will therefore be examining the ways in which his implied criticisms of system, quantification, mere force and formless matter tie into a much broader ethics of vitalism. Milton's poetry affirmed the divine life that expressed itself in different and distinct forms and that could only be corrupted by quantifying systems. He was therefore a proto-critic of technology: critical of the ways in which systems, such as language, politics, literary history and writing, can be divorced from the life which originally gave them form.[46]

Whereas a *techné* should, originally and properly, be a supplement to living praxis, or a way of extending and maximizing our life-expansive tendencies, *techné* can detach itself from life and become an automatic system. Language can become technical, in this sense, when words are no longer governed by intent or reference; language can become what Heidegger referred to as 'idle chatter',[47] and the world – rather than being experienced in its complexity – becomes 'standing reserve',[48] with man as mere manipulator. If capitalism has been condemned as a lifeless technical system devoid of ends or intent, it has also been associated with a reduction of language (in journalism, gossip, popular culture) to circulating noise without sense or subject.[49] The anxiety about a purely technical language is not new. Plato opposed philosophy, with its intuition of first principles, to sophistry and poetry – uses of language that supposedly no longer attended to the informing sense of words. What is important in that Platonic banishing of poetry and sophistry is the underlying rationale: language should remain close to intent, meaning, act and the soul. The criticism of language as lifeless system can therefore operate to produce the opposite argument, so that in popular works such as *Zen and the Art of Motorcycle Maintenance* it is the philosophers, not the poets and rhetoricians, who have taken the life and force of language and reduced it to logic. The idea of a language that has fallen away from the animating power of life, and the association of that detachment with corruption, has also been used to defend sophistry against philosophy.[50] It is the philosophers who have taken the active, forceful and passionate use of language as a social event and subjected it to a timeless and lifeless system of logic. In modernist poetics the deadening of life and the falling away from an originally fertile and productive relation to the world was often aligned with the mechanization of language. Not only did Ezra Pound place journalists in hell, along with the usurers who allowed money to operate in a similarly automatic and self-generating non-production, but a broader twentieth-century turn towards vitalism sought to retrieve a language deadened by science, metaphysics and other systems. The classic proponents of such a vitalism were Henri Bergson and William James, both of whom were critical of the ways in which the intellect and formal language had precluded the spirit of life from living fully. Bergson argued that while the intellect's formation of concepts had allowed it to operate efficiently, what had been lost in the mastery of the world was the creative spirit from which intellect had emerged. Bergson therefore appealed to mystical and religious experiences as a way of going beyond the utility of modern moralism.[51] James also, tellingly, insisted on the value of religious experience[52] as a way of enriching and expanding a life which had forgotten its once active and creative relation to language.[53] Where their vitalism differed from earlier and later versions was in its appeal to religious *experience* while desisting from making any claims regarding the true existence of any object of that religious experience.

In *The Matter of Revolution* John Rogers has looked at the ways in which seventeenth-century poetry appealed to vitalism against Descartes' reduction of the world to *res extensa*.[54] On the Cartesian model, relations among beings would be merely mechanical and could therefore be determined in advance. Vitalism posited a force that flowed through matter, animating relations and granting the world an immanent spirit. In its twentieth-century manifestation vitalism criticized the ways in which the creative difference and complexity of life had been reified by a language that allowed the world to be mastered and rendered efficient. Modern vitalism was perhaps less theological than its seventeenth-century versions, but it was no less spiritual in its resistance to the notion of a matter that was uniform and mechanistic. Henri Bergson defined spirit as one manifestation of life, which constantly evolves and strives to maintain itself *as difference*; the other manifestation of life is matter, which occurs when the flux of life is rendered relatively stable, lacking the responsiveness and perception that characterize the mind.[55] Vitalism, in this modernist form, was a commitment to a force or complexity beyond the seemingly stable world of quantifiable and technically masterable matter. For Henri Bergson, life's tendency towards intellect, or the mind's fixing of the flux of time into concepts that render time uniform, needs to be countered with intuition; intuition would work against uniformity and stasis and grant each perceived event its own inner life. Bergson was not alone, however, in tying vitalism to the duties of renewed perception. Blake famously set poetry the task of reanimating the world that had fallen into 'system' at the hands of the priests. It is this broad sense of vitalism, as an appeal to the dynamic, expressive and striving life of the world that dominates Milton's poetry, and the critical tradition through which Milton has been read.

Life is not one value among others but has always been the way in which value itself has been thought: the good is that which expresses and furthers life, while evil is the negation of life. Not only can we read the ways in which Milton defended his own politics and theology through images of proper life, we can also look at the ways in which life has functioned as a critical concept. I will argue that 'life' was a crucial value within Milton's poetry, and that some of his most 'wordy' and seemingly lifeless moments evidence a commitment to vitalism. Further, we should not accept and repeat the texts, values or figures of the tradition but see those figures again as though for the first time. This book will not replay the Milton problem – the problem of the life of his poetry – but it will point to the significance of that *value* of life in the very notion of what counts as good poetry. The life that was explicitly valorized in New Criticism's establishment of modern literary criticism still, I would argue, structures the commitment to literary history. For the notion that reading historically will locate the force or *act* of the text is one of the hallmarks of new historicism, with Jerome McGann insisting that we should see texts as social acts, and with Stephen Greenblatt arguing that we should look at texts as vectors of social energy.[56]

It is just this persistent dependence on life, which appears to resist historicization precisely because it grounds our concepts of history, which makes the reading of Milton so relevant today.[57] Those images which dominate Milton's theology – the goodness of relation, actualization, time and sense in opposition to detachment, inertia, chaos and the punctual – dominate literary theory and aesthetics. Literary criticism has, as its founding idea, an image of *reading* as the restoration of life and relations, whether that revivification be seen as the returning of a work to its context, or the retrieval of the original act that accounts for a literary work's force. Such images of actualization and reanimation are neither avoidable nor undesirable, for any act of reading necessarily attributes a sense that is not immediately given but may ideally be brought to presence. In this regard, history – or the connection of fragments, documents, texts and events into some narrative and meaningful order – is the ultimate method of all reading and criticism; for without the notion of what a text must have wanted to say there can be no reading. It was in this sense that Paul de Man argued that there could be no theory of narrative. Theory, or the explanation of how an event or meaning is possible, already orders elements into some temporal relation; narrative, sense, synthesis and ongoing life are transcendental.[58] To 'live' a world that was purely pointillist, without continuity, progression or experience of this world as determined in some way, would be impossible, would not be living, would not be 'life'. There could therefore, for de Man, be no escape from the subject as a condition for meaning and sense; whatever is posited as beyond sense, comprehension, relation and cognition can only be posited *ex post facto*, after the event of meaning. For de Man, the 'rhetoric of temporality' is just that inability to grasp a 'time itself' that would somehow be liberated from the *living* of that time as meaningful and oriented towards sense.

Jacques Derrida, whose work has been directed against the supposed purity and self-sufficiency of a life that could do away with all negation, loss, corruption and death, has provided a corrective to the metaphysics of presence through the figure of evil. Evil is not the corruption of spirit by body or matter, but the striving to free spirit from all taint of matter or the non-living. Derrida argues that a text that tried to eliminate any unintended, accidental, borrowed, accrued or mechanical traces would itself be a figure of evil.[59] One can only have life, spirit, history or 'living on' if meaning takes on, and expresses itself through, some body. The condition for life is also, therefore, a certain death. If I wish to speak and reason, then I must take on the structure of some language, but any language will also have its unthought, unintended, opaque and 'machinic' elements. Reading is the capacity to intuit the spirit that remains through time, a spirit that would subtend all the copies of a poem or text. Reading is therefore made possible through matter, but also precluded from full actualization because of matter. For matter can 'act' on its own: produce effects, create connections and establish temporalities which have no origin in sense, and which may never be rendered coherent. One needs to understand matter not merely as the dead weight through which spirit expresses itself but as the necessary remainder or internal resistance effected through the movement of spirit.

Throughout his poetry and prose Milton employs the figure of reading as intrinsically ethical: the world must not appear as fully actualized and determined, but as potentially the sign or expression of a divine life that remains different. But if this is so, and reading is always the attribution or anticipation of what is *not* present or given, then the text is essentially incomplete at the same time as it calls for completion. What we must confront, then, in our reading of Milton is the way in which his own opposition between good (as expansive life) and evil (as non-relation or absence of sense) underpins our own literary theories. If reading is necessarily a bringing into presence and an attribution of life, how does it negotiate all those elements that are devoid of animation and haunt the text, demanding to be read precisely because their sense is not apparent? It is the capacity of matter to free itself from animating reason – the tendency for texts to circulate without intent, spirit, or bounding context – that Milton figured as evil. The chapters that follow will detail Milton's continued use of images of the body, growth and nutritive consumption to signal good life, and his imagery of the formless, inertia, decay and automatic incorporation to figure evil.[60] Criticism ought not to affirm this axiology, but should attend to the ways in which *Paradise Lost* takes up the image of the body that is fully animated by spirit, falling into matter and death only accidentally. Such an affirmation of life as essentially expressive, requiring body and matter only to extend its own power, reinforces a tradition of regarding evil as having no real being.

As Milton tries to demonstrate in *Paradise Lost*, evil can only be parasitic, and will ultimately serve to bring forth order, life and relations. Evil can only be recognized, from the point of view of order and narration, as the failure to make sense, as an absence or lacuna in a time of realization and fruition. The following chapters will explore the vitalist assumptions of reading as history – reading as a bringing to life of a text's potential – but will do so alongside the no less necessary images of evil which dominate criticism and theory: the image of the system that operates without sense or intent, the body that remains alone, without relations, time or life.

1

Milton's History of Reason and Church Government

One way of understanding Christianity's relation to time is to follow neo-Platonism and see time itself as fallen, with this world of dispersed events as the falling away from an eternal One. Evil would then be a question of degradation and degree, an increasing distance from the origin. Although there are aspects of this notion of the world as essentially distanced from the proper origin in Raphael's Augustinian model of the increasing sublimation of matter towards its proper origin, and in Milton's more general commitment to 'one first matter' which partakes of varying 'degrees of substance', reading Milton as a *poet* requires attending to another relation between time and divinity. For the poem, understood in the sense of *poiesis*, is a creation that is distinct from its creative origin and bears its own proper life.[61] Milton's understanding of books, signs, words and names as bearing a proper sense and spirit is thus more in accord with an intrinsically temporal and Christian understanding of positive time than Platonic emanation. It is precisely because Christianity has a doctrine of incarnation[62] at its heart that it at once presents bodies and matters as properly and ideally spiritual, but also allows for an understanding of the spirituality of matter. Here, the time of this world is not a delay, deferral or deflection from a truth that would exist outside time, for becoming is itself divine. A more positive understanding of an eternal time is implied in contrast with Satan's symptomatic description of God as heaven's *perpetual* king. For Satan, God's perpetuity can only be figured as a lack of dynamism; such perpetual time is the absence of change, a monotonous continuity (that would then render the defiant Satanic will all the more vibrant and attractive). If, however, eternity is regarded as a form of continual creative accord that is always in harmony with itself, then eternity is no longer outside time but is instead understood as a form of time in command of itself. This mode of time is figured both in Milton's frequent use of music as at once a form of expressive motion and an image of a movement that has no end other than itself ('the dateless and irrevoluble Circle of Eternity' [CPW 1.616]), and in Milton's understanding of history, in which time, becoming, growth and realization are not unfortunate detours through which truth must be revealed but are intrinsic to the nature of truth as taking on its proper body and form.

As a Christian poet Milton worked with an ambivalent relation to life and evil, a relation that was essentially historical. Time is not a simple medium that contains the events of the world, for the world requires time in order to journey towards God and beatitude. It is the overcoming of time both in the focus on the pure present and in the absence of becoming that characterizes Satan, who is nothing more than his will, bearing no character that would give ongoing form or sense to his actions. If the mind is its own *place*, then it has no reliance on an orientation not its own; the mind is also, then, its own time. But if time is *more* than the mind's apprehension of its own syntheses and relations, this is because for Milton time is not a purely formal or quantitative measure but a trajectory in which beings come to fruition and are all the more possessed of beatitude because of the sense of their journey. A goodness that is apprehended as distant but attainable, and then freely chosen, is a *meaningful* goodness: not simply the proper form of a being but a form that is decided upon, worked towards and taken on as one's own. Time is required in order for the true meaning of the world to be disclosed; evil will be discerned not as an existence in itself but as a waywardness or fallenness that must be overcome through renewed perception. On the one hand, then, the status of the world as God's creation precludes its essential fallenness; neither as a poet nor as a Christian could Milton resign himself to the simple evil, worthlessness or corruption of matter. For the detour that truth must take in order to express itself in the worldly forms of art is hardly at odds with Christianity, a religion that has a doctrine of incarnation at its heart and sets itself the task of presenting the body of Christ as spiritual matter.[63] On the other hand, if this world possesses any worth it is only as an expression of God's divine light; matter in itself, divorced from all informing light, leads the soul astray and precludes human intelligence from ascending from the world of matter to the world of ideas. This theological problem of the journey towards true being then plays itself out historically: how will time progress to the apocalyptic moment when the earth will be paradise, and all the world's people prophets?

This historical theology, in turn, prompts a formal problem for art. Stanley Fish has already noted this problem in his reading of Milton, for the Christian poet must simultaneously present himself as the mediator of divine truth while at the same time creating poetry that is original.[64] For Fish this difficulty follows from the relation between the individual modern poet and his spiritual vocation, which is poised between the demands of poetic originality and religious fidelity. However, a more positive way of thinking about this problem goes to the heart of Christianity and its doctrine of the incarnation, and also allows us to approach the form of the art object more directly. Art presents the body of Christ and in doing so presents *spiritual matter*. This is particularly so in the case of poetry, for *Paradise Lost* gives a direct presentation of the word of God and Christ, along with a lived sense of paradise and unfallen man: not as tableaux or types but as lived realities with all the temporal vicissitudes of conversation, labour and eros, or 'sweet reluctant amorous delay'.[65] The notion of a divine and amorous delay marks Milton's poetry in general, where distance from the origin is not primarily a sign of corruption or fallenness so much as a felicitous placing into view of a paradise and holiness that we can recognize and take on as our own. The dimming of divine light,[66] the journey we take toward the good, the incarnation of God in Christ, and the divine similitude of Adam and Eve, are always more than mediations of a divinity that would otherwise remain unexpressed. Although Milton's theology will insist that God could have chosen not to create and still been divinely perfect, his having created – freely and without need or compulsion – expresses divine abundance and creativity all the more wondrously: 'It is, I say, a demonstration of God's supreme power and goodness that he should not shut up his heterogeneous and substantial virtue within himself, but should disperse, propagate, and extend it as far as, and in whatever way, he wills' (CPW 6.308).[67]

One common way of reading Milton historically is to see his prose and poetry as in line with a progressive internalization of law and spiritualization of matter, with both being outcomes of the radical puritan rejection of trans-cendent norms. On such an understanding, Milton takes up Edmund Spenser's vision but recognizes that his poetry is still too allegorical and so presents heaven and paradise directly. What this chapter seeks to do is problematize that notion of linear history by looking at the ways in which the forward move-ment of history always harbours remnants of persistent formal problems, prob-lems which will play themselves out in complex historical trajectories. Despite Milton's use of apocalyptic and teleological motifs, there will always remain material moments in his work which resist the transition from shadowy types to truth. Those formal snags in the trajectory of sense cannot be read as accidents which befall the poetic corpus from without, but are intrinsic to its possibility. We can begin to understand this by looking at the problem of the 'two-handed engine'. How might one decide, once and for all, the sense of such a phrase and image which presents itself at the moment of apocalyptic declara-tion in 'Lycidas'? There must have been some original sense or intent which put such a phrase into poetic circulation, and it is the labour of criticism to intuit the origin that would allow the 'two-handed engine' to become one with the progressive meaning of the poem. The history of criticism, however, testifies all too clearly to the necessary impossibility of such a task: necessary, because as long as one continues to read a poem one is committed to retrieving its sense or what it wanted to say, but impossible because all we have in order to retrieve that originating sense is the fragment or trace that has passed into circulation. This local problem can be confined neither to the problem of the 'two-handed engine' nor to the broader problem of, say, Milton's Satan, where a signifier seems to operate in ways at odds with the seeming intent of the poetic whole in which it is located. Such formal problems bring us to the essential problem of history. History is not a form we impose upon poems or signifiers, for there can only be sense or meaning on the assumption that one can retrieve, in the frag-ments of the present, the life or animation which originally gave birth to those signs. To read is to assume that one can in principle retrieve a sense once given over to the signs that are now its body. At the same time, it is precisely history that makes such a retrieval impossible: for a sense or work to go through time, or to live on, it must take on some embodied form or expression, some distance from its creator. It is precisely that living on through time in the form of the work that precludes the original sense from ever being at one with itself. One might say, then, that evil is the condition for the possibility of history: only with a detachment from the origin, and a release from the ground, can there be a work that goes through time and that must then be reread, re-inscribed, mastered and worked through. At the same time, evil is counter-historical and counter-temporal; for in its Satanic form evil is a refusal of all debt, origin, hope and recognition. What is played out in the reading of Milton's poetry is this double status of evil. For Milton will at the same time present the poetic work and the present moment as both enigmatic – requiring the labour of reading, thinking and working through – and as essentially harbouring a sense and origin that must always be retrievable in principle. This accounts for the more than moral status of evil in Milton's work: evil is at once both a threat of detachment, loss and fragmentation that must be warded off, and a necessary condition for the temporal process of trial and recognition. Before it is a moral concept in Milton's work, evil is ontological and formal: ontological, because poetry is an exercise in signs, in seeing the ways in which divine substance differs from and expresses itself; and formal, because the art of intuiting good from evil, the Satanic from the angelic, the originary from the parasitic, is an exercise in discerning proper modes of expression. Milton therefore deploys the notion of the world as an expression and efflorescence of a divine ground, and affirms that world as divine in its difference and distance.

Rather than see Milton's protestant affirmation of a paradise within as a modern reversal of a world once subordinated to the divine and transcendent, it would be more appropriate to see Christianity itself – in so far as it manifests itself in art – as always harbouring a double potential. History is not a straight-forward progression involving the increasing turn towards 'man' and imma-nence but a constant negotiation between the spiritualization of matter from some transcendent source and the potential divinity of matter itself.[68] Milton will therefore reject allegory and attribute a particular mode of life and politics to the allegorical tendency. If signs are distant and radically distinct from God, then their sense will require a labour of interpretation while the signs them-selves will be arbitrary or unmotivated. If, however, signs are the expression of a divine nature then poetry will still require reading, but that reading will not be an overcoming of the body of the sign so much as an intuition of the life from which language emerges. This explains Milton's intense commitment to ety-mology, to the point where the earth itself can sigh, and where acts of naming – such as the name given to 'Death' – flow directly from creation in general. It is important therefore to make a distinction between analogy, which is thor-oughly Miltonic, and allegory. Analogy allows all the signs and differences of this world to bear an essential resemblance and distance from their divine origin, allowing us at once to read all the signs and bodies of this world while recognizing their distinction from the true and essential being of divinity. Alle-gory can only approach the divine through a figure which is essentially distinct, and possibly arbitrary. A poetics of analogy acknowledges the difference of the divine, but nevertheless produces a work of art as expressive of divine life.

A matter that is different and distant from the divine but that has no life or spirit of its own raises the problem of dualism and Manichaeism; and it was just this idea of the utterly tragic – that which could not be taken up by history, sense or value – that once dominated the art of the Renaissance and Middle Ages but became a problem as theology sought to make its rational way in the world. The clearest articulation of this idea of a once tragic diremption that can now only be rationalized and historicized comes from Michel Foucault, who argued that prior to the modern age of incarceration and reason as a formal and universal principle, various modes of unreason existed as enigmatic, unfathomable but threatening 'others'. By the time we arrive at contemporary forms of psychology it is not only the case that forms of mental illness and even moral pathologies can be explained as disruptions of an otherwise general psychological survival mechanism of the human living organism (relying on the modern notion of 'life'), it is also the case that we begin to interrogate the brain's mechanisms through pathology. From Freud to Oliver Sachs, various psychic and neurological abnormalities allow us to perceive the brain's or mind's mechanism in its extreme forms, thereby enabling an understanding of normality. Rather than there being a potential for the absence of all logic, relationality, system or identity, the absence of reason is merely the potential for understanding and identifying the life of reason. Nothing is in principle outside the bounds of sense. If pre-modern presentations of the demonic and Satanic were concerned with nightmarish and chaotic images of grotesque destruction, Milton's imagery of evil and the Satanic is intensively rationalizing. Nowhere is this more evident than in Milton's hell which, far from being a nightmare vision of chaos, disorder, pain, non-being and the absence of all time and relation, depicts a corrupted form of debate and sociality. Even Milton's figures of chaos, darkness and death are negative versions of an order and structure which have failed to emerge, with chaos itself being the potentiality for the emergence of order: 'the Womb of nature and perhaps her Grave' (PL 2.911).

Milton's figuration of evil as a lapse or detour in an otherwise inevitable and flourishing reason resonates directly with his political theory. For however fallen, irrational and evil this world may appear to be, it must in principle bear the potentiality for redemption. If evil is negation then we also need to understand how a life that bears the potentiality for right reason falls back into the dark night of unreason. Before this becomes the theological theme of *Paradise Lost* it is exercised politically in the prose works, with the dominant motif of the relation between church and state allowing Milton to explore the relation between spirit and institutionalization. If the opposition between good and evil is the opposition between flourishing expressive life and its failed actualization, then the opposition between church and state is that of a spiritual institution that realizes reason, and a rigid law that impedes the process of self-recognition and internalization. Milton will therefore see history less as a sequence of events than as a vital and rational imperative: institutions in this world ought to be vehicles through which divinity restores, recognizes and realizes itself. If institutions stagnate or take on the form of an eternal law they become evil: detached from, and devoid of, the life which ought to be their animating principle. The history and reason of church government are therefore central concerns of Milton's prose and poetry, for the question and problem of theodicy is related to (and explained by) the fall of rational and expressive life into worldly and external systems.

History and Institution

The Christianity of the gospels deemed this world irrelevant to spiritual issues. Divine law was located in an other-worldly sphere, and justice could not be expected on this earth. There was a radical difference between spiritual and political realms: 'My kingdom is not of this world' (Jn 18:36). While obedience to worldly authority was encouraged 'Let every soul be subject to the governing authorities' (Rom 13:1–7); 'Therefore submit yourselves to every ordinance of man for the Lord's sake' (1 Pet 2: 13–15) such obedience should cease if a conflict between worldly and spiritual demands arose: 'We ought to obey God rather than men' (Acts 5:29). With the adoption of Christianity by the Roman Empire, there emerged a need for a greater tolerance towards the state. Tertullian (150–220) in his *Apology* emphasized the subordination of the temporal powers to God, but in doing so also subtly prefigured the theory of sacral kingship. As in Christian art, which negotiated the relation between body and spirit and had to do so without condemning body as spirit's radical other, theories of church and state had to attribute some worth to the state, but needed to ground that worth on a source not of this world. For Tertullian the king may be God's *servant* but he is nevertheless *God's* servant:

> For we, on behalf of the safety of the Emperors, invoke the eternal God, the true God, the living God, whom the Emperors themselves prefer to have propitious to them beyond all other gods. They know who has given them the empire; they know, as men, who has given them life; they feel that He is God alone, in whose power they are, second to whom they stand, after whom they come first, before all gods and above all gods. Why not? seeing that they are above all men, and men at any rate live and so are better than dead things. They reflect how far the strength of their empire avails, and thus they understand God; against him they cannot avail, so they know it is through Him that they do avail.[69]

Such appeals to divinity served both to justify and subordinate the state. In the political history of church and state, and in the question of the origin of law – is law an emanation of divine authority or a condition that follows from our fallen depravity? – a deeper issue is being played out. The world cannot be abandoned to itself in all its singular contingency but must be informed by some divine, animating and directing power. Disputes regarding kingship concerned the locus and extent of that divine expression; what could not be entertained was a material world that was not the sign or site of some transcendent and life-infusing divinity. For Eusebius of Caesarea (260–337) the emperor himself is not divine but one whom God 'receives': 'Thus outfitted in the likeness of the kingdom of heaven, he pilots affairs below with an upward gaze, to steer by the archetypal form.'[70]

It was this problem of the relation between divine law and its worldly expression that dominated Milton's political theory and his poetry. Despite the seemingly modern and radical nature of Milton's conclusions – arguing for divorce, republicanism, freedom of speech and the significance of poetry – his premises hark back to traditional problems of theology and its relation to the vagaries of matter. The theological resonance of these problems is not, however, resolvable by placing Milton 'in' a historical context but requires us to recognize that theology and its intrinsic problem of historicity is at the heart of all questions of art and politics: to what extent are political relations grounded or justified by some transcendent norm, and to what extent is this material world along with the bodies that inhabit it informed by a spirit or power not already actualized? These questions ultimately concern immanence. Is it possible to think of a life or world that has no law, logic or historical trajectory – no proper potential – which it is striving to actualize? Considering this question historically is itself question-begging. If we see Milton as moving ever closer to the recognition of the innate worth of the world, then we also see history as the gradual progression towards the world's proper sense. The only way to avoid beginning with a history of theology which will bear its own theology – in which 'man' arrives at the proper internalization of all that appears alien – is to pay close attention to those aspects that resist spiritualization, that will not be incorporated, rendered meaningful or allowed to work for a project of reanimation and self-recognition.

As I have already outlined in the introduction, goodness has always been figured through images of growth, actualization, fruition and self-realization, while evil has been figured as that which remains without relation and which resists any reference to what is beyond its own being. It was just this confrontation with the radically immanent which was so significant for Milton, who worked through the lure and insistence of evil. For Milton the tendency for life to resist its own proper historical trajectory could be partly accounted for through the doctrine of the soul: that aspect of the human self which is at one and the same time a site of 'ownness' and a receptacle of a divine light that is not its own. In working his way through the problem of the soul's tendency to turn away from its own proper potential Milton drew heavily upon Augustine.[71] Augustine had accepted, from Platonism, that the soul possessed a light and power that was not that of 'man' himself, but added to Platonism a sense of history and the capacity for the soul to work its way towards recognition of its proper being. This related directly to Augustine's, and later Milton's, politics.

The soul could at once guide life in this world, but must also always see the affairs of this world as having value only in relation to the divine.

The worldly involvement of the church is allowed for in Augustine but such accommodation is achieved only by stressing that the temporal affairs of the church should be subordinated to an ultimately divine order. In the *City of God* Augustine turns away from the demands of the empire and attends to the 'heavenly city'. It is the obligation of all Christians to bring the earthly city into as much conformity to the heavenly city as possible. Even so, Augustine exempted the state from the radical demands of the gospels; the kingdom of God was not expected to begin in history. Augustine's Platonism stressed that the soul was an aspect of God's light in human being, and this allowed for an aspect of transcendent value in the world. However, the divine reason of the soul no longer manifested itself in the practice of virtue in the city-state, as it had done for Plato and Aristotle, but in the activities of a separate institution – the church – whose orientation was other-worldly:

> the earthly city, that lives not by faith, seeks an earthly peace, and its end in aiming at agreement concerning command and obedience on the part of the citizens is limited to a sort of merging of human wills in regard to the things that are useful for this mortal life. Whereas the heavenly city, or rather the part of it that goes its pilgrim way in this mortal life and lives by faith, needs must make use of this peace too, though only until this mortal lot which has need of it shall pass away.[72]

Milton carries Augustine's concept of the soul further into the world. The soul's radical other-worldliness is retained in so far as its values and aims are transcendent, but the soul now dictates the foundation of political being. Milton restores the possibility of just government, which he regards as having been lost in the shift from the ancient concept of justice (where living well required a just polity) to the medieval conception of relative natural law (a conception that the fallenness of the world allowed for submission to tyranny).[73] Milton will tirelessly reiterate the history of this innerworldly fall, from the rational freedom of the ancients to the encroaching prescriptions of church government, and he will do so even in those texts (such as *Areopagitica*) which are not primarily historical. This explains why, even while acknowledging the primary truth of Christianity, Milton can on occasion appeal to ancient practice in the face of present evils (as he will do in *Areopagitica*). For Milton, the grace of God has willed that some vestiges of divinity should remain in the world. God's will acts in the cause of good in the temporal sphere; neither the state nor the human will is entirely fallen. Because the residue of divine goodness is located in individual souls, worldly justice can only be attained by freely reasoning individuals. This requires a radical separation of church and state. Modernity for Milton will therefore, as is so often the case for thinkers in his own time and now, be figured in the form of a retrieval of origin: the history of church government has overlaid the rationality and simplicity of the divine word with corruptions of worldly politics. The worldly institutions as they are must be recalled to their instituting principle, revivified by the spirit of which they ought to be the expression. However, this criticism of the church's politicization and the insistence on divinity is not a step towards political quietism. On the contrary: once the individual frees himself from the state that has used the church to sustain its worldly desires, he will be able to become truly spiritual and then, in turn, create a just polity. Only individuals whose spirit is free to reason will provide good citizenship, and only good citizens — those who master themselves rationally and are capable of self-rule — will develop the reason capable of attaining God's inner light. Milton's rejection of Christian empire, or the use of religion for political governance, is therefore radical at a temporal level, but strictly conservative at a spiritual level, relying as it does on the one true light that will emerge if reason is allowed to develop itself. Only a truly spiritual church, focused on God's light alone, provides the appropriate preamble for political freedom. A truly divine polity would, therefore, have to free itself from religious legalism, and this because the soul's divinity could only suffer from being reified by material institutions.

In addition to frequent references in the prose and poetry to an institutional encroachment of the polity into the spiritual sphere, Milton was more explicitly historical in his marking of the reign of Constantine as the commencement of the decline of church government, precisely because at that point the church became concerned with temporal affairs. A gain in power at the temporal level is a loss of spirit. Addressing the bishops in *Of Reformation* (1641), Milton saw Constantine as a figure who epitomized tyranny and poor church government:

> Stay but a little, magnanimous Bishops, suppresse your aspiring thoughts, for there is nothing wanting but *Constantine* to reign, and then Tyranny her selfe shall give up all her cittadels into your hands, and count ye thence forward her trustiest agents. Such were these that must be call'd the ancientest and most virgin times between *Christ* and *Constantine*. (CPW 1.551)

When Milton eventually demands a complete separation of church and state in *Of Civil Power* (1659), it is not only for the purposes of returning to the radical spirit of early Christianity in demanding a church free from temporal aims; once the church has freed itself from material power it can then provide the proper direction for politics. Separation must precede an ultimate unity. Milton's prose career begins by demanding a purification of the church from the corrupt and temporal influences of political government. Eventually, his vision of church government based on reason, the soul and its relation to transcendence provides a model for the state. In *A Defence of the People of England* (1651) Milton argues that the freedom enabled by the atonement is political as well as spiritual:

> I do not speak of inward freedom only and omit political freedom. The prophecy of [Christ's] advent foretold by Mary his mother, 'He hath scattered

the proud in the imagination of their hearts; he hath put down the mighty from their seats, and exalted them of low degree,' must indeed be but idle talk if his advent is instead to strengthen tyrants on their thrones and subject all Christians to savage power. (CPW 4.374)

In *Reason of Church Government* (1641) Milton allows the practice of jurisdiction (which rules by outward force) to continue in the political sphere. The moral sphere of religion, on the other hand, should be governed inwardly. To secure assent to doctrine through outward force is to corrupt the essentially inward character of Christian doctrine. Here, in *Reason of Church Government,* Milton argues that the spiritual affairs of the church should not be impeded by the bodily, temporal or material affairs of the state. The latter should be subordinated to the former. But later, in *The Tenure of Kings and Magistrates* (1649), Milton brings this argument regarding the internalization of law into the political sphere so that the temporal state, too, will benefit from the freedom from institutionalized and external law. The commonwealth will be a function of the free and independent exercise of reason without the impediment of arbitrary laws; but reason develops spiritually in an autonomous relation to the divine. Because religion is rightly a matter of the inner soul, there must be both an institution for the development of the spirit, and then a state where that spirit can be actualized. A state church can only impede the soul's inwardness because it governs spirit from an already decided system of political relations.

At the basis of Milton's initially separatist political theory of the church and state is a philosophical rejection of externally imposed laws; that rejection then precedes and enables the embrace of internally coherent and immanently valid laws of reason. Freedom, reason and spiritual autonomy can be achieved in the temporal sphere because we are innately divine and capable of a 'paradise within' (which would still, nevertheless, always be subordinated to, and directed towards, that transcendent paradise of the kingdom of heaven). Milton's appeal to a church/state division is therefore not quite a return to the parallelism of the gospels, which had in no way brought its religious concerns to issues of this world. Affairs of state, in so far as they are directed by reason and *always* have freedom of conscience as their aim, are still subordinated to the spirit which in the final instance is divine and transcendent. But the subservience to reason, to the inner light residing in all souls, need not be doubled by the subordination of legal practices to an institutionalized religion. If the spirit is allowed to work freely, the true practice of justice will emerge without the government of prelates entering the picture. Milton's belief in the singularity, plainness and attainability of truth (and truth's transcendence from all worldly difference and dispute) [74] is at the basis of this thought. Truth is attainable by each spirit; the state, therefore, does not need the 'spiritual authority' of the church. Political secularism − the freedom of government from the church − is justified on Christian grounds; it is because reason is God's inner light that we do not require a governing church to guide us. Truth is clear and attainable. Hence, in *Of Reformation* Milton remarks:

The very essence of Truth is plainnesse, and brightnes; the darknes and crookednesse is our own. The *Wisdome* of *God* created *understanding*, fit and proportionable to Truth and the object, and end of it, as the eye the thing visible. If our own *understanding* have a film of *ignorance* over it, or be blear with gazing on other false glisterings, what is that to Truth? (CPW 1.566)

If Milton argues for democracy it is not because souls acting together may form a conception of the good but because goodness and truth, which exist independently from the knowledge we have of them, have a better chance of emerging through free and rational discourse. What Milton desired was a form of government which enabled freedom of thought and the development of rational capacities, so that whatever political structure was achieved would be based on the inner power of reason. If Milton's demands yielded demo-cratic practice this was contingent; what was essential was the centrality of reason and the belief that justice would necessarily follow. If profoundly non-democratic means needed to be employed to achieve an ultimate freedom of the spirit, then Milton would advocate them, as he would do in *The Readie and Easie Way* (1660). Milton's political position was therefore curiously divided between a radical commitment to the spirit that – if allowed to reason freely – would arrive at the truth of politics, and an insistence that politics ultimately devolved on a single and plain truth that could only be corrupted if allowed to fall into the vagaries of an unthinking multitude. Milton would at one and the same time insist upon rational persuasion rather than brutal imposition (for individuals are rationally capable of accepting the law for its own sake) and insist that those who were doing the persuading would have to work against the obvious tendencies of the populace *not* to actualize the full potentiality of reason. Milton begins his *Reason of Church Government* by referring to Plato and the importance of persuasion in the education of government:

In the publishing of humane laws, which for the most part aime not beyond the good of civill society, to set them barely forth to the people without reason or preface, like a physicall prescript, or only with threatenings, as it were a lordly command, in the judgement of *Plato* was thought to be done neither generously or wisely. His advice was, seeing that persuasion certainly is more winning, and more manlike to keepe men in obedience then feare, that to such lawes as were of principall moment, there should be us'd as an induc-tion, some well temper'd discourse, shewing how good, how gainfull, how happy it must needs be to live according to honesty and justice, which being utter'd with those native colours and graces of speech, as true eloquence the daughter of vertue can best bestow upon her mothers praises, would so incite, and in a manner, charme the multitude into the love of that which is really good as to embrace it ever after, not of custome and awe, which most men do, but of choice and purpose, with true and constant delight. (CPW 1.746)

Laws should not be imposed; they should be seen to be good and adopted for their own sake. A true representation of these laws will be compatible with 'well tempered discourse', which will then allow the 'multitude' to see reason itself. So conducive is reason to life, happiness and becoming 'more manlike' that its exercise will be 'constant delight'. That seemingly casual connection between reason, happiness and masculinity is not, I would suggest, either accidental within Milton's corpus, nor out of character with the tradition within which he writes. His intense privilege of act, self-formation, autonomy and the spiritualization of the body will dismiss as secondary and parasitic all those radically material and *technical* elements which cannot be internalized as reason's own. As a rich tradition of feminist theory has noted, the division between active and passive, mind and body, form and matter and even self-conscious life and unreasoning *technē* has always reinforced a male/female gender binary. *Reason of Church Government*'s emphasis upon reason (and its manifestation in the immediacy of the gospel rather than textual tradition) relies upon the Platonic belief that laws should be valued in and for themselves and should be internally valid and not arbitrarily prescribed. This argument is reiterated in *Of Reformation*, when Milton states that 'Custome without Truth is but agednesse of Error' (CPW 1.561). Apart from their explicit Platonism, these arguments in *Reason of Church Government* and *Of Reformation* rejecting 'custome' rely upon an ethics of time and history; the reasons for a longstanding law ought to remain present, for the detachment of law from its founding justification is a loss of truth. It is not convention but truth that should be the basis for consent. Social structure is therefore founded upon and directed towards the interests of inner experience, for it is the inward self that can always (throughout history) intuit the reason from which historical institutions and conventions emerge. What unites all sections of *Reason of Church Government* (including the autobiographical 'digression') is an argument about the relations between the inward and outward spheres of human being. The inward spirit is identified with reason, the eternal, the divine and the essential, while outward corporeality is aligned with the contingent and the temporal.

Whereas radical protestant thought more often than not rejected church government of any form as essentially a contamination of the pure individualism of the inner light, Milton at this point still conceives the worldly practice of Christianity as appropriately embodied in a trans-individual structure such as the church. When Milton eventually demands church/state separation he is still not opposed to institutions per se, for the practice of civil law and magistrates is valid. But the condition for their legitimate existence is the attainment of the knowledge of virtue, which can only be achieved by the individual examining scripture and their own heart. When Milton considers the role of the state in individual flourishing, it is essential for him that laws be framed in accord with the truth and reason which is God's will; this accord is achieved through self-reflection so that law 'if it be at all the worke of man, it must be of such a one as is a true knower of himselfe' (CPW 1.753). Self-knowledge, therefore, is at the heart of sound government; but this is not because of any modern 'Cartesian' commitment to man as a reasoning substance set over against a world of matter.[75] The self to be known is a portion of that divine, creative life that also expresses itself in the natural and material world.

By beginning *Reason of Church Government* with a reference to persuasion, Milton invokes the Platonic tradition of demanding an understanding and internalization of law. Law should remain proximate to spirit; the progressive circulation, habituation and systematization of law rob it of its original justifying force. Whereas the good and rational law can be referred back to the unity of an animating intent, the fallenness of law is associated with its becoming plural and diffuse. Milton claims that when the 'multitude' embraces justice and honesty through 'custome and awe' it cannot truly be happy. It is when a 'love of that which is really good' leads to a 'choice and purpose' that justice is appropriately conceived (CPW 1.746). Act, here, is privileged over reception, the singularity of reason over a dispersed multitude, and the relation of love and recognition over the rendering passive of 'awe'.

Milton will even defend Old Testament law as compatible with, if not reducible to, reason. Old Testament law, he insists, gave humanity the bare form of rational government. Now that the atonement has installed an inner light in the human soul the necessity for internalized law should be imperative:

> If then in the administration of civill justice, and under the obscurity of Ceremoniall rites, such care was had by the wisest of the heathen, and by *Moses* among the Jewes, to instruct them at least in a generall reason of that government to which their subjection was requir'd, how much more ought the members of the Church under the Gospell seeke to informe their understanding in the reason of that government which the Church claimes to have over them: especialy for that the Church hath in her immediate cure those inner parts and affections of mind where the seat of reason is; having power to examine our spirituall knowledge, and to demand from us in Gods behalfe a service intirely reasonable. (CPW 1.747–8)

Milton's rejection of 'contracts and mutual rights of man' in favour of an internalized law derived from thoughts of God and true human nature, can be contrasted with modern social contract theories of law. The idea of 'contracts and mutual rights of man' (where contracts defend property and rights exclude encroachment from others) sees law as negative. Contract theory begins from pre-social individuals who then enter society in order to achieve rights, with rights guarding against exploitation by others. Such a social theory not only presupposes a competitive notion of the individual and a law imposed upon selves, it also begins from an understanding of the subject divorced from any normative understanding of nature; although such subjects may harbour implicit norms of capitalism and individualism,[76] these are quite distinct from the norms of a more general flourishing life of which rational man would be a privileged expression. By contrast, for Milton the achievement of reason and law is a fulfilment and realization of the self. Social relations express, rather than impede, a self who ultimately desires to become rational.[77] Although Milton uses a form of contract theory to explain the origin of kingship in *The Tenure of Kings and Magistrates*, his conception of a contract only explained the *conditional* handing over of power to a king in order to safeguard the interests of reason. Unlike Hobbes, Milton did not see reason as fallen (nor the self as a pre-social and atomic unit) and therefore did not see kingship as an unconditional handing over of rights. Indeed, Milton makes clear that there is an original and natural 'autoritie' in every individual that constitutes kingship 'unitedly . . . for ease and order'. Prior to the handing over of power to a sovereign, a commonly agreed social arrangement is constructed; the social whole, therefore, precedes and governs kingship:

> they agreed by common league to bind each other from mutual injury, and joyntly to defend themselves against any that gave disturbance or opposition to such agreement. Hence came Citties, Townes and Common-wealths. And because no faithe in all was found sufficiently binding, they saw it need-full to ordaine som authoritie, that might restrain by force and punishment what was violated against peace and common right. This autoritie and power of self-defence and preservation being originally and naturally in every one of them, and unitedly in them all, for ease, for order, and least each man should be his own partial Judge, they communicated and deriv'd either to one, whom-for the eminence of his wisdom and integritie they chose above the rest, or to more then one whom they thought of equal deserving: the first was call'd a King; the other Magistrates. Not to be their Lords and Maisters . . . but to be their Deputies and Commisioners, to execute, by vertue of thir intrusted power, that justice which else every man by the bond of nature and of Cov'nant must have executed for himself, and for one another. (CPW 3.199)

Milton insists that law is not a result of fallenness and thus disagrees with the history of relative natural law, which explained away worldly inequality and the difference between individual good and legal right as due to some postlapsarian condition. Law only appears alien to desire when its origin in human reason and the natural superiority of reason have been forgotten. Milton is therefore advocating neither unquestioning obedience to authority nor a radical and unlimited freedom. True freedom entails recognizing the value of law in willing and reasoned obedience, so that as created beings God's law is our own good. Law, order and limit are intrinsic to human being as such and not merely in our postlapsarian state, because 'man' is at one with a more general order and harmony:

> And certainly discipline is not only the removall of disorder, but if any visible shape can be given to divine things, the very visible shape and image of vertue, whereby she is not only seene in the regular gestures and motions of her heavenly paces as she walkes, but also makes the harmony of her voice audible to mortall cares. (CPW 1.751–2)

The soul has a determined and structured character which accords with law and virtue; it is in recognizing and achieving this essential being that freedom is attained. Were human nature to be purely open, undefined and characterless, law would have no essential basis and would be alien rather than essential. For Milton, goodness itself is limited, defined and marked out, while discipline plays a role even in paradise, as *Reason of Church Government* goes on to argue:

> The state also of the blessed in Paradise, though never so perfect, is not there-fore left without discipline, whose golden survaying reed marks out and measures every quarter and circuit of new Jerusalem. (CPW 1.752)

The link between goodness and limit is not unique to Milton, although it is intensified in his poetics and politics.[78] If imagery of evil begins from corruption, degradation, lack and the failure of potentiality, it is associated intrinsically with an absence of form and limit: both a loss of a body's proper borders (loss of physical limit) and a loss of definition and essence (loss of metaphysical form). Milton will constantly stress the harmony of borders, bounds, demarcations and lines, and he is thus in accord with an understanding of paradise in its etymological sense (of walled enclosure) as essentially limited – not in the sense of being deprived of an ever increasing goodness, but of being perfectly formed and self-contained.[79] There is, therefore, a law which is divine and eternal, and which is not a restriction of the flourishing of the soul. In fact, divine law is the condition for the soul's fulfilment. In his reform tracts of the early 1640s Milton uses the distinction between divine and human law to argue for a certain type of church government grounded on inner experience. *Of Prelatical Episcopacy* (1641) opens with the question whether episcopacy 'is either of Divine constitution, or of humane' (CPW 1.624). This distinction between human and divine value underlies and enables the further distinctions which are articulated in Milton's prose tracts: between outward and inward human experience, between state law and church government, between magistrates and ministers, between the temporal and the eternal, between jurisdiction and censure, between the texts of the Fathers and Holy Scripture and between sophistry and true reason. It is only if there can be a divine law, and not merely human law, that human beings have access to transcendence and are, in turn, capable of elevating themselves above any given tyranny to a higher humanism. Ultimately, the foundational value and that which decides and determines all other values is that of the life of reason.

Milton, accordingly, imagines the Christian commonwealth as a projection of a living being whose form is reason. It is this notion of the proper, unified and living body which is expressive of normative life in general: if the human body is the proper image of a commonwealth this is because the body is an image of harmonious and self-governing relations, informed by a reason which is its internal law.[80] A similar image will also underpin Milton's defence of the living book in *Areopagitica,* and his overall insistence on self-formation and expressive form:

a Commonwealth ought to be but as one huge Christian personage, one mighty growth, and stature of an honest man, as big and compact in vertue as in body; for looke what the grounds and causes are of single happiness to one man, the same yee shall find them to a whole state, as *Aristotle* both in his ethicks, and politicks, from the principles of reason layes down. (CPW 1.572)

Milton's emphasis upon the historical importance of Constantine in *Of Reformation* reveals his recognition that it is after the state is Christianized that the church loses its inward character and becomes worldly and outward-directed.[81] The appropriation of the church by the state is, for Milton, a loss of original purity and a move towards the material body – from inherent value to the *appearance* of value. Furthermore, the forgetting of the spiritual and inner origin of Christianity is the condition for a seizing of political power; here, as elsewhere, Milton will use metaphors of digestion and consumption to figure an increasing becoming-brutal of a body that ought to be directed towards ideal and spiritual nourishment:

But when through *Constantine's* lavish superstition they forsook their *first love*, and set themselves up two Gods instead, *Mammon* and their Belly, then taking advantage of the spiritual power which they had on men's consciences, they began to cast a longing eye to get their body also and bodily things into their command, upon which their carnal desires, the Spirit dayly quenching and dying in them, they knew no way to keep themselves from falling to nothing, but by bolstering and supporting their inward rottenes by a carnal and outward strength. (CPW 1.576–7)

The idea of a 'lavish Superstition' which enslaves the spirit continues Milton's earlier condemnation of Constantine's fixing of fasts and feasts (CPW 1.556). Outward display and theatricality emerge when inner spirit weakens and atrophies. Attention to the body is both symptomatic of, and causally related to, a loss and forgetting of 'inward Sanctity' (CPW 1.556). It is important to realize that this is not a simple denigration of the body but is part of a tradition insisting upon an ethical spiritualization of the body by the soul. Against a Pauline denigration or subordination of the flesh (and its concomitant political theory of a radical break with worldly systems[82]), Milton is closer to a classical tradition of spiritual exercises which progressively – through temperance, contemplation and dialogue – brings the whole self into accord with a reason that transcends any individual.[83] That process of spiritualization is the trajectory of life; a body should live in such a way that it becomes soul. This progressive spiritualization applies both to the human body and to the world. For Milton history as such should be an ongoing rendering-spiritual of the earth.

In keeping with this, Milton acknowledges the importance of bodily action when it accords with spirit. In Book Three of *Paradise Regain'd*, once Satan is 'confuted and convinced / Of his weak arguing' he is compelled to admit the integrity of Christ's character. Christ's virtue entails the realization of inner good with outer action, the manifestation of spirit in words and deeds:

> Thy actions to thy words accord, thy words
> To thy large heart give utterance due, thy heart
> Conteins of good, wise, just, the perfect shape. (PR 3.9–11)[84]

The 'shape' of goodness lies in the heart. The origin of outer value is inward in character. In Book Four, when Satan tempts Christ with worldly power, claiming that it is a condition for the emancipation of the people, Christ claims that power may be a necessary but is certainly not a sufficient condition for freedom. Just as *Of Reformation* states that spiritual enslavement is the first and most important loss of freedom, Christ stresses that the 'degenerate' are 'by themselves enslav'd' and asks rhetorically, who 'could of inward slaves make outward free?' (PR 4.144–5). This is not a denial of the significance of bodily enslavement; rather, imprisonment of the body *presupposes* a loss of spiritual autonomy. The condition for political tyranny is an abnegation of inner strength. And it is in this sense that Christ claims that the people are 'Deservedly made vassal' (PR 4.133) because frugality and temperance have given way to 'lust and rapine' (PR 4.137). Bodily excess, individual desire and the denial of limits lead to a corporealization of the spirit. Once the self is imbruted it becomes nothing more than its actual body within the world, and so has no insight into a law above and beyond the warring relations of material forces. Excessive self-regard within the world leads to a failure to see the truly other-worldly dimension of the self. The church since Constantine, according to Milton, has exploited this process of embodying the spirit as a means for enslaving its members.

Milton, therefore, saw reflection upon church government by individuals as a moral duty, for only an institution grounded upon individual reason could be valid: 'how much more ought the members of the Church under the Gospell seeke to informe their understanding in the reason of that government which the Church claimes to have over them' (CPW 1.747). It is with the development of theocracy after Constantine that value is derived from a mediate body of the emperor and the other-worldly individualism of early Christianity gives way to a subordination to divine right. In the opening of *Of Reformation* Milton compares the history of the church and Christian doctrine with the body of the resurrected Christ, again allowing the figure of the unified and integrated body to provide a norm of proper form:

> after the story of our Saviour *Christ*, suffering to the lowest bent of weaknesse, in the *Flesh*, and presently triumphing to the highest pitch of *glory*, in the *Spirit*, which drew his body also, till we in both be united to him in Revelation of his Kingdome: I do not knowe of any thing more worthy to take up the whole passion of pitty, on the one side, and joy on the other: then to consider first, the foule and sudden corruption, and then after many a tedious

age, the long deferr'd, but much more wonderfull and happy reformation of the *Church* in these latter dayes. (CPW 1.519)

When Milton likens the church to the body of Christ that emerges from 'foule and sudden corruption' he de-institutionalizes and re-individualizes the church; for the figure of the body of Christ allows each member a direct orientation to the divine, of which they themselves are already expressions. This sentiment is heightened in *Reason of Church Government* with the depiction of the reformed church as analogous to the resurrected Christ. It is through examination of the soul that we shall 'accomplish the immortall stature of Christ's body which is his Church in all her glorious lineaments and proportions' (CPW 1.757).

True values are still 'internal' for Milton in so far as their basis is the inner sanctity of the soul but they are transcendent precisely because the soul is divine in nature, oriented to what is not itself and not of this already constituted world. *Reason of Church Government* therefore argues that church discipline is 'beyond the faculty of man to frame' and should not be 'left to man's invention' (CPW 1.756). Though transcendent, the rules for church government should not be seen as alien. The foundation of law is the will of God, which reveals itself in the human soul:

the soule of man . . . is his rationall temple and by the divine square and compasse thereof [it can] forme and regenerate in us the lovely shapes of vertues and graces. (CPW 1.757–8)

The church in its true foundations is grounded upon the act of inward reflection, is centred upon the soul, and in itself is a projection of the 'greater man' whose soul and virtue is a model for individual existence. The church, ideally, is not a disciplining *force* but an exemplar of that internalized discipline which is the individual's true nature, and which reveals itself in 'lovely shapes' or 'glorious lineaments and proportions'. There is a direct relation between politics and aesthetics; the true order of the world expresses itself in well-bounded form, where each living part depends upon and sustains the whole.

If law is merely 'politicall', according to Milton in *Reason of Church Government*, 'than no Christian is oblig'd in Conscience' (CPW 1.764). If the origins of law are worldly no citizen can be inwardly impelled. In a world of positive law reasons for obedience could only reside in expediency and prudence; law would therefore be non-universal and contingent. However, Milton identifies another possibility whereby law would be 'morall'. In this sense the law would be 'substantially and perpetually true and good' (CPW 1.764). There are two means of attaining 'morall' law. The first is by 'what we fetch from those unwritten lawes and Ideas which nature hath ingraven in us', and the second is through gospel law (CPW 1.764). Milton thereby identifies innate human law, the law 'ingraven in us' with divine (or gospel) law and sets this law over and against a tradition which 'copies out' from 'borrow'd manuscript' (CPW 1.764). This extends the opposition between evil as corruption and goodness as proper vital life to an opposition between a merely copied and borrowed manuscript and an original engraving. What is 'ingraven' within human hearts has the same status as the moral law of the gospels, as that which is divinely ordained. The aspect of human nature which is eternally and substantially true is divinity, the divine law harboured within. The soul is other-worldly and therefore provides 'morall' law. The writing of true law is therefore a transcription of the soul's proper order, an order which is itself engraved by a power not the soul's own. In this series of copies, engravings and manuscripts, the relation between writing and origin is one of *extension*, allowing the original word to further its reach and power without any breach or noise. What must not occur is a writing that operates without that relation to informing spirit. The notion of proper reading, or tying signs back to their animating and divine spirit, is essential for Milton's politics and poetics, with evil constantly figured throughout his work as that which has become detached from harmonious and ordering relations to become mere noise or formless matter. Human law, which is 'politicall', relies upon constructed hierarchies within the world and not the natural law of the soul's subordination to God. 'Politicall law' not only lacks the validity of 'morall law' but contradicts the doctrine of Christian individualism. Political law comes into conflict with individual moral law because it is corporeal; its justification relies on outward force rather than inward assent, on arbitrary worldly hierarchies of power: 'For the ministration of the law consisting of carnall things, drew to it such a ministery as consisted of carnall respects, dignity, precedence, and the like' (CPW 1.766).

A worldly hierarchy of power based on 'dignity and precedence' leads, according to Milton, to a 'pomp and glory of the flesh' (CPW 1.766). Milton acknowledges and approves of only one hierarchy – the subordination of the worldly to the inner sanctity of the soul, and (in turn) the soul's natural subordination to its Creator. Hierarchy in the world, by contrast, is a condition for the loss of spiritual autonomy and depends upon the forgetting of the true hierarchy which would subordinate human to divine value. If there has been a tradition of vitalism in literary theory – urging us not to forget that the signs of language are *signs* and refer back to some sense or reference, urging us to read the very life from which sense emerges[85] – such an insistence on the primacy of spirit over matter is also the driving force of Milton's politics. Whereas the early church allowed radical spiritual individualism and equality in the eyes of God to exist alongside worldly hierarchy, Milton demands that worldly practice be governed by the doctrines of the soul, because inward freedom is corrupted by an attention to mundane honour. For Milton, the simple parallelism of early Christianity is inadequate precisely because a resignation of the self to worldly and irrational hierarchy can only lead the self away from its proper spiritual condition. Political reform is therefore both necessary for, and enabled by, the renovation of the spirit:

if the forme of the Ministry be grounded in the worldly degrees of autority, honour, temporall jurisdiction, we see it with our eyes it will turne the inward power and purity of the Gospel into the outward carnality of the law; evaporating and exhaling the internall worship into empty conformities and gay shewes. (CPW 1.766)

Milton's critique of the effect of worldly power on inner experience underlies his distinction between jurisdiction and ministry, a distinction which in turn privileges the living body over the institution. Jurisdiction deals with *imposition* and with the negative aspect of law in the form of restraint and punishment. (This is the role of magistrates.) Ministry, on the other hand, deals with 'censure', the promulgation of virtues for their own sake and the constitution of the good in individual discipline. Ministry entails sustaining 'the person of Christ' (CPW 1.767) in the role of preaching. Prelacy, on the other hand, introduces the worldly 'politicall' role of jurisdiction (such as ecclesiastical courts) into church government. What first appears as an event of religious empowerment – episcopacy's appropriation of juridical practices – ultimately results in a contamination of the spiritual sphere with external constraint. The prelate who governs but does not preach, has put the temporal before the spiritual. Again, the same problem presents itself. The world is valueless without the influx and influence of divine spirit, but as spirit makes its way in the world it is increasingly drawn down to the level of mere body; the prelate should work against this tendency by concentrating on the more noble office of preaching:

why should the performance of ordination which is a lower office exalt a Prelat, and not the seldome discharge of a higher and more noble office which is preaching & administring much rather depress him? (CPW 1.767)

Milton accepts the role of jurisdiction in the political sphere but wishes to subordinate this exercise of outward law to spiritual truth. The original teachings of the gospels claimed an equality of souls before God but did not allow that equality to ordain political equality. By contrast, equality for Milton also applies to the temporal sphere; worldly inequality cannot be irrelevant because of the soul's temporal nature. The soul's becoming-rational and its journey towards God are enabled by an exercise of justice which recognizes the true and the right. The soul must perceive the true principles of life and being, and so must act in this world in accord with the eternal forms of divine life – forms which this world can bring into being. Milton presents the problem of the detachment of the temporal world from the divine in terms of form; this world can either reflect the divine relations of a life in which each being is holy *or* it can take the form of a hierarchy, where one body determines and orders other bodies. It is in this sense that Milton not only argues that goodness has a form and shape, but that such a shape can be understood through a quite specific geometrical figure. Against the pyramid, which would subordinate bodies through a mere increase in power, Milton argues for the more just 'forme' of the globe or cube, where each point in the whole is related to the centre:

So that Prelaty if she will seek to close up divisions in the Church, must be forc't to dissolve, and unmake her own pyramidal figure, which she affirms to be of such uniting power, when as indeed it is the most dividing, and schismaticall forme that Geometricians know of, and must be faine to inglobe, or incube her selfe among Presbyters. (CPW 1.790)

Significantly, it is that image of the globe which will dominate *Paradise Lost*, with its imagery of bounded spheres, the pendant world, balance and circumference (in comparison with the 'depth immeasurable of hell'): the world is 'the firm opacous Globe ... enclos'd From Chaos' (3.418–21). As Satan journeys towards heaven, the narrator admits that heaven is neither square nor round but is nevertheless a 'circuit', and it is from that ordered heavenly circuit that the geometry of the world emanates. The circuit is therefore a *form itself* that is not yet determined as this or that specific shape; it is the potentiality for shape in general: 'Farr off the Empyreal heav'n, extended wide / In circuit, undertermined square or round ... And fast by hanging a golden Chain / This pendant world' (2.1047–52). In *Reason of Church Government* Milton argues that 'our happinesse may orbe itself into a thousand vagancies of glory and delight, and with a kind of eccentricall equation be as it were an invariable Planet of joy and felicity' (CPW 1.752). Even though the cube has less resonance in the poetry, the idea of a proper geometry that is aligned with a natural and divine law is also given in Milton's depiction of the creation, which is the bounding and delimiting of matter. The *potential* for that order of creation (the compass) is eternal and therefore pre-exists the enacting of order and time:

> He took the golden Compasses, prepared
> In God's Eternal store, to circumscribe
> This Universe, and all created things:
> One foot he centr'd, and the other turn'd
> Round through the vast profunditie obscure,
> And said, Thus farr extend, thus farr thy bounds,
> This be thy just Circumference, O World. (7.225–31)

William Blake's image of Newton the geometer mapping the order of the world is well known (used on the cover of popular science text books, and as a statue in the forecourt of the new British Library in London). Blake's association of such geometrical order with tyranny is made clear in *The Four Zoas*, but this is because Blake, too, will associate imposed and external order with a certain lifelessness. Milton regards eternal geometry as the very soul and reason of the world, while Blake will regard such systems as a consequence of our forgetting that orders are a consequence of the originally 'enlarged and numerous senses' of the first animating poets. Blake's description of Urizen's great building adopts the discourse of geometry which atomizes the world into a uniform aggregate of discrete entities: 'Quadrangular the building rose the heavens squared by a line. / Trigon & cubes divide the elements in finite bonds'.[86] Blake then describes the order of Urizen's universe, again using the discourse of geometry; not only Urizen's building but the movements of his sons and daughters have become enslaved to 'mathematic motion wondrous':

> Others triangular right angled course maintain. others obtuse
> Acute Scalene, in simple paths. but others move
> In intricate ways biquadrate. Trapeziums Rhombs Rhomboids
> Parallelograms. triple & quadruple. polygonic
> In their amazing vast subdued course in the vast deep.[87]

Blake's poetry and engravings constantly present the lure and seduction of images of fixed order; the fall into system, law and limitation is not a simple accident but a tendency – a consequence of the wondrous and 'amazing' power of those forms to 'subdue'. Well before Blake lamented the fall into systems and fixed relations, Milton had also warned against mistaking the actual forms of the world for the true potential for form – the divine compass, or the circuit which is neither square nor round. It might appear that Milton's invocations to liberty, spirit and the capacity of each individual to find truth for themselves would also tend towards a recognition that systems belie the world's complexity, but this is not the case. Milton rejected the radical puritans of his day who appealed to the divinity of the body and the individual spirit; the body is divine only as expressive of the incorporeal light and forming power of which it is one particular emanation.[88] There is a just and true order of the world, a divine geometry, which should dictate both the form of government – as an inclusive globe – and the way in which order is known.

Just as government must be subordinated to spiritual ends so Milton hierarchizes knowledge. The 'contemplation of naturall causes and dimensions' is a lower wisdom compared to the knowledge of God. Christian discipline is grounded in the higher aim. Milton refers to 'the only high and valuable wisdom' as knowledge of God which entails 'the improvement of these his entrusted gifts' which are 'summes of knowledge and illumination' (CPW 1.801), again stressing that self-cultivation is an expression of, and homage to, holiness.

The light that illuminates the world and gives it order, the light that is God, is also the light that allows for human knowledge. Evil is the absence of light or 'darkness visible'. It is when we do not recognize the *emanating* nature of light that we fall into error.[89] In 'L'Allegro' the dazzling light of day allows all things to be seen clearly, with no sense of the hidden; the poem's dominant use of the connective 'and' presents the world in a connective series, and the repetition of 'while' reinforces the sense of everything being simultaneous and laid out for view or consumption. Darkness is presented as easily dispersed and as capable of being scattered or drowned out simply through the attention to physical objects: 'While the Cock with lively din, / Scatters the rear of darknes thin.' 'L'Allegro' presents a mode of perception in which the world is fully and completely present, self-sufficient and dazzlingly multiple – with no sense that all the presented differences are differences of some prior or hidden power:

> Wher the great Sun begins his state,
> Rob'd in flames, and Amber light,
> The clouds in thousand Liveries dight,
> While the Plowman neer at hand,
> Whistles ore the Furrow'd Land,
> And the Milkmaid singeth blithe,
> And the Mower whets his sithe,
> And every Shepherd tells his tale
> Under the Hawthorn in the dale.
> Streit mine eye hath caught new pleasures
> Whilst the Lantskip round it measures,
> Russet Lawns, and Fallows Gray,
> Where the nibling flocks do stray,
> Mountains on whose barren brest
> The labouring clouds do often rest:
> Meadows trim with Daisies pide,
> Shallow Brooks, and Rivers wide. ('L'Allegro' 60–76)

In 'Il Penseroso' it is the shielded light emanating from a God too bright to be seen without mediation that leads to wisdom. It is in not seeing immediately, in not being fully informed by our bodily, commanding and desiring vision, that we are compelled to take the weaker spiritual view which would recognize worldly vision as analogous to, or reflective of, a higher truth. Where 'L'Allegro' is dominated by 'and' and 'while' or a conjunctive logic, 'Il Penseroso' uses 'or', as though images will be alternative but inadequate ways of expressing a preceding truth:

> Hail divinest Melancholy,
> Whose Saintly visage is too bright
> To hit the Sense of human sight;
> And therfore to our weaker view,
> Ore laid with black staid Wisdoms hue.
> Black, but such as in esteem,
> Prince *Memnons* sister might beseem,
> *Or* that Starr'd *Ethiope* Queen that strove
> To set her beauties praise above
> The Sea Nymphs, and their powers offended.
> Yet thou art higher far descended,
> Thee bright-hair'd *Vesta* long of yore,
> To solitary *Saturn* bore. ('Il Penseroso' 12–24)

Milton unites his discussion of Christian wisdom and light with the political issue of prelacy by claiming that the worldly power of the prelates has been achieved by directing attention away from inner truth through the allure of 'the fals glitter of deceitfull wares'. Originary light requires a dimming or contemplative mediation to lead to truth; a physical light that is perceived by humans as bright unto itself allows the soul to remain within itself, forgoing its journey towards the source of emanating light. Milton's light imagery, like his image of the flourishing body, sets a dependent and proper dualism against a fall into immediacy. The light of day and lure of this world is valuable only as an expression of divine non-physical light; the bodies we inhabit are worthy only in so far as they express true virtue grounded in reason. It is when we fall away from the originary light that mediates this world, and the true form which ensouls the body, that we become subjected to worldly mediation and hierarchy. If we lose light and spirit then the only way we can reach law and truth is through bodily and worldly means. We lose the proper relation to the divine, and are drawn to the mediate signs of the divine.

The prelates' ecclesiastical mismanagement has as its basis a forgetting of the divine origin of value: 'it consists in a bold presumption of ordering the worship and service of God after man's own will in tradition and ceremonies' (CPW 1.826). The 'traditions and ceremonies' which have obscured the primordial truth are merely human; the 'pure simplicity of saving truth' is lost due to a false immediacy. We have taken the signs and emanations of truth for truth itself. Truth is now mediated by the worldly institution of the church and its tradition, but we do not recognize that mediation *as a mediation*, for we remain at the level of the body of the law, not its generating spirit:

> mistrusting to find the autority of their order in the immediat institution of Christ, or his Apostles by the cleer evidence of Scripture, they fly to the carnal supportment of tradition. (CPW 1.827)

There is a confusion in church government between true and false hierarchies – a confusion between the ontological hierarchy of the spiritual and temporal and the political hierarchy of episcopacy. The ontological relation between spirit and body is one of realization – the body becoming what it properly is in its orientation towards soul, while the political hierarchy is a form of usurpation, with one body taking command of another through force rather than reason. This confusion of modes of hierarchy stems from a failure to acknowledge the finite nature of human experience in its relation to the divine: 'instead of shewing the reason of their lowly condition from divine example and command, they seek to prove their high pre-eminence from humane consent and autority' (CPW 1.827).

It is important therefore to distinguish between two structures of reason and individuality. A modern, Cartesian and (for Milton) Satanic mode of selfhood establishes the world's law and relations from itself. For Descartes the world is extended substance available for representation by a distinct viewing subject; relations among bodies, on this picture, are themselves purely material or mechanical. Because the subject is a separate substance defined by 'thinking', the world itself is devoid of thought, and therefore receives sense and representation only through the mental activity of the subject. It is not surprising, therefore, that from its very beginning 'Cartesian individualism', or the detachment of the self from animating life, was associated with all the evils of modernity, of a subject or life no longer possessing norms or meaning.[90] Of course the Cartesian subject can be saved theologically by endowing reasoning substance with its own internal postulates of good thinking and common sense,[91] but it is telling that the extreme possibilities of Cartesianism from Milton to the present have been figured as evil:[92] for the subject who is nothing other than himself, who is pure will, is beyond good and evil. For Milton's Satan the 'will' or selfhood is set over and against the world; it then follows that any opposition, otherness or resistance to the individual's will appears as force. It is against that form of atomized or self-sufficient modern individualism that Milton sets his emphasis on the soul, inwardness and right reason. Milton does not wish to devalue the divine potential of human being. It is, rather, a sense of *worldly* individualist autonomy which he sees as the cause of error. It is essential that the possibility for the attainment of truth be awakened within each individual. However, the self-reflection which leads to truth should reveal the dependence and finitude of the individual alongside the self's divinity. The knowledge of that which is most divine in human being relies upon distinguishing that which is merely mundane and secondary – the body, positive law, sophistry and temporality – from what is divine:

> ye think ye by these gaudy glisterings to strive up the devotion of the rude multitude; ye think so, because ye forsake the heavenly teaching of *S. Paul* for the hellish Sophistry of Papism. (CPW 1.828)

Milton's denigration of the 'hellish Sophistry' which appeals to the 'rude multitude' reinforces his extra-mundane individualism. When the self is part of a worldly multitude it is led into error; truth is achieved when the self turns away from the world to its personal relationship with God. Only then can the self become a true citizen, for then disputes among persons will be debates among those who recognize themselves as finite. Just as individuals are led astray by falling into corporeality, so it is when the church as

> a decay'd nature seeks to the outward fomentations and chafings of worldly help, and external flourishes, to fetch, if it be possible, some motion on her extream parts, or to hatch a counterfeit life with the crafty and artificial heat of jurisdiction. (CPW 1.833)

By referring to 'artifical heat' Milton raises the question of how one might distinguish between good and evil modes of force or energy, for Milton's vitalist metaphors will continually contrast a living and active body (as good) with a wasting, corrupted and rotting body (as evil); and while he will also use apocalyptic imagery of rising up to burn away the fleshly veils that distance us from truth, he will warn against a force or heat that is a 'counterfeit life' or 'artificial heat'. One must not only distinguish between the life of spirit that informs the body, and mere bodies detached from spirit, but also those bodies that appear animated or endowed with life. Perhaps this is why Milton's most vital and forceful figure will be Satan, whose body will be the testing ground for proper reading. Far from presenting evil as absolute corruption, Satan will be a constant deflection and simulation of true life, testifying both to goodness's insistent power and to the potentiality for goodness's appearance to separate itself from its proper substance. In the passage above, Milton regards jurisdiction as just such a detached force, for the church that thinks to give itself life and reformation by using worldly law will only further its self-alienation.

Milton's rejection of jurisdiction as an ecclesiastical function restricts worldly or bodily discipline to the realm of the state, with the church devoted to 'the mighty operation of the spirit'. In some ways we can see Milton as a proto-critic of modernity's managerial encroachment on the soul. If selves are regarded as so much substance to be organized in relation to each other, then the world is led inevitably into 'biopolitics' or – in contrast to man as a political being who also has a bodily life – a sense that political and social being proceeds directly from bodily nature or forces.[93] Whereas Michel Foucault will later contest biopolitics by referring to the self not as a substance to be managed but as a potentiality for experimentation,[94] Milton will look back more nostalgically to a prelapsarian subject capable of recognizing its spiritual potential in divine transcendence, a self that cannot be reduced to the body manipulated by pragmatic and positive law. Milton stresses the independence of the church, for the worldly activity of the state can only contaminate the ideals of the gospels. The state as it stands at the moment must not bring inward experience into its service: 'the Magistrat hath only to deal with the outward part, I mean not only the body alone, but of the mind in all her outward acts' (CPW 1.835). However, Milton later argues for a more revolutionary position; the spirit that has been left to think freely by a church liberated from politics, will be able to discover a more just form of politics. *The Tenure of Kings and Magistrates* argues that the inward demand for justice, which rightly grounds church government, should also apply to the temporal sphere for 'Justice is the onely true sovran and supreme Majesty upon earth' (CPW 3.237). In the earlier *Reason of Church Government* Milton stresses the importance of civil peace and sound government as 'undoubtedly the first means to a natural man' who might then 'open his eyes to a higher consideration' (CPW 1.836). Justice in this world creates an environment conducive to 'higher considerations'. Milton's earlier rejection of any interplay between church and state practices, in *Reason of Church Government*, follows from his vision of the political sphere as based on temporal, external and contingent values. But even temporal government must be such that it allows the free working of the spirit in the church. The church does not embrace secular institutions for its purposes; it merely requests that these relative institutions do not interfere with its progress and do not provide conditions which preclude its development.

What the very form and figures of Milton's political theory indicate is that oppositions between good and evil, the divine and the temporal, spirit and body, and inner law and outer jurisdiction all follow from the very nature of God. If 'Justice is the onely true sovran and supreme Majesty upon earth', this suggests that God's being in this world takes the form of a balanced ethical order, for it is certainly not the case that we labour under conditions of unreason while awaiting redemption in a world beyond. If Milton's poetics and politics is one of waiting, the delay is historical − a faith and hope for worldly justice that will evidence our spiritual growth and our nature as expressive of divine reason. It is that original commitment to the one God who is expressive light and life which allows for quite specific arguments and subordinations. God must not be seen as a judge set over and against life; God is 'now no more a judge after the sentence of the Law, nor as it were a schoolmaister of perishable rites' (CPW 1.837). Milton derives the nature of true church government from God's benign paternalism and the emanating light: 'in the sweetest and mildest manner of paternal discipline he hath committed this other office of preserving in healthful constitution the inner man, which may be term'd the spirit of the soul to his spiritual deputy the minister of each Congregation' (CPW 1.837).

The image of God as father, and as form-giving inseminator of divine light, is central to the very mode of Western metaphysics, where the logic of the world is neither external nor arbitrary; the world possesses an intrinsic logic or living normativity which it is the task of human beings to disclose. God expresses himself in a worldly creation whose being is not separate and disjunctive, but continuous and expansive. Not surprisingly, images of gender and self-fathering are not accidental distortions of a theory that might otherwise be sexually neutral. We cannot, I would argue, see gendered images and biases in writings such as Milton's as peculiar accretions of an otherwise neutral theory;[95] without the distinction between a spiritual, form-giving, actualizing and inseminating force, and a dependent, potential, material receptivity, we could not have a distinction between what the body properly is or strives to realize, and what bodies actually are in their contingent relations. It is only the image of man, as a body whose personal being is also the natural law of the world, that can provide the correct starting point for political theory.[96] For Milton, as for rationalist vitalism in general, life is not a realm of chaotic, divergent and contingently related forces. Relations flow from a proper, and self-organizing life, and that life is properly recognized by man as a political animal who in turn recognizes his own body as the vehicle for spirit.

It is for this reason that law should not be seen as the imposition of relations on chaotic matter. Positive law would not be necessary if each individual attended to their own self, where they would find the very law of life 'ingraven' in their hearts. Jurisdiction in general would be supererogatory if humans bore an 'inward reverence for their own persons'. Such 'inward reverence' would not be an attention to *personal* selfhood but would lead away from self-interest to love of God − precisely because of the divine nature of the soul: 'And if the love of God as a fire sent from Heaven to be ever kept alive upon the altar of our hearts, be the first principle of all godly and vertuous actions in men, this pious and just honouring of our selves is the second' (CPW 1.841).

One needs, therefore, to create a polity conducive to this appropriate inward reverence, where the self is not a law unto itself detached from all others, but recognizes itself as a member of humanity and life in general. It is through political activity and relations that the self becomes what it ought to be, realizing its proper potential, so that the soul will attain 'the true likenesse and visage of what she is indeed' (CPW 1.844). The use of the feminine pronoun to refer to the soul, like Milton's reference to 'vertue' and the 'forme' of the self as also feminine, testifies to the essentially masculine nature of the subject. For those qualities through which the self becomes – virtue, form, visage – are media through which spirit returns to itself. Masculinity is not any one of these qualities, but the ground or *subject* through which these features are expressed.[97] The self, therefore, achieves its essence by rejecting tradition, external government, corporeal desires and positive law. It attains its likeness by a vigorous participation in the activity of reason through taking part in a church founded on spirit. This is why, according to *Reason of Church Government*, 'the functions of the Church government ought to be free and open to any Christian man' (CPW 1.844). Intervention and participation in church government is not so much a duty as a necessary condition for spiritual edification, because the church should be composed of individuals and not be an institution for the distribution of sacraments.

The radical distinction of the primitive Christian church between this world and God's kingdom is replaced by Milton with an application of divine law to this world. The established church's tradition of relative natural law, which had justified the involvement of the church with temporal issues by referring to the fallen nature of this world, is also at odds with Milton's insistence that this world and humanity are imbued with God's being – both 'endu'd / With Sanctitie of Reason' (PL 7.507–8) and suffused with grace (PL 11.23). The transcendence-in-immanence of the human soul should not therefore accommodate itself to mundanity; rather, the temporal sphere – the world of government, religion, marriage and literature – should aspire to the spiritual. Although Milton's doctrine of accommodation in *Christian Doctrine* insists that we distinguish between the literal and figural, the problem of an anthropomorphic presentation of God is solved by his insistence that a 'human' God would be no less divine:

> if God attributes to himself again and again a human shape and form, why should we be afraid of assigning to him something he assigns to himself. (CPW 6.135–6)

The similar suggestion in *Paradise Lost* that the 'Earth / Be but the shaddow of Heav'n' (PL 5.574–5) does not contradict Milton's valorization of spiritual over temporal being; it maintains the possibility that the earth may be a realm of divine rather than merely mundane value so that the prelapsarian earth which 'Seemd like to Heav'n, a seat where Gods might dwell' (PL 7.329) may be regained when 'God shall be All in All' (PL 3.340). Milton's Christian humanism is connected with this belief in the achievable divinity of the world. Just as the fall is a consequence of forsaking their 'Makers Image' (PL 11.515) so redemption lies in an adherence to the 'Divine similitude' (PL 11.512) which is retained after the fall.

2

Capital Time, Production and Generation

It is not by having flesh, which the devil does not have, but by living according to his own self, that is according to man, that man has become like the devil. For the devil too chose to live according to his own self when he did not adhere to the truth, and thus the falsehood that he told had its source not in God but in himself.[98]

Throughout *Paradise Lost,* in contrast with the continual recollection of their divine origin by Adam and Eve, Satan declares his self-origination, along with his absolutely self-sufficient being. Despite Satan's subsequent claims that it is God's priority which causes his subjection ('The Gods are first, and that advantage use / On our belief' [PL 9.718]), prior to the war in heaven he alleges total self-creation:

> . . . who saw
> When this creation was? remember thou
> Thy making, while the Maker gave thee being?
> We know no time when we were not as now;
> Know none before us, self-begot, self-rais'd
> By our own quick'ning power, . . .
> Our puissance is our own, our own right hand
> Shall teach us highet deeds, by proof to try
> Who is our equal. (PL 5.856–66)

Satan's discourse here exploits the epistemology of an extreme modern rationalism – a rationalism that has in the twentieth century been associated with modernity's loss of life, its fall into technology and systems, the disenchantment of the world, and the detachment of human existence from a world once considered meaningful and possessed of aura.[99] If something is not known, its existence is open to doubt; only what is apodictically present to the self is certain and foundational.[100] Adam in Eden receives revealed knowledge and accepts Raphael's word because of the limits of his knowledge: 'for who himself beginning knew?' (PL 8.251). Satan, on the other hand, transposes his epistemological finitude into his ontology. If his creation by God cannot be known, seen or remembered (because it is transcendent to experience) he will reject God's creation: 'The mind is its own place, and in itself / Can make a Heav'n of Hell, a Hell of Heav'n' (PL 1.254–5). Hell is, accordingly, just this predicament of self-enthralment: it is precisely because Satan reduces all life and being to states and determinations of the self, with no transcendent reference, that he suffers from self-enclosure. The belief in the absolute power of the self *is* hell, for that belief is a refusal and a negation of the life and power beyond the self that would grant life meaning and orientation. It is Satan, whose 'puissance' is his own, and who will bring to the fore Milton's imagery of evil as self-involution; for once power is considered to be the power of selves opposed to other selves, and not power as potentiality from which selves draw, the self becomes nothing more than its negation of other powers. The triumph of a will that knows nothing other than itself in Book One becomes the reactive self enslaved to negation of Book Four:

> And like a devillish Engin back recoiles
> Upon himself; horror and doubt distract
> His troubl'd thoughts, and from the bottom stirr
> The Hell within him, for within him Hell
> He brings, and round about him, nor from Hell
> One step no more than from himself can fly
> By change of place: Now conscience wakes despair
> That slumberd, wakes the bitter memorie
> Of what he was, what is and what must be
> Worse; of worse deeds worse sufferings must ensue.
> (PL 4.17–26)[101]

Here, in Satan's hell of absolute self-determination and self-reference, we can glimpse the nightmare vision of Cartesian modernity that is also an intensification of the traditional image of evil as a loss of divine time and order. Satan's self-sufficiency is, as Milton makes clear, a struggle against his better nature; his quantification of all force, and his reduction of power to differences of degree in relation to himself, is constantly thwarted by the return of conscience. It is after a troubling return of conscience in Book Four that Satan acknowledges that his mind is not only an inner hell amidst a spatial hell but an increasingly greater and 'lower deep':

> Which way I flie is Hell; my self am Hell;
> And in the lowest deep a lower deep
> Still threatning to devour me opens wide,
> To which the Hell I suffer seems a Heav'n.
> (PL 4.75–8)

That use of 'devour' here not only adds to the images of Sin and Death as concerned with self-consumption but reinforces Milton's more general vitalist poetics which will contrast the nourishment of relations that are directed beyond the self to the evils of redounding self-relation. Eating is a profoundly important figure in the axiology of good and evil.[102] If the good self must be neither rigidly enclosed nor chaotically formless, then it must have some measured and proper relation to the world: that relation can take the form of consumption, in which that which is ingested becomes food for thought. Alternatively, what is devoured can corrupt and even consume the self; relations with what is outside the self would not be genuinely other but involuting rather than evolving. The self does not expand and flourish by relating to what is not itself; instead, all that is outside the self is determined in advance through the self's own measure. Self-relation is viciously circular rather than expansive.[103] It is because Satan's rhetoric and comportment are dominated by force or relations of quantitative power that his relation to his own self does not proceed by way of an image of a virtue or excellence within himself that he ought to realize. Conscience returns in *Paradise Lost* just at those moments when Satan aims to be absolutely self-determined. When he manages to free himself from all transcendent reference and relation he falls back into a mode of self-devouring. It is significant that at this point Satan's economic or quantitative conception of God's power is rhetorically tortuous. Although he still uses an economic metaphor, Satan sees that his error lay in interpreting obedience to God in terms of quantitative difference – thinking that,

> ... one step higher
> Would set me highest, and in a moment quit
> The debt immense of endless gratitude,
> So burthensome still paying, still to ow;
> Forgetful what from him I still receivd,
> And understood not that a grateful mind
> By owing owes not, but still pays, at once
> Indebted and discharged; what burden then?
> (PL 4.50–7)

Satan, at this moment of reawakened conscience, acknowledges that God's position as creator places him qualitatively higher and that his continual sovereignty is due to the fact that creatures owe their existence to their maker. However, Satan's irreparably self-devolving character induces him to see this as a 'burden' and 'debt immense', even though he goes on to assert that it is *not* a burden and that such owing 'owes not'. Satan's rhetoric is here straining at its limits. He is still using quantitative metaphors to express essentially qualitative distinctions. His rebellion was prompted by an economic conception of value – by seeing the presence of the Son as doubling the honour he would have to pay to God: 'Knee-tribute yet unpaid, prostration vile, / Too much to one, but double how endur'd' (PL 5.782–3). Consequently, when Satan considers repentance he knows he would be unable to sustain reconciliation. He calculates such a return to obedience as of little worth, again in economic metaphors: 'so should I purchase deare / Short intermission bought with double smart' (PL 4.101–2). When Satan returns to hell after tempting Adam and Eve he proclaims that the rebellion has in the end proved a worthwhile bargain: 'A World who would not purchase with a bruise' (PL 10.500). Raphael has already cautioned against such a concept of exchange value. Adam should not see Eve's 'shows' as exchangeable with 'realities' (PL 8.575); there should be a hierarchical relationship of recognizing difference, where value and profit are based on just and right and not on free exchange:

> ... weigh with her thy self;
> Then value: Oft times nothing profits more
> Then self-esteem, grounded on just and right
> Well manag'd; ... (PL 8.570–3)

So much of *Paradise Lost* will depend upon contrasting two notions of economy: one in which relations are determined by nothing more than competing forces (Satan's notion of God as one whom 'thunder hath made greater') and an economy of true weight, in which something bears its own value and proper relation. The problem, of course, is that the proper economy of weight is still an economy, even though the value of each term is derived not from relations among elements but from a transcendent source. God may not be reducible to Satanic notions of force, power and thunder, but the task of *Paradise Lost*, and Milton's politics in general, will be to argue that although divinity cannot be reduced to worldly life and efficacy, it is nevertheless the point from which all value and system emerges. Raphael here endorses a conception of value in which each being can be weighed and its value decided, because the scales of justice are extra-worldly. Here, self-esteem is contrasted with Satan's self-reference, precisely because the weighing of the self is grounded on just and right; the self possesses a reference to measure not its own (conscience or God's installed light). Divinity is, therefore, both the soul's true essence, but also something *other*. The soul refers outside itself (to God) to become what it truly is: 'For God wisheth to make thee a God; not by nature as He is son in Whom He hath begotten; but by His Gift and Adoption.'[104]

The image of justice and order as balance, also employed in the war in heaven, is not one in which the scales may tip either way, for each being has its measure in relation to the God who sets the scale of justice. A purely economic conception accounts for value only through a system of relations. All entities are exchangeable and hence no one being (virtue or good) has any *a priori* merit over any other. The modern doctrine of economy rejects the limits and inherent qualities of particular beings, and thereby entails a loss of centre, value, being and life. In an economic conception no being has a proper trajectory which it must fulfil, it simply goes through time. Time itself has a history; with time once being considered as the time through which each being arrives at its proper form (with forms themselves not being subject to change). In modernity time is no longer the duration of each being (nor is space the proper locale for each essence); time becomes the measure of movement, with movement being determined mechanically as the interaction of forces.[105] It is therefore possible to contrast two conceptions of value – the economic conception of warring forces in relation and the intrinsic conception where beings are situated in relations according to their nature – with two conceptions of time. Once the world becomes extended matter devoid of proper potentiality, then time is no longer the time required for a being to journey towards its proper potential. Instead, time is merely the sequence in which we map movements across a uniform space. The self is no longer essentially within time, requiring time in order to arrive at what it ought to be; instead, as Immanuel Kant will make explicit, time is the form through which the subject knows and represents the world.[106] The world, in itself, is no longer temporal. The pure subject of modernity, in knowing only itself, becomes a ghost in a machine; all external life is then rendered contingent and devoid of sense, for time is lived only from the self, as a mere sequence of 'nows'. Well before Enlightenment science had internalized time as a form imposed by the subject, or rendered time into a 'container' within which change as movement takes place, Milton had presented Satanic and fallen time as devoid of qualitative becoming. Satan is always already fully actual. His being is completely self-present and given; there is no transcendence towards which his spirit is directed, no past origin which grants him a sense of proper form and genesis, and no inner potentiality which requires a journey of time to come to fulfilment. By contrast, for Milton, redeemed and divine time retains the past into the present, and anticipates the future from the now. One can only be a defined and essential self through meaningful time.

Well before Michael escorts Adam through the drama of human history in the final books of *Paradise Lost,* Milton presents the life of paradise as one of narrative time. Here, the present is lived with a sense of the origin, while the origin signals a potential that awaits fulfilment. Before the fall, Adam and Eve know each other through narration; Adam narrates his awakening and self-questioning to Eve, who in turn narrates her turn from narcissistic capture to sociality to Adam. It is their possession, and then shared relation, of a past that allows them to live and enjoy dialogue and requires them to work through their relations with each other. Although the labour and rest of the garden are given in the form of cyclic natural time, Milton presents a life of the mind in which learning and rational development are required even in paradise.

This is not only to mark that Milton regards education, discourse and reason as properly unfallen activities along with sexuality and gender differences; he also gives a specific image of paradisiacal time. This is a time of meaning. In order to have meaning – to be able to say that something *is* something – we must mark something identifiable that is repeatable through time. To say that something has a certain essence or identity is to determine it in some way, and it is for this reason – as twentieth-century philosophers have recognized – that there can be no private or purely punctual language.[107] As meaningful – seeing or living this present *as* this or that being – language must have the capacity of repeatability. Meaning requires a time in which the present is connected to the past and future. Concomitantly, time, as the ongoing and sustained life of experience, requires meaning or some identifiable order. Without this synthesis of time, without the maintenance of the past into the present and the anticipation of a future, we would be left with the chaos of disconnection and fragmentation. To *be* this or that essential and defined being requires time: one must actualize one's potential, arriving at the proper form that defines oneself. This is so not only for human beings who have the freedom either to live according to their reason or become 'imbruted' by falling back into their bodies; it is also the case for all living beings, for all life.

It is this fundamentally Aristotelian conception of life as inherently meaningful or directed to self-realization which entered into Christian philosophy with Aquinas, and which still informs Milton's ontology.[108] Just as Raphael defines the one matter of creation that expresses itself variously in degrees of substance,[109] so Milton will insist upon the duty of each individual to take his or her own free path towards achieving reason. Whereas all being is in a process of divine becoming, it is in the nature of human being to be able to decide upon its becoming, to choose rational freedom.[110] The understanding of reason as a state or purely procedural set of rules, or as a capacity that is simply given and fixed as a law, is a denial of the *life* of reason, in which the journey and attainment are intrinsic to the end attained. Milton's ontology of life therefore allows a direct transition from the being of the world to the art of reason, with a further transition to ethics. The world, as God's creation, is ordered and structured in such a way that each being can realize itself as an expression of divine life; this principle of divine and creative life can be intuited by man, who is a being empowered with the art of definitions or seeing the true being or principles that give each being its identity. That capacity for knowing or intuiting the life of things is also a recognition of the divinity that flows through the world and is, therefore, definitive of man's proper being. For while each being is defined according to its highest potential, man's good or highest potential is self-actualization as one of God's rational creatures. While the good is that which does not remain within itself but realizes its proper potential only in relation to what is not yet fully given – and we can think of love in paradise as just this free submission either to a being who is differently embodied or to one who is possessed of a more refined reason – evil remains within itself. Indeed, divine life is a life of meaning, while life falls into evil only with that loss of sense, relation and meaning.

Milton will therefore present chaos as the absence of number and time and as devoid of all synthesis, orientation and relation. At a more specific level, Milton not only presents paradise as a site of growth, progression and narration; he also presents human reason as a narrative power. Whereas the fallen angels try to reason by passing from a definition of their own being to what they ought to do (PL 2.147), Adam and Eve define themselves and their relations to each other through narration. It is in hearing each other's story of their own emergence that they establish their hierarchy of marriage. But lest this passage from narration to the present looks too much like a divine right of kings argument, where an originally bestowed power dictates the present, Milton also allows narration to open onto divergent futures. Eve and Adam discuss the possibility of a division of labour, both after Eve has narrated her dream of the fall – which may occur and allow reason to remain untainted – and after they have fallen and must decide how to live on. Bearing in mind that their first deliberation about how to proceed is prelapsarian, we need to see the ways in which collective decision making is not, as it was for the fallen angels, a question of passing logically from definitions to decisions, but a narrative and relational art in which disputants consider their created nature and entertain possible futures. Time is therefore essential to the life and being of reason, but it is also definitive of love and relations in paradise. According to Raphael, 'love refines / The thoughts, and heart enlarges, hath his seat / In Reason, and is judicious, is the scale / By which to heav'nly Love thou maist ascend' (PL 8.589–92).

It is time and deferral that also allows Milton to place sexuality and labour in paradise: because human beings live with a sense of their life as a whole they do not submit to present pleasures but order all bodily desires into a chosen life. The 'sweet reluctant amorous delay' (4.310) of paradise is both a remnant of the tradition of the Petrarchan love sonnet in which the desired body becomes more valued in its *not* being immediately given, while Milton also acknowledges that there is a time when the body and its pleasures can be fulfilled. This is when the other body is *read*. Shoshana Felman has astutely argued that all sexual relations are literary: ways in which we are submitted to another person's desire that we must read. This in turn allows us to think of all literary relations as in some sense sexual, for we have to read the text as 'wanting to say' (*vouloir dire*): not a thing to be consumed, but a body that bears a sense that is not yet present.[111] It is not surprising that Milton begins his poetic career with the significance of a desiring and ethical relation to signs, with poetry both tending towards apocalyptic revelation and also bearing in mind the distance and waiting in relation to the disclosure of sense. As in 'Lycidas', the Nativity Ode begins with an image of nature as directly reflecting and participating in divine sense:

> Nature in aw to him
> Had doff't her gawdy trim,
> With her great Master so to sympathize:
> It was no season then for her
> To wanton with the Sun her lusty Paramour. (4–8)

The poem then goes on to narrate a music emanating from angelic light that will suggest an overcoming of the difference between heaven and earth – 'Harping in loud and solemn quire, / With unexpressive notes to Heav'ns new-born Heir.' But just as this vision is entertained, the poetic voice warns that one must wait for such harmony: 'But wisest Fate sayes no, / This must not yet be so.' There cannot be a direct and willed passage from nature and signs of life to full and unmediated life. Milton presents his poetry as just such an art of reading and waiting (or reading poetry *as* waiting): 'But see the Virgin blest, / Hath laid her Babe to rest. / Time is our tedious Song should here have ending.' Nature is a sign of a divine life to come, but as signs or expressions of divinity one must relate to bodies not as they are in themselves but as expressions of a spirit not yet revealed.

Adam relates to Eve not as a property to be consumed or managed but as one who has her own life and reason, and it is through narration and relation that Eve becomes more than a mere body. Similarly, Eve's relation to Adam is not one of corporeal submission but one in which she recognizes that there is reason, even if the full presence of that reason cannot – because of her different nature – be given. Without the working and discoursing together that allows Adam and Eve to live their time meaningfully, so that the present carries over what they know of each other's past and looks towards a future that is not yet known or discovered, Adam and Eve would be mere bodies in relations of force, rather than dialogue and love.

After the fall this reciprocal relation of paradise is temporarily lost and Adam does see Eve as nothing more than a corrupting lure or object to be consumed. The time of delay, decision, discourse and seduction – the time in which selves recognize each other through relation – becomes a mechanical time in which elements follow each other without hesitation. The naked majesty of Adam and Eve which expresses lordly rule in Eden is replaced by a controlling and usurping body. The discourse of postlapsarian sex is permeated with compulsion: 'in Lust they burne', 'contagious Fire', 'Her hand he seis'd', 'sleep / Oppress'd them' (PL 9.1015–45). This sense of compulsion is coupled with the contamination of the faculty of reason and the intrusion of error: 'that fallacious Fruit, ... / About thir spirits had plaid, and inmost powers / Made erre' (PL 9.1046–9). But Milton also makes clear that it is not reason itself that has fallen; where the will had once followed understanding and reason, there is now a loss of reason's sovereignty:

> For Understanding rul'd not, and the Will
> Heard not her lore; both in subjection now
> To sensual Appetite, who from beneathe
> Usurping over sovran Reason claimed
> Superior sway. (PL 9.11271–31)

Whereas Adam and Eve's earlier discourse in paradise had been deliberative, after the fall they merely exchange accusations that have no shared or reflective end: 'Thus they in mutual accusation spent / The fruitless hours, but neither self-condemning; / And of their vain contest appeared no end.' We have moved from a narrative time of relation to a time in which accusations are exchanged without any sense of commonality; and all this because the will – the will Satan celebrated as inconquerable no longer directs itself to reason.[112] Without that rational orientation of the will Adam and Eve react to each other, rather than negotiating each other.

A more intense version of this compulsive time is given in the emergence, rather than creation, of Sin and Death. The first point that needs to be noted about this aspect of *Paradise Lost* is that Milton's use of this drama of origins and origination, in which creator and created are no longer placed in a temporal sequence of progression and emanation, is itself a use of literary and theological time. Much has been written and noted of Milton's subsumption of the mythic and literary tradition, and the ways in which the pagan tradition appears in *Paradise Lost* as a derivative and belated expression of the divine Christian truth.[113] The very form of the epic, in its mode of taking up literary materials, creates a new mode of time. Fragments from the past are not simply used but repeated in such a way as to reveal their deeper and eternal logic. In order to explain this, we can draw an analogy between Milton's radical Christianity and twentieth-century phenomenology: both movements were insistent that full reason and responsibility could be achieved not by simply repeating and maintaining the past, but by intuiting the original logic that the past could only dimly perceive. It is in this sense that vitalism, or the insistence that all signs and systems can be traced back to an animating, original and retrievable life, is fundamental to Western metaphysics.

Vital Signs

Jacques Derrida has argued that in this regard twentieth-century phenomenology is an intensification of the metaphysics of presence that has dominated the West. No element or being should simply be accepted or allowed to remain external and contingent, but must be rationalized, brought to presence and intuited as reason's own.[114] For Edmund Husserl this entailed a critique of any logic or system that operated in an unthinking or mechanical manner, such as the logician's or mathematician's technical skill and manipulation of symbols without a sense of the truth of which those symbols are a formalization. Against a time as a mere sequence in which signs are repeated mechanically, phenomenology requires that every given sign should, in principle, be intuited as an expression of a once-conscious presentation that could once again be renewed. Euclid's geometry should not simply be accepted as a workable system, for we should be able to see – in concrete and lived space – those very features that allowed Euclid to formalize relations that would be true for any subject whatever. For Husserl this reliving of the past in the present is a bringing back to life of all those elements that circulate in an automatic manner in current scientific thinking; it is a renewal of the present by a reliving of the past.[115] This method of phenomenological *Destruktion* is an overcoming of the present in its given, inert and irrational systematicity in favour of an intuition of the life from which present systems emerged. At the heart of such an ethic of time – that the sedimented logic of the present may always be retrieved – is an ethic of active creation: reason is not the dead weight of law that one must accept passively, but is a power to discern in the present and particular what would be true for all time. It is a commitment to the active creation of the universal.

It is perhaps this aspect of Milton's poetics that renders him at once modern – refusing to accept the mythic transcendence of systems – and avowedly anti-modern: lamenting the fall into evil days in which one no longer bears a relation to the divine. Milton does not simply want to accept reason and the law as given and imposed, but argues that each living spirit should be able to intuit the truth of law for himself, and can do so genealogically – recognizing that the present is the outcome of human acts and decisions. At the same time, while recognizing that truth and reason have a genealogy and can be derived or deduced by looking back from the present, Milton also maintains that truth and reason are eternal and not mere conventions adopted for the sake of social convenience or power. Milton's poetry and politics will continually emphasize a dynamic notion of temporal retrieval: all those contingent, received, lifeless and seemingly external laws that weigh upon life should either be internalized and recognized as reason's own or rejected as accidental corruptions of the one reasoning life of which we are all expressions. This is also why Milton appears to offer a proto-critique of capitalism at the same time as he endorses a realm of proper and orienting value.

On the one hand, any idea of a system of exchange and circulation that operates in its own right without reference to the creative logic from which that system emerged is the very image of evil: a system of relations with no end beyond itself, no form towards which it develops, and no reference to a value or measure that would ground and centre the system.[116] On the other hand, a life that expresses itself in different forms and that enters into relations in order to create ever more difference and production is the very essence of divine being. There is, underpinning the embrace and denunciation of capitalism, a distinction between two ways of conceiving systems: a divine world in which relations are subtended by the breath of life on the one hand, and a detached and fallen world in which elements circulate without fruition or expansion on the other. Such a distinction between good and evil systems follows directly from the theological definition of God's being. God could have chosen to remain within himself, without creation. However, having entered into creation God could not have produced a world that was fully actualized and devoid of qualitative becoming. For a world in which matter becomes ever more formed and ever more substantial – enters into change and relation in order to arrive at what it *ought to be* – is a world in which being recognizes divine life as a good that would be freely adopted and affirmed.[117] A mechanical system in which there is no potential for the realization of a good is a system devoid of the time of recognition, and without recognition God would not have been affirmed as that to which all life freely and joyfully progresses. Regina Schwartz has placed this time of recognition at the heart of her reading of *Paradise Lost*. Adam and Eve in prayer, and the angels in hymning chorus, are images of a worldly creation and expression that serves to recall original and divine genesis.[118] Life in this world does not simply go through time, for it is only with a complex time of remembering and repeating that a true development or growth towards the future can occur. Mechanical time is opposed to organic time, and the latter is not only expressed within Milton's epic; it also organizes its mode of composition.

Accordingly, when we look at the two borrowings that mark the episode of Sin and Death in *Paradise Lost* we can see that Milton does not simply use the pagan and literary past; he also gives a new temporal logic to the original sources in his rendering of both motifs. One borrowing that displays Milton's temporal logic clearly is his use of Athena springing from the head of Zeus (the second source, Spenser's, *Fairie Queene,* will be considered in the next two chapters). Originally the tale of Athena and Zeus is devoid of the strong moral binaries that inflect Milton's narration of Sin's emergence from Satan. Unlike the pagan original, Milton places this scene after a description of divine creation, so that we can distinguish between active, form-giving and actualizing creation on the one hand and contingent emergence on the other. A created being is matter that has been given form, essence and limit by a divine and immaterial God; the form or model precedes the coming into being of the created. A created being therefore bears its own temporality, and has the potential to move away from matter to become increasingly formed, ordered and bounded – more divine – or to remain as undeveloped potential and mere matter. Creation, in which a being is produced according to some pre-existing form or idea, is opposed to emergence, in which change yields a being by chance, without a prior governing essence. (We could also draw an analogy here with two ways of using one's literary past: either to read that past as an expression of the truth of divine creation, thus drawing the literary archive closer to its spiritual condition, or allowing that past to remain as it is, as a series of texts and fragments with no connection to a deeper truth. A *created* text must have been the act of some reasoning subject and therefore bears a potential spiritual life; to regard a text as having *emerged*, however, would be to render its being accidental and contingent.) Sin in *Paradise Lost* is just such an emergent rather than created being. Whereas creation requires an author who perceives a form that will govern matter – a form which is the created being's essence, and the ideal towards which it ought to live and become – an emergent property occurs through a chance encounter or relation and has no pre-existing or governing form or *telos*. Satan does not intend, actively create or even consciously experience Sin's emergence; he recalls her existence only after the fact. The production of Sin does not occur in a time in which the future is imagined or intended in accordance with the being of the present. Instead, Sin is the effect of a 'swerve', perturbation or deviation. Although this emergence is the beginning of theodicy, or the point from which all later deviations and evils will follow, it occurs not as a decision or act but as an eruption that is only recognized as such after having been.

Paradise Lost's status as a theodicy is nowhere more evident than in the episode narrating the emergence of Sin from Satan's head, and the subsequent family triangle played out between Satan, Sin and Death. A theodicy, after all, has to account for the existence of evil in a world created by God. And if we take God, as Milton does, to be life – a principle of creation, fruition, positive diversity and expansive connection – then the account of the emergence of evil is also an explanation of how a principle opposed to life comes into being from within life. For Milton, this problem is also a political problem: how is it that free, active and rational or imaginative human beings continue to choose their enslavement? What is at stake for Milton's theodicy is the problem of the binary, or the problem of what is other than life. As we have seen in the preceding chapter on *Reason of Church Government*, Milton argues for a world of binaries that are distinguished from fruitful contraries: good and evil are not distinct forces so much as a power and its negation. Male and female in their proper form would be fruitful contraries, as in the love evidenced between Adam and Eve, while good and evil would be binaries: the good is sufficient unto itself, but may be deflected and create evil or opposition which would not be its proper other. This distinction, though, breaks down as soon as it is articulated, for it is also the case that goodness will seem to require the trial of evil and adversity to achieve its highest expression. The paradise within, following the journey of grace and redemption, will be 'Paradise, far happier place / Then this of *Eden*, and far happier daies' (PL 12.464–5). Similarly, while the feminine and matter ought to be enabling contraries for the development of masculinity and reason, Milton will often suggest matter and femininity's diabolical potentiality if detached from forming masculinity. The theodicy of *Paradise Lost* will be explicated through a contrast between Adam and Eve as prelapsarian contraries that are mutually enhancing, and Sin and Death as a corrupting power generating an even more intense tendency to further corruption. Thus there are two theses regarding the logic of opposition: on the one hand, life requires difference, trial and relation in order not to remain within itself and devoid of spirit; on the other hand, that necessary condition of trial and relation may always fail to go out towards a genuine otherness and merely turn back or redound upon itself. Two economies are given form in two sexual relations.[119] Paradisiacal love and labour presents bodies in relations of difference that are subtended by a tendency towards divine and flourishing life.[120] One does not consume the other – as a thing that has no soul – but *reads* the other's body as possessing a spirit disclosable through discursive relations. In Sin and Death, the other's body – both Sin's emergence from Satan, and Death's generation from Sin – does not possess a genuinely different soul to be read so much as material that enables further self-involution.

Eve is not a mere body subordinate to Adam's reason, but a soul possessed with a different mode of spiritual recognition. Adam becomes a more rational being by relating to and governing a fellow being whose soul is different and distinct from his own. Milton will insist in *Areopagitica* that a 'fugitive and cloistered virtue' is less robust than one that has encountered trial. While good and evil are not the outcome of a competition of forces – for good is not simply what is asserted to be good by a powerful God but is asserted by God because it is good – relations of contraries do enable a strengthening of distinctions. Contraries have their logic in a single divine life which gives form and bound to each being, but those bounds and limits are exercised in a contrariety that (unlike Satan's reduction of all relations to power) recognizes distinction.

Milton dealt explicitly with the question of contraries in his prose tracts concerning divorce and in his writing on logic. In *Doctrine and Discipline of Divorce* Milton argues that incompatible partners in marriage should not be forced to remain together. To support this argument he invokes a notion of cosmological harmony defined through the concept of contraries:

> there is indeed a twofold Seminary or stock in Nature, from whence are deriv'd the issues of love and hatred distinctly flowing through the whole masse of created things, and . . . Gods doing is ever to bring the due likenesses and harmonies of his works together, except when out of the two contraries met to their own destruction, he moulds a third existence, and that . . . is error, or some evil Angel. (CPW 2.272)

Milton goes on to state that a refusal to act in accordance with either the natural attraction for like to meet with like or the repulsion of contraries is 'against the fundamental law book of nature' (272). It is when different forces, which are themselves innocent, are mistakenly coupled that evil emerges. A power or life can turn back upon itself if it fails to enjoy a proper relation to what is not itself. Evil is not something present and created by God, but follows from an improper coupling. In the case of *Paradise Lost,* when a perfectly divine female form is uncoupled from 'manly' virtue and combined with aspirations to knowledge and mastery – becoming a law unto itself without relation – true reason is deflected from its proper aim. This deflection of reason from itself is, for Milton, *the* problem of evil: if man is rational and created in God's image then he must have the potential to be good, but this potential may also fail to realize itself. Deflection is non-actualization: reason failing to come to presence. This occurs when reason remains within itself – remains indifferent – and fails to make a proper and fruitful coupling. Milton's clearest expression of this distinction between evil and virtuous couplings is given figuratively, in *Paradise Lost,* in the emergence of Sin from Satan's head.

Sin springs from Satan's head, but not through any decided act or willed production; and it is just this lack of conscious decision, or mere allowing to be, that characterizes Sin's non-being. Sin and evil are not positive created qualities but digressions that occur when the mind does not act on its own power, does not take command of itself. Satan becomes enamoured of Sin who, though initially abhorrent, becomes narcissistically appealing: 'Thy self in me thy perfect image viewing / Becam'st enamour'd, and such joy thou took'st / With me in secret' (2.763–5). Sin then gives birth to Death, whose 'life' is divided between consumption and rape, for he is perpetually raping his own mother, whose womb is then continually gnawed at by the 'yelling monsters' to whom she has given birth: 'Before mine eyes in opposition sits / Grim *Death* my son and foe, who sets them on, / And me his Parent would full soon devour / For want of other prey, but that he knows / His end with mine involv'd' (2.803–7). Evil, figured in this scene, is self-consumption, incest and the circulation of sameness without progress, production or any true relation.

Satan's forgetting of his created being – his refusal to acknowledge that *as created* his life emanates from a logic and law not of his own making – enables Sin's emergence. Sin occurs as the generation of a difference or deviation that is not the production of a formed and ordered being but occurs through mere replication that is not oriented towards a governing end. Throughout *Paradise Lost* a distinction is made between the swerve or deviation of emergence and the genuinely formed act of creation. In a similar manner, in his repetition of literary history Milton does not simply include or wander through the texts of the past; that past is recreated and activated, oriented towards disclosing its inner condition. Those images of pagan emergence, such as Athena springing from Zeus, should be recognized as deviant and derivative *and* as harbingers of a true logic of creative order. As long as we see difference and becoming as contingent and devoid of any *telos*, we are condemned to formlessness, forgetting and chaos. It is because there is no clear sense of the active authoring of difference – no sense of creation – that Satan can forget that Sin is one of his own emanations. Satan falls into relation with his own simulacrum. This then produces a closed cycle of repetition and circulation without production or exit.

Eating Well

Milton uses metaphors throughout his poetry and prose of the evils of a consumption that merely ingests without converting usage into further creation. This distinction between two modes of incorporation is indicated as early as 'Lycidas' with the images of swollen sheep taking in mere air: 'The hungry Sheep look up, and are not fed, / But swoln with wind, and the rank mist they draw, / Rot inwardly, and foul contagion spread' (125–7). This imagery of incorporation uses the mouth, both the organ of consumption and the organ of speech/singing, to make a complex link between a properly nutritive and harmonious life, in opposition to a disordered life devoid of sustenance: the 'swelling wind' and 'rank mist' are oral incorporations that have no real nutritive worth, and are the very opposite of an inspiration that would issue in something other than the 'lean and flashy songs' that grate on 'scrannel pipes of wretched straw' (123–4). The notion of the 'blind mouths' that begins the apocalyptic break in 'Lycidas' captures a distinct relation between empty consumption and disorder that runs throughout Milton's poetry. Consumption and incorporation ought to be acts of feeding, which will then yield the production of song, speech and harmony.

In 'Lycidas' and in the scene of Sin and Death we see a consumption that merely incorporates without production, a relation that is *blind*, or has no sense of that which it consumes. True music that is ordered harmonically and expresses the relations of the cosmos feeds the soul; the basis of the metaphor of music as sustenance lies in a commitment to poetry and art that in their proper form would allow the spirit to grow and develop. Mere noise, by contrast, is not expressive of anything other than itself, and has no basis in a system of relations not its own. Thus in 'Lycidas' there is a contrast between an inspiring breath that allows for the music of the earth ('that singing in their glory move') – that feeds the expansion of life – and the noxious gas that swells the unfed sheep, who are rotting inwardly. Images of devolving decay are opposed to expansive nutrition and are in turn intertwined with two modes of sound: accidental noise with no orderly relations is opposed to harmony, order and balance.

Much has been made in discussions and distinctions of modernity about the relation between closed and opened worlds and economies. According to a standard motif in the history of ideas, the pre-modern world is characterized by reference to some transcendent order and is, to that extent, 'closed'. By contrast, modern societies do not order elements according to some external logic but are immanently generated and therefore open, infinite or economic.[121] At first glance such a dichotomy would allow us to locate the capitalist ethic within modernity, for relations and systems are no longer determined by some transcendent pre-given law and hierarchy. Law and society are produced through relations; the world has no inherent order or quality and is blank matter or raw material. If we were to place Milton in a pre-modern worldview or cosmology we would draw attention to all those images of balance, hierarchy, order, due reverence and essential difference that occur throughout his poetry and that allow us to read Satan with all his economic rhetoric of will and power as the harbinger of modernity. Alternatively, we could read Milton as a rationalist prophet of modernity, appealing to the free circulation of texts in *Areopagitica*, to the right for reasoning individuals to determine their own law in *Reason of Church Government* and to the self-determination of women and the private sphere in his divorce tracts.

Following the first line of reasoning, where Milton would be a proto-critic of capitalism, it might appear that Milton attributes an exchangist, economic and equalitarian mode of thinking to Satan, who reduces God's difference in kind – as creator and form of reason – to a difference in degree. God for Satan simply possesses more force and is quantitatively superior. Reason for Satan is not a substantive faculty, endowing the self with some innate law, but is a purely procedural and equalizing power. Reason is calculative and instrumental, a capacity for any rational being to evaluate from the present. Satan regards the self, and therefore his rational being, as devoid of content: reason is not each being's proper form but simply that which renders all beings equal: 'Whom reason hath equald, force hath made supream' (1.248). While it is possible to see Satan as a proto-capitalist – viewing what is other than himself as so much material awaiting appropriation – and also therefore view Milton as appealing to a world of forms and essences that has not yet been disenchanted, we also need to recognize the ways in which Milton's world is anything but 'closed' and the positive ways in which he also uses economic and capitalist metaphors. The distinction is not, then, between a closed world characterized as a 'great chain of being' and an open society produced solely through immanent relations. Such an opposition is too crude to gauge the complexity of Milton's poetics and too crude for history. Rather, the supposedly closed and hierarchical world of pre-modernity was always already open and infinite; the divinity of God's creation lies in its potential for further formation and actualization, so that freedom is the hallmark of creation: the happy and willing movement towards form and substance. Similarly, the open and infinite world celebrated in capitalism has always been properly centred upon a value or life that provides circulation with a productive rationale. Capital exists properly for the sake of human exchange, based on mutual advantage. Indeed, a system of relations that was purely immanent – that possessed no law, logic or life other than that of circulation and exchange – would be both open in a nightmarish sense (possessing no limit, border or definition) and closed in a lifeless manner (mere mechanical interaction without intent or act).

We can therefore contrast the productive relations of love in paradise, where Adam and Eve relate to each other in a mode of reading such that each body is a sign of divine expressive life, to the centripetal closure of Sin and Death.[122] In the latter case the other body is given the minimal life required for ongoing existence, and not productive expansion. Relations are closed in upon themselves, repeating a consumption that yields no production, and a birth that yields no life, time or difference.[123] We can also see these two modes of relation, time and economy in *A Masque at Ludlow Castle*.

A Mask Presented at Ludlow Castle

In *A Mask*, Milton does not – as he will do in *Paradise Lost* – present two economies in morally dichotomous terms, with evil being identified with involution, consumption, non-production, cyclic stasis and repetition without difference, and good as outward relation, growth, progression and dynamic time. In *A Mask* Milton presents two economic worldviews as rhetorical strategies, thereby foregrounding the extent to which the moral path towards virtue depends upon a certain interpretation of life, or a certain way of viewing relations. The *Mask* is, like *Paradise Lost*, dominated by images of compelling and necessary harmony. Just as Satan will be struck 'stupidly good' by the divine image of Adam and Eve and can never completely lose all trace of virtue and conscience, Comus recognizes in the lady that 'somthing holy lodges in that brest, / And with these raptures moves the vocal air / To testifie his hidden residence' (245–7). There are two ways of interpreting this divine compulsion to harmony. One is Comus's own appeal to the lulling seduction and value of nature in itself, so alluring as to dull thought of anything beyond itself: compared with Circe's sirens that 'in pleasing slumber lull'd the sense, / And in sweet madness rob'ed it of it self,' the music prompted by the lady awakens reason to itself: 'But such a sacred and home-felt delight, / Such sober certainty of waking bliss / I never heard till now' (259–63). Like Satan, Comus cannot but recognize virtue, which has a compelling and essential force. Even so, he fails to read the lady's beauty as a sign of divine life, and also fails to allow that music to awaken his reason. Instead, he regards the lady and nature as property, with property bearing both the (capitalist) sense of that which is to be acquired and (the metaphysical sense) of property as that which has no essential or substantial being (properties as added on to substance). Comus's view of the world as mere matter for unthinking manipulation and consumption is clearly presented as a privation, as a path taken by Comus away from the world's inherent tendency towards balance and form. Throughout his poetry Milton will constantly present the path of virtue as compelling, with Comus, like Satan, struggling to turn away from the call to reason.

As Milton's most neo-Platonic work, *A Mask* deploys a language of imbruting and defilement which befalls the soul as it moves away from reason. The elder brother will articulate this philosophy explicitly. Indeed, his logic of creation is built on a conditional. *If* creation were not opposed to involution, *if* there were no essential and necessary movement away from what already is given to a higher form, then the world would be without foundation:

> Vertue may be assail'd but never hurt,
> Surpriz'd by unjust force, but not enthrall'd,
> Yea even that which mischief meant most harm
> Shall in the happy trial prove most glory.
> But evil on itself shall back recoyl,
> And mix no more with goodness, when at last
> Gather'd like scum, and setl'd to it self
> It shall be in eternal restless change
> Self-fed, and self-consum'd, if this fail,
> The pillar'd firmament is rott'nness,
> And earths base built on stubble. (COM 588–98)

The brother's earlier neo-Platonist appeal to chastity, as a movement away from the body towards rational and animating life, is therefore grounded on a strict logic of how the earth must be structured if it is to have any being. If there were no order towards which life were tending, and if mere enjoyment or the pleasures and whims of the present were to have overriding force, then we could not have the harmonious cosmos as we know it, and could not have life as we see it in its natural and developing form. Milton does not, then, simply allow a character to state the way of the world, and does not simply mention neo-Platonist doctrine, but grounds that divine philosophy in a deduction of the virtues from the perceived order and balance of nature. The earlier speech made by the brother does appear at first as a straightforward encomium to chastity:

> So dear to Heav'n is Saintly chastity,
> That when a soul is found sincerely so,
> A thousand liveried Angels lacky her,
> Driving far off each thing of sin and guilt,
> And in cleer dream and solemn vision
> Tell her of things that no gross ear can hear,
> Till oft convers with heavenly habitants
> Begin to cast a beam on th' outward shape,

> The unpolluted temple of the mind,
> And turns it by degrees to the souls essence,
> Till all be made immortal: but when lust,
> By unchaste looks, loose gestures, and foul talk,
> But most leud and lavish act of sin,
> Lets in defilement to the inward parts,
> The soul grows clotted by contagion,
> Imbodies and imbrutes, till she quite loose
> The divine property of her first being. (452–68)

The virtue of chastity – so different from the joys of productive wedded love in *Paradise Lost* – is already in *A Mask* in accord with Milton's vitalist ethic of expansive production. As the elder brother notes, chastity precludes wasteful sexual spending; a promiscuous attachment to bodies takes the soul away from its more fruitful journey towards its own proper being. Milton's virtue of chastity here does not take the form of fetishized courtly love, where the chaste lady is desired precisely because she is disallowed. On the contrary, the lady's chastity is a form of saving for the sake of later production and fruition, a properly bourgeois form of the originally Catholic virtue. Further, in its Miltonic version, the material body is not negated or suppressed in chastity but renovated and renewed, and thereby brought closer to the condition of spirit. This movement 'by degrees to the soul's essence' is not achieved by a mortification of the flesh but an illumination of the 'outward shape'. Thus to Comus's wasteful and profligate sensualism of use and consumption, Milton will oppose a 'divine philosophy' that tempers its sensual enjoyment in harmony with the world. The second brother responds, dialogically and responsively, to the elder brother's description of hierarchy, with the rejection of 'crude surfeit'. This is not a rejection of the body per se, but a measuring of enjoyment according to the proper trajectory of the soul:

> How charming is divine Philosophy!
> Not harsh, and crabbed as dull fools suppose
> But musical as is *Apollo*'s lute,
> And a perpetual feast of nectar'd sweets,
> Where no crude surfet raigns. (COM 475–8)

To refer to philosophy as 'musical' is to oppose its art of persuasion – which is in tune with the order of the world – to the 'barbarous dissonance' of Comus's rout. Whereas the lady's harmonious music is enlivening – 'strains that might create a soul / Under the ribs of death' – Comus's bacchanalian celebration is of a mixed, unruly dance. Comus must therefore refuse to read the production, fruition and order of nature as an expression of creation and must instead present the world in economic terms. For Comus, if we do not enjoy nature then we are turning, ungratefully, away from creation's gift. From his consumerist perspective the only proper relation to nature and life is one of unbounded enjoyment. This follows because, as Patrides notes, Comus can make no distinction between abstinence – the rigid denial of pleasure – and temperance, the enjoyment of pleasure in order and measure.[124] In his attempt to seduce the lady Comus puts forward a *carpe diem* argument regarding nature, and anticipates Satan's later seduction of Eve which also appeals to the idea that nature requires, and not merely allows, our use:

> Why should you be so cruel to your self,
> And to those dainty limms which Nature lent
> For gentle usage and soft delicacy?
> But you invert the cov'nants of her trust,
> And harshly deal like an ill borrower
> With that which you receiv'd on other terms,
> Scorning the unexempt condition
> By which all mortal frailty must subsist,
> Refreshment after toil, ease after pain,
> That have been tir'd all day without repast,
> And timely rest have wanted, but fair Virgin
> This will restore all soon. (COM 678–98)

In response to this argument that the natural body requires sustenance and that one would accuse and abuse nature if one were to remain self-enclosed, the lady puts forward the idea of a 'wise appetite'. In contrast with the 'blind mouths' of 'Lycidas' (where a bodily organ is closed off from relation to an outside world) a 'wise appetite' presents a bodily force (appetite) ordered by an incorporeal power (wisdom). In this highly Platonic poem Milton places a more Aristotelian emphasis, not on the negation or non-being of matter, but on the positive capacity for the material body or the appetite to become wise, to take on the form and order of the world.[125] By contrast, Comus will maintain an argument that is both proto-capitalist in its presentation of nature as material for use, and also tyrannically feudal in its inability to recognize a certain intrinsic reason and measure in nature, so that order must be imposed. In *Paradise Lost* Adam and Eve's gardening of nature is not solely for their own use, but allows the pruning back of growth to enable further fruition. By contrast Comus, like Satan, presents nature as 'man's' own raw material, possessing neither spirit nor any value independent of its appropriation:

> Wherefore did Nature powre her bounties forth,
> With such a full and unwithdrawing hand,
> Covering the earth with odours, fruits, and flocks,
> Thronging the Seas with spawn innumerable,
> But all to please, and sate the curious taste?
> And set to work millions of spinning Worms,
> That in their green shops weave the smooth-hair'd silk

To deck her Sons, and that no corner might
Be vacant of her plenty, in her own loyns
She hutch't th' all worship ore, and precious gems
To store her children with; if all the world
Should in a pet of temperance feed on Pulse,
Drink the clear stream, and nothing wear but freize,
Th' all-giver would be unthank't, would be unprais'd,
Not half his riches known and yet despis'd,
And we should serve him as a grudging master,
As a penurious niggard of his wealth,
And live like Natures bastards, not her sons,
Who would be quite surcharg'd with her own weight,
And strangled with her waste fertility;
Th' earth cumber'd, and the wing'd air dark't with plumes,
The herds would over-multitude their Lords,
The sea o'refraught would swell, & th'unsought diamonds
Would so emblaze the forhead of the Deep,
And so bestudd with stars, that they below
Would grow inur'd to light, and com at last
To gaze upon the Sun with shameless brows.
List lady be not coy, and be not cosen'd,
With that same vaunted name Virginity,
Beauty is natures coyn, must not be hoorded,
But must be currant, and the good thereof
Consists in mutual and partak'n bliss,
Unsavoury in th' injoyment of it self
If you let slip time, like a neglected rose
It withers on the stalk with languish't head.
Beauty is natures brag, and must be shown
In courts, at feasts, and high solemnities. (COM 709–45)

From a certain way of viewing the world – from an ontology – Comus passes directly to a moral imperative. Natural growth has no internal limit; left to itself nature would turn in upon itself: 'surcharg'd with her own weight, / And strangled with her waste fertility'. Comus therefore accepts the prima facie value of production, and argues that if nature's production is not allowed to feed and be enjoyed – if nature does not refer beyond itself – then it will become self-corrupting.

This passage raises the question of just how one passes from an observation regarding natural growth and abundance to a moral theory. For Comus growth and consumption are adjudicated in quantitative terms; excess and abundance require consumption. His nature has no *internal* ends or limits. If nature requires human representation and consumption to mark its value this is because nature itself is devoid of direction, always threatening to fall from limit into chaos: 'The earth cumber'd, and the wing'd air dark't with plumes, / The herds would over-multitude their lords.' What this sequence of reasoning reveals is the similarity of logic that ties an unbridled capitalism with a brutal feudalism. If nature has no inherent value or normativity, then this means that it can either be reduced to raw material for appropriation, or that its lack of inherent limits requires some lordship that would stem the swelling of multitudes. By contrast, an ethical and liberal capitalism will always temper exchange and the use of nature with some notion of a normative centre, whet'er that be natural law or natural human dignity. We will see just such an ethic in the lady's response to Comus, where she argues for nature's 'sober laws'.

Like Satan, Comus is a nominalist, acknowledging no reality other than that of conventional terms: 'that same vaunted *name* virginity'; and like Satan also, Comus's relation to the world is exchangist. The value of nature lies in its circulation alone, with no intrinsic goodness or function directing nature's proper use: 'Beauty is nature's coyn, must not be hoorded, / But must be currant, and the good thereof / Consists in mutual and partaken bliss.' That use of the word 'current' draws attention to the deeper sense of 'currency'; there is no value other than that of the system of circulation, nothing that would ground, stabilize or maintain exchange through time. Value is given only in the present, in presentation, or what something is taken to be. It is because of nature's reduction to a medium of exchange that value becomes simulation; the worth of a term is given through its display. Something is desired because it is exchangeable and commodified, rather than becoming a desired commodity because of what it is.

Comus's evil is not yet as radical as Satan's will be. If radical evil is, as defined by Kant, not a simple error of judgement but a direct exception of one's own will from duty or law, then it is Satan's 'Evil be thou my good' that is wickedness in a radical sense.[126] For Kant, humans can only be good or evil, either acting in conformity with the law, or rationalizing their self-interest through a flouting of the law for themselves. What Kant refused to acknowledge was the possibility of a being who bore no relation to law or maxims; for even the choice of self-interest over the law places one in relation to a duty one has foreclosed. One of Milton's achievements in *Paradise Lost* is to combine the earlier Augustinian sense of evil as privation or non-being – a falling away from the good rather than a positive existence – with the modern Kantian conception of evil as an act of the will that freely decides to will particularity and exception.[127] What Milton will stress throughout all of his poetry is both the sense that life tends towards realization and actualization of its highest potential – and so evil would be a falling away – and the more modern sense of Kantian evil that such a falling away requires a positive will that actively and defiantly denies right reason. Both Satan and Comus are constantly struck or affected by the good and then turn back to their rigid self-interest in order to swerve towards an evil which negates that presented good. Milton maintains the theological tradition's conception of evil as having no real being, or as being a privation of life's proper tendency, but then presents the renegade individual's swerve away from the good as an act of will. Evil is at one and the same dependent or reactive (requiring a goodness it will refuse or negate) and isolatable in the will as the capacity each body has to take *itself* (rather than the universal) as a law, selfishly construing all the world's relations as reducible to the will. The world for Satan and Comus is not lawless, but their conception of law or relations is one of the will: competing forces in which each body strives to maximize its own power without any reference to a transcendent or informing life.

Comus's arguments, like Satan's, are parasitic upon certain assumptions regarding the good. What cannot be admitted, either by Comus or Satan, is a world that would be devoid of any relation, recognition or value. Both appeal to values of quantity which will, supposedly, allow life's expansion and flourishing. Satan will accuse God of jealously guarding and limiting a life and goodness that could be enjoyed and maximized by all. Comus, similarly, regards virtue, virginity and delay as limiting production. The Miltonic reply to this idea that life can be increasingly enjoyed, used and exchanged without limit, is the introduction of a notion of quality into quantity. While exchange, use and expansion are essential to life, that circulation and use must be subtended by some measure. The problem with a purely relational economy for Milton is that measure is achieved through money which is (or ought to be) nothing more than a mechanism of exchange. Yes, nature must be enjoyed, used and consumed but that does not entail that there is no proportion to our relation to nature. In contrast with Comus, who presents a nature as mere quantity that would 'over-multitude' itself, the lady attributes an agency and *meaning* to nature: 'With her abundance she good cateress / Means her provision only to the good.' Like Comus the lady will also warn against a nature that turns in upon itself, but this is not the result of excess production but excess consumption:

> Impostor do not charge innocent nature,
> As if she would her children should be riotous
> With her abundance, she good cateress
> Means her provision onely to the good
> That live according to her sober laws,
> And holy dictate of spare Temperance:
> If every just man that now pines with want
> Had but a moderate and beseeming share
> Of that which lewdly pamper'd Luxury
> Now heaps upon som few with vast excess,
> Natures full blessings would be well-dispens't
> In unsuperfluous eeven proportion,
> And she no whit encomber'd with her store,
> And then the giver would be better thank't,
> His praise due paid, for swinish gluttony
> Ne're looks to Heav'n amidst his gorgeous feast,
> But with besotted base ingratitude
> Cramms, and blasphemes his feeder. Shall I go on?
> Or have I said anough? (COM 761–79)

The failure to recognize a measure beyond consumption imbrutes the soul and directs attention away from transcendence: 'swinish gluttony / Ne're looks to Heav'n'. We see, between Comus and the lady, two modes of relation. For Comus, the gift of nature is that of an object without meaning that *then* requires value, display and exchange to yield sense and worth. For the lady, the relation is reciprocal; only if we receive nature with a sense of its intrinsic properties do we really acknowledge its gift: 'And then the giver would be better thank'd.' These two economies also mark out the miracle of grace in *Paradise Lost*: it is precisely because God's mercy is *not* already there at our disposal, and because we require something other than our own will to arrive at beatitude, that our relation to the divine is that of a gift economy. We are finite, dependent, fallen and created; the grace that would restore us can never be earned, and can be achieved only by a free and unwarranted bestowal of divinity, which occurs with the incarnation. The incarnation, in turn, is also that one miraculous moment when instead of spirit becoming increasingly sublimed, it freely takes on a body, but does so in order to allow carnal life to ascend once again by degrees to heaven.[128] It is this act of grace, of spirit sacrificing itself to matter for the sake of a retrieval of spirit, which is also the logic of the Christian work of art. Spirit takes on word or material body in order to circulate, be read and spiritualize readers in turn. Just as grace and the incarnation are superlative logics, whereby divine life gives what is not owed, so the submission of spirit to the letter is a taking on of a body which – as Milton will insist in *Areopagitica* – allows for a certain immortality of the word that can, nevertheless, be brutally slain and dismembered through censorship. Milton will therefore acknowledge both the divinity of embodiment and the divine possibility of economic circulation (of debts, gifts and sacrifice) only if those relations and taking on of tokens are animated by life and a greater law of creation.

There can be no equilibrium or equivalence between the ransom paid by the Son and our dependence. Far from being a cause of lament, this economy of dependence is what allows for life. If we were already self-sufficient, fully actualized and at one with the divine, then there would be no time or journey required to actualize our potential. This time of meaning and actualization is wilfully spurned by Satan who sees himself as fully self-present. Satan's economic metaphors are, therefore, those of a debt economy in which any relation to what is other than his own self-referring system is calculated negatively. To draw a modern economic analogy: Satan's economy has not yet arrived at the point of development where exchange and interaction can be productive. His point of view is isolated and self-present, incapable as he is of recognizing a broader system of balances. By contrast, the economy of seeing each term as bearing a worth or measure in accord with a value that is outside the system of exchange, giving that system order and sense, is directly tied to a vitalist ethic whereby each body *is* and has value only in terms of a broader life and spirit which flows through it. Vitalism is not opposed to economy and system, for it is simply the underwriting of economic and systemic terms by a higher, creative and transcendent value.

What these two modes of economy – closed with no reference versus open but measured by some value – bring in train are competing views of language. For Comus and Satan language is a system of pure convention that has no reference or measure beyond itself. Accordingly, to step outside that system of convention would result in pure chaos. It was just this sort of strongly conventialist way of seeing the world that allowed the Royalists to argue that without the monarchy there could be no social order. Originally Milton acquiesced in that way of seeing relations. He argued, against the 'No Bishop, No King' cause, that reform of the church would not lead to a collapse of order in general. Increasingly, though, Milton and the regicides appealed to a natural law which would allow for the evaluation of a system of conventions and relations. Any such positive or contracted system should not be read as a sign of fallenness – as in relative natural law, where the laws of the polity swerve away from true order to take account of our corrupt reason – but an expression of the world's potential to aspire to divine justice. For both Comus and Satan the law is nothing other than a force that negates and regulates will, and language is nothing more than a system of conventions that might just as easily take on another form. For the lady, however, language and communications are expressive of natural law. Unlike Comus's seductive 'false rules prank't in reason's garb', the lady's rhetoric is grounded in the very being of the world. This is so much the case that only a body that is appropriately tempered or attuned to the way of the world can respond to the justly measured message:

> To him that dares
> Arm his profane tongue with contemptuous words
> Against the Sun-clad power of Chastity;
> Fain would I something say, yet to what end?
> Thou hast nor Eare, nor Soul to apprehend
> The sublime notion, and high mystery
> That must be utter'd to unfold the sage
> And serious doctrine of Virginity,
> And thou art worthy that thou shouldst not know
> More happines than this thy present lot.
> Enjoy your deer Wit, and gay Rhetorick
> That hath so well been taught her dazling fence,
> Thou art not fit to hear thyself convinc't;
> Yet should I try, the uncontrouled worth
> Of this pure cause would kindle my rap't spirits
> To such a flame of sacred vehemence,
> That dumb things would be mov'd to sympathize,
> And the brute Earth would lend her nerves, and shake,
> Till all they magick structures rear'd so high,
> Were shatter'd into heaps o'er thy false head. (COM 779–98)

Morality, then, is not a question of competing arguments or propositions but a capacity to recognize a law beyond one's own will. Only a morality that has a reference beyond itself is able to measure its relations 'in unsuperfluous eeven proportion'. If this were not the case the good would be nothing more than a relation between acquisition and consumption; the good would be whatever one desires and not the goal towards which desire ought to tend. So powerful is this natural law that whereas the lady can resist and reason against Comus's rhetoric, her own doctrine strikes Comus with a force beyond mere words: 'I feel that I do fear / Her words set off by som superior power' (799–800). Comus, though, returns to his nominalism; but we are made aware that this takes some effort: 'Com, no more, / This is meer moral babble, and direct against the canon laws of our foundation' (805–7). Tellingly, while the lady refers to sober laws of nature, Comus will refer to canon laws; the lady's precepts are grounded in nature as a benevolent guide and cateress, suggesting a dynamism and growth. Comus, by contrast, refers to a law established once and for all, not as a cateress or benefactor but as a rigid foundation, a simple imperative to consume.

Whereas *A Mask* presents the opposition between good and evil as a dialogue concerning two ways in which we might comport ourselves towards a world of clearly natural goodness and abundance, *Paradise Lost* will offer a more direct image of radical evil. This radical evil is hinted at in *A Mask* in the notion of both a canon law that is simply accepted as a rigid foundation, and in the images of self-consumption and inward-turning swinish gluttony. But whereas Comus and the lady will dispute the best ways to avoid the corruption of life – through unlimited or limited use – *Paradise Lost* offers a figure of evil that is not merely deluded as to how one might best maximize life, but has avowedly turned away from life. This wickedness is not a deviation from the good, nor a failure to recognize the proper form of the world and time; rather, it is the negation of form, law, order and time *as a principle*. It is here that Milton begins to present evil with all the positivity that much later figures, such as Schelling, would do. Evil would be more than failure, corruption, deviation or even a making an exception of oneself from a law one nevertheless recognized as valid (as in Comus's and Satan's attempts to use moral rhetoric for self-interest). With the figures of Sin and Death, and at times in the Satanic declarations that evil be now one's good, Milton entertains the possibility of a principle that not only deviates from life, or fails to realize itself, but that works demonically against life, recognition, identity, time and all being.

In this sense I would argue that it is important to consider the ways in which the scene of Sin and Death is not an allegory. To claim that a literary scene is not allegorical – that it simply *is* what it presents – is perhaps the impossible aim of all discourse that tries to overcome mediation, and to that extent all writing is at least in part allegorical.[129] If writing and life are possible only as distance or doubling, for something can be or have identity only if it recognizes itself as this or that nameable and repeatable form through time, then allegory is an inescapable condition. Something *is* only in its taking on of a form or name that remains the same through time, and is therefore necessarily different from its purely punctual or actual being. How would non-allegorical presentation be possible? And how could one argue that the scene between Sin and Death in *Paradise Lost* is not allegorical? The first point to note is that Sin and Death are not personae or types; instead, Milton tries to present Sin as a specific form of life, a style of time and relations. Second, if we were to think of Sin and Death as allegories we would need to consider just what they are allegories of. If they represent psychological or moral possibilities then we can acknowledge to a certain extent that giving such ethical modes an embodied existence is a type of allegory.[130] However, to do so would require distinguishing between a moral possibility – a virtue or vice – and a style of embodied life. This is where we can contrast Milton with his other precursor, Spenser. Spenser will distribute the virtues and vices into historical and mythological personae, allowing virtues to be presented both as mythic figures and historical and social types. Milton neither distributes the virtues or vices into personifications, nor do any of his characters – despite attempts to liken Satan to Cromwell – double as allegories of historical types.[131] Rather, just as Milton will insist that Christ's body is an expression of his virtue, and that virtues entail a specifically embodied being, so it makes sense that if he wants to present Sin and Death *as such*, they will be presented as bodies. In that regard Milton's poetry is certainly analogical, for it presents every created being as expressive of a divine life that gives itself in various forms of virtue – where virtue is better considered in its original sense as excellence or power, and not as a moral or psychological quality. For that reason, though, Milton's poetry is not allegorical, for the analogical expressiveness of the world does not require the poet to present either history or ethical life as distinct doubles of an otherwise ideal spiritual sense. Milton, then, is less Platonic – less inclined to see truths and values as radically distinct from this world – than neo-Platonic, allowing this world to be an emanation from a divine and informing life. The Christianity of Milton's poetics will not see this world as essentially distanced or degraded from its governing idea or form, for it is the very nature of this historical and temporal life to progress towards the original spiritual order of which it is a creation.

3

Allegory, Analogy and the Form of the World

Milton presents human life and nature in general as matter blessed with form. Each being created from that formed matter has a proper potential, true being or substance which it strives to actualize. Evil is possible, therefore, precisely because as a created being blessed with reason, humans are capable either of moving towards their more divine potential or of falling back into matter and immediacy. If 'reason is also choice' (3.108), then falling away from the good is, to a certain extent, *not choosing*. When Adam and Eve fall they do so not because they recognize and decide upon something they mistakenly believe to be good, but because they decide not to decide. Instead of acting upon her own reasons, which Milton has Eve rehearse, he shows the way in which she is drawn away from voice, relation and decision towards being an object of speculation and enjoyment. Satan argues that she should not be placed in a position of decision and moral choice. Instead, he makes two appeals. The first is that she is already sufficiently good and complete, such that she should be the object of admiration of the world and not a responsible subject who must make her way in the world:

> Wonder not, soveran Mistress, if perhaps
> Thou canst, who art sole Wonder, much less arm
> Thy looks, the Heav'n of mildness, with disdain,
> Displeas'd that I approach thee thus, and gaze
> Insatiate, I thus single, nor have feard
> Thy awful brow, more awful thus retir'd.
> Fairest resemblance of thy Maker faire,
> Thee all living things gaze on, all things thine
> By gift, and thy Celestial Beautie adore
> With ravishment beheld, there best beheld
> Where universally admir'd ... (PL 9.532–42)

Satan presents Eve to herself as a body, as an object of delight and wonder, and not as a subject. Second, suggesting that Eve should better conceive of herself as a spectacle – as remaining unto herself rather than being observant – Satan goes on to argue that a world without law or prohibition would be more appropriate for her being; she should not have to decide between her own will and the law: 'Why then was this forbid? Why but to awe' (9.703–4). In both respects, Satan robs Eve of her subjectivity and her reason, for reason is also choosing and subjectivity is essentially tied to subjection or recognizing oneself as a being possessed of law.[132] Adam's decision to follow Eve is also a retreat from reason, responsibility and decision. As the narrator of *Paradise Lost* will later stipulate, necessity is the tyrant's plea. We become tyrannical when we abandon our reason, when we cease to decide and instead become beings whose life is fully determined, either by compulsion or by our bodies as they already are.[133] The fall, then, is a fall away from decision and the delay that is constitutive of reason – the delay or pause that allows us not to be objects that react compulsively but subjects who act with a sense of possible outcomes not yet given.

It is because Eve's fall occurs through a swerve or deflection of her right reason, and not through evil elevated as a principle, that she can also receive grace and be redeemed. By contrast, Satan's sin occurs not through a deflection of the proper path of becoming but through a destruction of creative time; he refuses all time before his own being: 'we know no time when we were not as now' (5.859). In abandoning hope he also refuses the possibility of a future.[134] Satan's abandonment of hope is not only a sin in traditional theology,[135] it is also an anticipation of the radical evil that will lie at the centre of Kant's enlightenment ethics and its intersection with rational theology. According to Kant, we view the world as an ordered, lawful and harmonious unity, and do so because our reason aims towards an Idea of ultimate organization, which we can think but never intuit. When it comes to scientific judgement, we assume that the world's being is in accord with our concepts, and that the ongoing understanding of the world by others will also harmonize with our own understanding.[136] We perceive the world not only as lawful, but as lawful for others, and for future understanding. In terms of ethics, when we will an action we imagine that action as being in accord with other wills who are also free, and who recognize themselves both as capable of ordering their actions, and of imagining or desiring a world in which each will recognizes its lawgiving and 'supersensible' power. Hope, though a traditional Christian virtue, still structures Kant's bridge between a theory of knowledge and aesthetics and morality. Ideas of reason, for Kant, are future oriented; we may never be able to experience the world as an ordered totality, nor experience ourselves as free subjects, nor experience God. But even though we are always placed in *relation* to such ultimate and completing Ideas, we can – practically – act as if we were free and not determined by nature. We may imagine ourselves as not governed by the desires, pleasures and happiness of this world, but as capable of thinking of ourselves as members of a kingdom of ends. In our relation to nature, we may imagine the world as ultimately in accord with our rational striving for morality and harmony. Without the image of a world in accord with our reason, neither our personality nor our morality would have any meaning. Radical evil turns away from reason's striving towards humanity as a kingdom of ends and makes an exception of itself, placing finite desires before the capacity of reason. Wickedness in its even more radical form has no norm or law other than itself; its absence of relation is its being and principle.

In addition to the myth of Athena springing from the head of Zeus – a reference Milton draws upon to establish both the moral distinction between generation and creation and the ethical time of his own appropriation of his sources – the scene of Satan's encounter with Sin and Death also recalls Spenser's allegory of holyness and error in *The Faerie Queene*. Spenser explicitly presented *The Faerie Queene* as an allegory, and has also placed himself avowedly within the epic tradition, offering his own work as a suitable next step in the epic sequence. Spenser is also clear that the task of literature is that of enabling self-fashioning: allowing the reader to discern in the historical past the virtues or excellences of character that are true for all time. This gives his allegory a general referent: all the positive historical figures within *The Faerie Queene* are examples of the virtuous man. Spenser thus reads the past as embodying a general truth, a generality that can also be expressed in his own particular allegory:

> Sir knowing how doubtfully all Allegories may be construed, and this booke of mine, which I have entitled the *Faery Queene*, being a continued Allegory, or darke conceit, I have thought good as well for avoiding of jealous opinions and misconstructions, as also for your better light in reading thereof, (being so by you commanded,) to discover unto you the general intention and meaning, which in the whole course thereof I have fashioned, without expressing of any particular purposes or by-accidents therein occasioned. The generall end therefore of all the booke is to fashion a gentleman or noble person in vertuous and gentle discipline: Which for that I conceived shoulde be most plausible and pleasing, being colored with an historicall fiction, the which the most part of men delight to read, rather for variety of matter, than for profite of the ensample: I chose the historye of King Arthure, as most fitte for the excellency of his person, being made famous by many mens former workes, and also furthest from the danger of envy, and suspition of present time. In which I have followed all the antique Poets historicall, first Homere, who in the Persons of Agamemnon and Ulysses hath ensampled a good governour and a vertuous man, the one in his *Ilias*, the other in his *Odysseis*: then Virgil, whose like intention was to doe in the person of Aeneas: after him Ariosto comprised them both in his Orlando: and lately Tasso dissevered them againe, and formed both parts in two persons, namely that part which they in Philosophy call Ethice, or vertues of a private man, coloured in his Rinaldo: The other named Politice in his Godfredo. By ensample of which excellente Poets, I labour to pourtraict in Arthure, before he was king, the image of a brave knight, perfected in the twelve morall virtues ...

Spenser's understanding of literary history is clear. There is a truth that remains the same for all time – the truth of the virtues – which can then be given separate form; and it is for this reason that allegory is entirely appropriate. If there is an ethics of time in Spenser's use of history and the literary past, it is that truth remains as the referent to which various literary products are signs.

The youthful Milton also considered Arthur as a possible hero of the epic he would write. Spenser's choice of Arthur places the English epic in what Joseph Wittreich has referred to as the 'line of vision', a prophetic tradition in which the poet takes up a literary historical sequence and becomes, once again, like the visionaries of old but does so for his own time ideally moving closer to apocalyptic revelation.[137] Milton, however, does not have this allegorical approach to literary history. Rejecting a literature of self-fashioning, where the self is both the agent and scene of composition, Milton presents a logic of creation, in which the one first man (and the 'one greater man') and the efflorescence of virtue are expressions of an original and originary logic: the genesis of form and order from chaos. We do not begin from a general model of 'man' which can then be varied or repeated through time; there is a transcendent divine life, which is then 'substantially expressed' or given image and form in Christ and humanity. Human norms refer back to a more general rationale of life. If Milton is in some respects, like Spenser, neo-Platonic in acknowledging the eternal and distinct nature of truth and goodness, he is nevertheless distinctly vitalist in insisting that the bodies and selves we experience in this world are expressions of a divine and creative life that exists expansively and productively through those bodies. Thus in *Paradise Lost* virtue emanates from the order of the heavens, so that we can see the excellence of each being as dependent upon a preceding order of life: 'and to each inward part / With gentle penetration, though unseen, / Shoots invisible vertue even to the deep' (3.584–6).

At the level of literary form, Milton does not write an allegory, but gives God, Satan, Sin, Death, Chaos and Old Night a direct voice and presentation. The truth, then, cannot be given as it is by Spenser, in a formal model of conduct, as a manual of virtues which would then be fleshed out in literary form or given aesthetic presentation. On the contrary, Milton presents certain formal or aesthetic modes and styles as true, others as false; more importantly, Milton gives evil a direct image. He does not imagine good and evil as abstractions which might then be given concrete and aesthetic form – eternal verities which might then be placed in time. Rather, good and evil are modes of life and time. The proper ethical mode of the epic cannot be allegorical, for the commitment to truth and light must be a commitment to thinking of the good itself, as intuited in the very being or life of creation.

In contrast with Spenser, Milton presents the very genesis of signification, the passage from God's divine light to the body of Christ who is the substantial expression of the divinity.[138] It is this image of God – God as expression – which then provides the aesthetic logic for the depiction of Adam and Eve as 'the human form divine' through which 'the image of their glorious maker shone'. Rather than compose an allegory, which would present the literary object as distanced from its truth and origin, Milton writes an epic about origination and produces framing passages – such as the invocations – in which light itself descends to illuminate the scene of first causes. If there is a circularity to the form – where the content of the epic (light) also acts as a formal device or framing narration – this circularity is not the centripetal force of Sin and

Death. The circle is centrifugal: God is the very form of matter, the divine act that brings matter to its state of true being. All that flows forth from God therefore becomes what it ought to be when it properly expresses its origin. Creation moves beyond what it already is to arrive at the immanent end that was there all along, in potential. The cycle of Sin and Death, by contrast, remains closed in upon itself, repeating only itself, and allowing nothing other than itself. The other (virtuous) circle − of light as that which is described in the poem and that which generates the poem − is an image of divine harmony in which repetition only serves to create complexity and add richness to the one expressive score.

When Stephen Greenblatt defined Renaissance literature through the idea of self-fashioning, he did so by looking at the literary past through the insights of Machiavelli.[139] The idea that there is not a truth that one should then use as the basis of self-development, but that there is no truth or being outside the creation of oneself as a forceful character is a motif in Western thought that runs from Plato's Thrasymachus through to certain interpretations of Foucault and Nietzsche.[140] Spenser presents his own epic as a manual for an ideal self: placing Raleigh as the norm and his own typical characters as persuasive defences of that norm. One might also see the mode of address, in the author's letter, as a performative in which Spenser presents his literary work not as a description of the true and the good, but as the production of social relations. The allegory will 'fashion' a noble character in the sense of 'fashioning' as both presentation and creation. It is just this literary model of self-creation, in which the work produces what it refers to and the act of literary creation is an allegory of self-creation, that Milton's model of literary time subverts.

It is Satan in *Paradise Lost* who is the proto new historicist, rejecting the idea that certain beings are intrinsically or qualitatively powerful (acting to express their power); for it is only through performance or act that one creates oneself as a power. Satan appears to have read his Foucault, Greenblatt, Nietzsche and Butler; there is not a self who acts and then establishes social relations.[141] Rather, there is an act of force which produces positions and relations (of disequilibrium) and this effect of differential force is all that selves are. As Rogers makes clear, it is just such a notion of a world that is nothing more than the effect of differences in quantity that Milton and other seventeenth-century vitalists sought to challenge.[142] We can see this in the first book of *Paradise Lost* where Satan is presented as an artful rhetorician, as one who regards power as productive of law ('Who now is sovereign can dispose or bid'), and as a character whose being *is* his performance ('The mind is its own place'):

> Is this the Region, this the Soil, the Clime,
> Said then the lost Arch-Angel, this the seat
> That we must change for Heav'n, this mournful gloom
> For that celestial light? Be it so, since he
> Who now is Sovran can dispose and bid
> What shall be right: fardest from him is best

> Whom reason hath equald, force hath made supreme
> Above his equals. Farewel happy Fields
> Where joy forever dwells: hail horrours, hail
> Infernal world, and thou profoundest Hell
> Receive thy new Possessor: One who brings
> A mind not to be chang'd by Place or Time.
> The mind is its own place, and in it self
> Can make a Heav'n of Hell, a Hell of Heaven.
> What matter where, if I be still the same,
> And what I should be, all but less than he
> Whom Thunder hath made greater? (PL 1.242–58)

Rejecting his position as a created being who has been given a form that might be actualized or illuminated through a journey towards divine light, Satan interprets the world as the outcome of competing forces: 'Whom thunder hath made greater'. The self is no longer an expression of a celestial light that might lead to some greater end. Rejecting that notion of informed becoming, Satan's relation to the world becomes one of ownership: 'Receive thy new possessor.' Satan here is at once the image of the modern subject, having no being other than his power of appropriation and dominance, and at the same time also an exemplary feudal tyrant, for his governance of the fallen angels relies on an essential confusion of political principles.[143] Despite his constant appeals to the 'mind and spirit [that] remains invincible' (1.139–40), Satan also relies on conflicting metaphysical appeals to angelic substance, which is supposedly destined to reascend to glory. This is further combined with a curious amalgam of rights logic, appeals to merit and fixed laws. Satan's use of language suggests that, far from the isolated Cartesian subject being *opposed* to traditional political claims of merit and right, it is only once the self is nothing more than 'its own place' that it can take on any political discourse whatsoever, for there is no grounding reason. Having spurned the celestial light, Satan's arguments now contain 'semblance of worth, not substance' (1.529), for he uses the language of intrinsic properties (celestial virtues) without the rationale that would yield consistent first principles. The narrator states that Satan sits on his throne 'by merit raised' (thereby suggesting that worth precedes and produces relations of power), in contrast with Satan who will accuse God of being nothing more than domination by force 'upheld by old repute' (1.639). The narrator's description of Satan's merit also reinforces the negative, parasitic and inessential nature of evil; for all Satan's hatred of the sun's beams he cannot detach himself from the source of light and life: 'his form had not yet lost / All her Original brightness, nor appear'd / Less than Arch Angel ruind, and th' excess of glory obscur'd' (1.591–4). The use of the female possessive to describe form – 'her original brightness' – emphasizes also the distinction of form; Satan's form is something he takes on, that shines regardless of his will.

Satan therefore struggles to live up to that principle articulated by Mammon: 'to seek / Our own good from ourselves, and from our own / Live to our selves'

(2. 252–3). Again and again Milton will show Satan desperately declaring an absence of light and a mind sufficient unto itself, 'self-raised, self-begot', only to fall back upon a language of reason, substance, law and right:

> Powers and Dominions, Deities of Heav'n,
> For since no deep within her gulf can hold
> Immortal vigor, though opprest and fall'n,
> I give not Heav'n for lost. From this descent
> Celestial vertues rising, will appear
> More glorious and more dread than from no fall,
> And trust themselves to fear no second fate:
> Mee though just right and the fixt Laws of Heav'n
> Did first create your Leader, next free choice,
> With what besides, in Counsel or in Fight,
> Hath bin achievd of merit, yet this loss
> Thus farr at least recover'd, hath much more
> Establisht in a safe unenvied Throne
> Yielded with full consent. (PL 2.11–24)

By turning away from the light Satan is departing from a reason grounded in the way of the world. His arguments become *ad hoc* and sophistical, so that he can appeal to 'merit', 'just right', 'free choice,' and eventually argue that he need not justify his governance at all, for hell is so lacking in light and joy that it also provides no desire for possession: 'Where there is then no good / For which to strive, no strife can grow up there / From Faction' (2.30–2). In a world without quality or value there is no reason why one should desire either one's own proper place or one's own apportioned share. Reason for Satan is nothing more than 'ratio', a calculating and measuring power, rather than a governing form: 'Whom reason hath equalled, force hath made supreme.' Satan must therefore be an exemplary rhetorician and performer, must be nothing other than his performance, and must also be constituted through the relations that such performance creates.

Satan will therefore reject light: the very source of form that Milton will both describe within *Paradise Lost,* and call upon as the forming power *of* Paradise Lost. It is with light that matter takes on form: 'Bright effluence of bright essence increate' (3.6). Light is itself not created but the vehicle of creation, bestowing essence through God's voice: 'as with a Mantle didst invest / The rising world of waters dark and deep, / Won from the void and formless infinite' (3.10–12). By calling on that same light to write his poem, Milton presents his epic as the world's coming into further form, becoming more rational:

> So much the rather thou Celestial light
> Shine inward, and the mind through all her powers
> Irradiate, there plant eyes, all mist from thence
> Purge and disperse, that I may see and tell
> Of things invisible to mortal sight. (PL 3.51–5)

Milton's poem is therefore not an inessential or accidental addition to the world and its history, but an illumination, coming from the source of the world's own creation. *Paradise Lost* both is, and describes, a turning towards light as a realization of form. That turning to celestial light is made possible by a rejection of literalism, a rejection of any one of light's expressions or figures as final or definitive; it is therefore requisite that one move from a received image of light to the light through which images are given. This journey from given terms to the genetic source of terms is presented in Milton's grammar, and his use of the word 'or'.[144] The invocation to Book Three opens by entertaining two mutually exclusive theological possibilities:

> Hail, holy Light, offspring of Heav'n first-born,
> Or of th' Eternal Coeternal beam (PL 3.1–2)

Light is either heaven's offspring or co-eternal, either the very source of all genesis or the primary genesis. Some lines later 'or' appears again, after the proposition that 'God is light': 'Or hear'st thou rather pure Ethereal stream, Whose Fountain who shall tell?' The call to inspiration is multiple, conceding that we approach the source of life through its expressions. These figures of expression have – until the composition of Book Three, which will approach God's own voice and logic – proved adequate: 'I sung of Chaos and Eternal Night, / Taught by the heav'nly Muse to venture down / The dark descent, and up to reascend' (3.19–20). The figural relation deployed by Milton is one of analogy, not allegory. Just as divine light gives form to night, so must Milton, through the production of poetry, give form and reason to our relation to chaos. But analogy must be seen as analogy, as a figure of that truly original divine light. This method will not do for Book Three, which no longer takes its place within literary history, and can no longer work with an analogy between physical light and divine light. Instead, the inability to see the world in its full immediacy allows one to turn to the divine light. Milton's physical blindness has its precedents:

> nor somtimes forget
> Those other two equal'd with me in Fate,
> So were I equal'd with them in renown,
> Blind *Thamyris*, and blind *Maeonides*,
> And *Tiresias* and *Phineus* Prophets old. (PL 3.32–6)

Literary tradition and the line of prophetic vision yield a poetry that is both active – 'thoughts, that voluntary move' – and that might be seen as part of the natural cycle of time. As in Spenser, each era will bring forth its appropriate song:

> Then feed on thoughts, that voluntarie move
> Harmonious numbers; as the wakeful Bird
> Sings darkling, and in the shadiest Covert hid

> Tunes her nocturnal Note. Thus with the Year
> Seasons return. (PL 3.37–41)

However, it is only when worldly wisdom and the cyclic time of renewal is 'quite shut out' to present a 'universal blank' that the poet can leap over worldly time to the very source of that time. It is the 'celestial Light' that allows the poet to adopt the point of view of God, a looking that no longer receives light but a 'beatitude past utterance'. The narration breaks with the cycle of natural renewal and presents the pure presence – or 'Now' – of the divine gaze enjoying its own image; that pure now also transcends space, sitting in a height above all height:

> Now had the Almighty Father from above,
> From the pure Empyrean where he sits
> High Thron'd above all highth, bent down his eye,
> His own works and their works at once to view:
> About him all the Sanctities of Heaven
> Stood thick as Starrs, and from his sight receiv'd
> Beatitude past utterance; on his right
> The radiant image of his Glory sat,
> His only Son; On Earth he first beheld
> Our first two Parents, yet the onely two
> Of mankind, in the happie Garden plac't,
> Reaping immortal fruits of joy and love,
> Uninterrupted joy, unrival'd love
> In blissful solitude. (PL 3.56–69)

Only in turning away from expressions of light to the light itself does the epic move to the viewpoint of God, a viewpoint that both bestows life, and then allows that life to become fruitful in turn: 'His own works and their works at once to view'; 'Reaping immortal fruits of joy and love'. The poetry here follows the order of expression from the pure 'now' of God's gaze, to the firmament, to God's image in Christ, and then to Adam and Eve whose relation of love is regarded, in contrast with Sin and Death, as fruitful. It is when God then surveys hell that he communicates with his Son about the structure of Satan's fall and the potentiality for evil. It is as though only a recognition and expression of that 'Uninterrupted joy, / unrivalled love' could provide the preamble for a discussion of evil. Milton's order of composition thereby denies evil any positive being, for Satan and hell are placed in God's purview beyond the bounded world. God's gaze moves from observing Satan's original freedom – 'whom no bounds prescribed' – to considering the potential for the fall of man: 'Ingrate, he had of me / All he could have; I made him just and right, Sufficient to have stood, though free to fall' (PL 3.97–9). By taking on the voice of God, this section of the epic looks into the very being of justice, or what form justice must take if it is to be just.

Milton is, therefore, neither a voluntarist nor nominalist: God cannot be a being who arbitrarily determines some qualities as good, others as evil; nor can these terms of good and evil be merely conventional. It is important, then, that God's speech takes the form of syllogisms, conditionals and definitions. Milton refuses allegory, analogy and figure, presenting God as the voice of reason. His voice is in accord with the very order of the world. We are therefore given the poetic playing out of a conditional: if God were to create, his world would be expressive of that free creativity, and could not be subjected to necessity; a world without that freedom would neither be worthy of God, nor allow for the maximum life for his creatures: 'What praise could they receive? / What plea-sure I from such obedience paid' (PL 3.106–7). This conditional then yields a definition; reason could not be blind adherence to law but must be a divine capacity to choose what is just and right in one's nature: 'reason also is choice' (3.108). From that conditional (if God were to create, his world would need to be divine) to the definition (only a reason of choice is free and therefore in tune with the divinity of the world), God offers a syllogism: if we accept that a divine world is a free world, and that reason must therefore be the power of choice, then we must conclude that God could not do otherwise than allow man to fall. This does not subject God to necessity, but follows from what it is to be a divine creative being; freedom follows from man's form, which is also ordained by the very logic of creation:

> I formd them free, and free they must remain,
> Till they enthrall themselves: I else must change
> Thir nature, and revoke the high Decree
> Unchangeable, Eternal, which ordain'd
> Their freedom, they themselves ordain'd thir fall. (PL 3.124–8)

The one thing God cannot do is *not* be God. God is the very being of the world, the one thing that truly *is*, not requiring a process of becoming to arrive at this or that form of being. To 'revoke the high degree' or alter his free and divine crea-tion would require that God be now one way now another, at once creating freely, and then creating mechanistically. This principle of non-contradic-tion – something cannot both be and not be – is not merely rhetorical but the very condition for saying that something *is* at all.[145] (By contrast Satan is torn by contradiction: 'Vaunting aloud though racked with deep despair', at once a being of pure self-determination and indomitable will.)

The key point of this use of logic, syllogisms and consequences at this point in the epic is twofold. First, it establishes a *substantial* distinction between good and evil. Good and evil are not two properties of being; nor are they two beings. Rather, good or justice is the very logic of the world and therefore demands a style of reasoning in which one moves from first principles to the definition of nature; nature is then defined as the potentiality for the fulfilment of reason. By contrast, Sin and Death are not expressed through propositions, definitions and conclusions – not through voice – but are presented in the image of a body that multiplies from itself alone, then turns back and devours itself. The distinction between Sin/Death/Satan and God is not – as Satan would have it – between one body and another, between competing forces. It is, rather, an ontological distinction of kinds, between an ultimate subject that underlies all being and aspects or emanations of that being (God as the very form of substance or what truly is) and accidents (for Sin and Death are nothing other than processes of deviation and impotentiality or failure). This ontological distinction then yields a difference in style, between God's language of logic and first principles and the creature's language of analogy and likeness. This passage from ontology to logic then allows for a proper sense of the relation between good and evil, for they are not symmetrical qualities, such that one might compare a good being to an evil being. No being is in itself evil or marked by evil as a quality, for evil is that capacity for any being to turn away from its proper potential. In this sense, evil is defined by Milton as a false contrary: as the result of a being not becoming according to its proper kind or definition. The principle of divine life as pure voice and reason may progress to fulfilment or, if negated, leave a remainder of non-being, anti-production and privation. The correct style for dealing with good and evil in poetry would not be to present a battle of two different beings, but a relation between true being and a force that operates against being.

In addition to establishing two modes, genres and styles for dealing with good and evil, Milton also gives an internal account of those styles. Literary history has dealt with figures of chaos and night, and to take part in that tradition one can call upon the world as it has been expressed; but *Paradise Lost* will not be one more text within literary time and relations, for it will also give voice to the very distinction between figure and reason, cyclic time and creative time, emanated light and divine light. The epic is both the narration of the genesis of the world and an account of the poem's own coming into being, achieved by turning away from figures of creation to the light and life of creation itself. Milton will not take two figures, one to represent good, the other evil. Instead, he will regard good as the illuminating source of all figuration, and evil as the remaining-within-itself of a body that simply *is*. Adam and Eve are his figures of the 'human form divine', capable as they are of seeing each other as expressions of divine light; but they can also reject expressive relations, for they will remain free, 'Till they enthral themselves'. The way out of such self-enthralment, and the way out of reason's failure to actualize its proper form, is poetry: the creation of both a narrative and a style that gives reason an image of its proper being and power.

Paradise Lost offers an argument about the relation between light and history, insisting that we must see the fall as a swerve away from the light, and not an intrinsic property of corruption that condemns humanity to passivity. But *Paradise Lost* is also an activation and internalization of literary history; only through reading Milton's theodicy and thinking in the style it demands can we see all literary productions as figures that stand in for the one creative life. Milton's invocation in Book One presents preceding literary history as a series

of illuminated scenes, which *Paradise Lost* will suspend by appealing to the
source of prophecy rather than epic:

> Sing Heav'nly Muse, that on the secret top
> Of *Oreb*, or of *Sinai*, didst inspire
> That Shepherd, who first taught the chosen Seed,
> In the Beginning how the Heav'ns and Earth
> Rose out of *Chaos*: or if *Sion* hill
> Delight thee more, and *Siloa*'s Brook that flowed
> Fast by the Oracle of God; I thence
> Invoke thy aid to my adventurous Song,
> That with no middle flight intends to soar
> Above th' *Aonian* mount, while it pursues
> Things unattempted yet in Prose or Rhime. (PL 1.6–16)

Like Book Two, Book One deploys the Miltonic 'or', which allows a number
of figures to stand in for the creative and genetic power itself: 'Of Oreb, or of
Sinai'; 'or if Sion hill'. Rejecting literalism, the 'or' allows for a series of terms
to exfoliate from the expressive source, just as God's creation expresses itself
through harmonious difference, which can only become dissonant when any
single term is detached from its expressive origin. The 'barbarous dissonance' of
Comus in *A Mask* or the scraping of scrannel straw in 'Lycidas' is opposed to the
divine harmony that refers beyond itself to an eternal order which is also the very
movement of the world ('That sing, and singing in their glory move' ['Lycidas'
180]). The use of 'or' commits the narrator and the reader to *reading*, and to
intuiting the life from which different terms emanate. Book One rejects the
'middle flight' and aligns its voice with the very forming power of creation, but
does so by requesting illumination: 'what in me is dark / Illumin' (1.22–3).
Book Three takes on the point of view of light itself, 'things invisible to mortal
sight'. Milton's literary newness is not simply one of novelty, but is essential and
formal. That position above middle flight, to 'things unattempted yet', is
achieved not by adding one more term to literary history, but by giving form to
the creative power itself. Milton will therefore refuse allegory in order to define
God as light, both the source of all form and that through which form is known.

By contrast, in rejecting light Satan sees only what is present and not
its coming into being. This is directly disclosed in Satan's rhetoric, which is
dominated not by 'or' – a term which allows us to take one figure, now another,
as expressing the one life – but by the conjunctive logic of 'and': 'Me though
just right and the fixed laws of heaven / Did first create your leader, next free
choice / With what besides.' Satan will seize just right, and fixed laws, and
free choice. His logic is accumulative, using whatever terms are at his disposal,
with his connective principle being nothing more than an opportunistic list.
This is the style and logic of evil: chaotic terms and relations collected without
principle or order. If all we see are already given terms, then we fail to question
how those terms are given. Turning away from the light to relations among
forces, as Satan does, entails turning away from genesis – or how things are

given – to the given. The antidote to that fall back into chaos is poetry, not a poetry that creates order *ex nihilo* from itself, but a poetry that aligns its own order with the creative harmony of life.

Milton is clear that turning away from light is also a turning away from happiness, for happiness can only be achieved when the soul arrives at the light that is the source of its proper being. Satan farewells the 'happy fields / where joy forever dwells' to become nothing more than his own mind that is at forceful war with all that is not itself. The rejection of light is also a rejection of origins. One moves from an ontology where the contraries of good and evil can be explained by referring back to the creative potential of life (and this is what Milton will do in his epic) to an ontology where there are simply competing forces, with no way to discern the difference among forces other than quantitatively. Satan's governance of the rebel angels is one of degree, not of kind, and must therefore be achieved by taking on ventures that constitute him as the most forceful. His power takes the form of 'power over' (*potestas*), and not power as each being's virtue or potential (*potentia*). The scenes in which Satan is the central character are scenes of performance, in which he produces himself through acts of speech, persuasion, soliloquy and oration. Rhetoric is not tempered by, grounded upon, or read as, the expression of some prior substance, for there is no self beyond effective rhetorical creation.

A different mode of power – power as *potential* – governs the form of creation that Milton uses in *Paradise Lost,* and contrasts directly with power as self-fashioning. This is why the scene of Sin and Death is so important; Milton will show that Sin emerges from Satan's selfhood: his capacity to remain within himself, to become enamoured of himself, to forget all that is not himself, and even forget his own past that produced his contrary present. Considered properly – that is, historically – the self is not pure force, but a potential. A being may remain within itself, turning back upon itself to be nothing other than 'its own place', or it can take the journey of time: progressing from recognition of creation to fulfilment. It is not the case, as Spenser's defence of allegory might suggest, that power is effected by creating oneself as a noble person, or by presenting a style of person as noble. Literary texts are powerful not because of their force – not as performances which establish relations – but because they actualize those potentials that are grounded in divine life itself. Milton will therefore write *Paradise Lost* not as an allegory, but as an intuition of the very genesis of order out of chaos, and will then – in the trajectory of the narrative – explain how it is that at a certain moment in literary history it is possible for a poet to discern the form of the good itself – the form that has, until now, only expressed itself in shadowy types.

History and Truth

We can only understand and see ourselves as bearing a 'paradise within', or a reason capable of moving beyond derivative images to intuit the imaging power itself, once we become historically self-aware. In the concluding historical books of the epic Michael will explain to Adam that it is only prior to the New Testament that human beings have a reason so flawed that God will impose upon them a power of pure force. We might say that if one is neither historically self-aware, nor aware of the very structure of the fall as a turn away from our divine potential as rational, then Thomas Hobbes' argument holds true: man is simply not rational enough to prevent his desire operating in a brutish and violent manner and therefore he requires an external authority. However, once that 'one greater man' freely allows his life to be spent for the sake of a life that did not recognize any life beyond its present desires, then human beings will become capable of working their way towards truth. History for Milton has its own formal requirements; it is not a series of distinct moments, but a progression, and one in which the historical power itself comes into being. After the vision of Old Testament history disclosed by Michael, Adam no longer suffers from either the despair that follows from seeing human beings as dispossessed of the potential for rational self-governance, or from the illusion that the future will follow in a determined or mechanical fashion:

> O thou who future things canst represent
> As present, Heav'nly instructer, I revive
> At this last sight, assur'd that Man shall live
> With all the Creatures, and thir seed preserve.
> Far less I now lament for one whole World
> Of wicked Sons destroyd, than I rejoyce
> For one Man found so perfet and so just,
> That God voutsafes to raise another World
> From him, and all his anger to forget. (PL 11.870–8)

History produces and requires the 'paradise within' that allows 'man' to recognize his created being, and thereby to move forwards to rational self-governance. History requires narrative reflexivity, not because literature creates or brings into being relations of power, but because true power – the power that is the realization of our divine potential – requires the passage and the act of time. Milton will therefore oppose a time of growth, progression, increasing complexity, creativity and revelation, to a time in which everything is already given and one can only create new relations through force.

Paradise Lost is itself both a meditation on how history might have an order and what role poetry might play in that order. This historically self-conscious mode of composition does not use history for moral purposes but presents different modes of historical understanding as good or evil. If we make the most of our rational being and live up to our potentiality, then we will not simply accept the order of the world, nor will we present poetry and figuration as adornments of the world. Rather, accepting that we are created and that creation is divine, we have two options. The path Milton chooses is to create in such a way that all one's works might be in accord with the creative power of life, thereby bringing the rational power in general to a proper understanding of itself. Rational man becomes a historical agent capable of choosing his own free self-governance.[146] The other path is to see time as having no trajectory and no intrinsic potential. The scene of Sin and Death is therefore an image of a time which cycles around meaningless repetition. The generation of that mode of time is traced back to Satan's resistance to form; far from acting or reasoning in accord with relations of harmony beyond his known being, Satan regards all relations and events as reducible to forces measurable against his own will. Satan is, however, not evil itself – for Milton insists constantly on the vestiges of virtue, reason and angelic being that Satan retains – but he is a being who chooses or tends towards evil. Satan is not an image of evil, but one possible historical relation to evil.

Satan operates in *Paradise Lost,* not as a contrary to God, nor as a distinct principle or being. Rather, Satan is expressive of all those qualities that both Milton and the Christian tradition had celebrated – qualities such as self-affirmation and dynamic striving – but at the same time he represents the incompletion of those qualities. Satan is not evil as such; he possesses all too evidently the spirit of life, but a life that swerves from its proper potential. Part of the rationalism and vitalism of *Paradise Lost* lies in the continued presentation of *all* life – however fallen – as participating to some degree in divine light. For all his declarations, Satan can neither become fully evil, because he always evidences some degree of brightness and virtue, nor, despite all his efforts, can he ever bring about the negation of life; all his designs pervert and delay but ultimately serve the good. What we see in Satan is a particular corruption of life, a vital force that has not realized its fullest potential. Satan will use all the rhetoric of creation, activation, production and growth, but these are all divorced from their enabling condition: thus Satan's self-affirmation, self-creation, self-production and self-definition all begin from Satan himself. Satan derives all relations, all force, all quantification and value from himself. One term in the system of relations generates relations in general, and this is what leads Satan into contradiction. On the one hand he affirms the active, productive, creative and relational, while on the other hand allowing his own mind or self to be a point irreducible to relations, a point of conjunction or coagulation. In his affirmation of forces, the one point not subsumable by relations is his own subjectivity.

This 'Satanic' subject – which we might also liken to the subject of contemporary new historicism – is in a paradoxical position. On the one hand, by affirming forces, performance, creation and relations the subject no longer has an essential nature, and can therefore no longer be subject to definition or some transcendent moral law. On the other hand, those forces, relations, performances and acts are executed *by the subject.* So we might say that we are left with nothing other than a world of forces, even though there are some forces (subjects) who take themselves to be at one and the same time causes and effects, agents and outcomes. The subject is at once subjected to power relations – nothing more than an effect – at the same time that power relations are produced through competing and performing subjects. Such a notion of the subject and power is given in Satan's own affirmation of his fellow fallen angels. On the one hand he strives for re-ascension through power, while on the other hand claiming that such a process of ascension (power over) would be nothing more than the self's own autochthonous power: 'For who can beleeve, though after loss, / That all these puissant Legions, whose exile / Hath emptied Heav'n, shall fail to re-ascend / Self-rais'd, and repossess thir native seat?' (1.631–4). There are two ways in which we can deal with this conundrum. The first, Miltonic, way is to assert that relations, forces and the power to perform are not the subject's own, and that our recognition of the light and life through which we are effected is the only way in which we can escape the inner hell of a mind that can only find itself. The mind is not its own place but is the effect of a dynamic and living world, a world which the vitalist ethic behoves us to consider. The other, modern historicist, way is to argue that the mind is its own place, and that the world, history, texts and relations are effects of subject relations, even if the subject is nothing more than those relations. There are not selves who act, but actions from which selves are effected. What I will suggest in the concluding chapters is that reading Milton counter-historically offers us a path beyond both these conceptions of the subject. This is because Milton's poetry, like all art, also offers us that which resists both a rhetoric of interacting forces and a rhetoric of emanating life. For it is in poetry *as poetry* – a created and detached object – that we come face to face with the non-living, the ineffective, the non-relational and the inert.

What we need to consider for now is the way in which, despite the Milton debates, a certain history is adopted by both parties: vitalism. For Milton, the source of life and light is God; to turn away from the light is to negate life, to be drawn away from knowledge, becoming, reason and one's own proper being. Satan recognizes no source of life beyond competing forces, no intrinsic being that would govern relations, for being is effected from relations. Satan is the first new historicist, recognizing nothing other than self-creation. Like Stephen Greenblatt, when Satan looks to find the subject he looks for an interior and self-present truth; he, not surprisingly, finds nothing and a hell opens within him. For Milton, however, it is just this turn to an isolated interiority that draws Satan away from life towards evil. Satan's mistake is to look inwards to find himself, when reflection should properly be directed to God's inner light 'ingraven' in our hearts. There are, therefore, two modes of introspection. The Platonic, Christian and ethical modes examine the self in order to discover an inner light which is not the self's own. The Satanic version is Cartesian: the look inward finds nothing other than itself, thereby reducing the truth and the self to a capacity to doubt, to not be what is simply given or present.[147]

For Milton, truth does not take the form of looking inward to find a self that is already there and fully actual. Truth is achieved only by tracing the signs of our genesis from the present, in order that we might then intuit what we ought to become. If we have any force this is not because power is achieved through relations – 'power over' – but because power is the actualization of potential. Our reason, our history, our present: all these are actualizations of our potential.

This allows us to make a number of observations with regard to Milton's own response to history and literary history. As I have argued, Milton argues from a position of rationalist vitalism: reason is the very order of the world, and any deviation from that order is a negation of life. In his pre-revolutionary writings this commitment to the inevitable life of reason – that reason would, through its intrinsic force, come to the fore – underpinned Milton's writings on government, the private sphere and the reading of texts. Only with the unimpeded exercise of the spirit would the proper political order of the world appear. The church and state must be separated, not to limit the power of the church, but because a spirit liberated from a merely worldly and contingent power would eventually discover the truth of reason required for good government. Similarly, divorce should be allowed, not because the values of the private sphere were personal and up to individual decision, but because only the development of reason – liberating women from being corporeal chattels to become spiritual helpmeets – would allow for a rational public sphere. Accordingly, a freedom of debate and publication would allow the one true light of the world to flourish; distortion and error emerge when the natural life of the mind is restricted.

If Milton's theology aligns God with reason, and the created world with the potential to become rational, how does he cope with the failure of reason that occurs when individuals turn their backs on liberty? One answer is given within *Paradise Lost*: with the transgression of God's one sole command we have turned our backs on law, and in the irrationalism that follows God allows temporal government to be imposed. Another answer is given in the very act and existence of *Paradise Lost*: once God's grace has allowed the Son to redeem our sin we are given the potential to journey once more to the light of law and reason. But this requires a recognition of where we are historically, and of the tendencies of history. One of those tendencies is forgetting; if we know no time when we were not as now, and if we regard government, law and morality as ways of managing the world *as it is*, then we will turn to political expediency. This, indeed, is the attitude towards time taken by the opportunist and relativist Satan, and by those who allowed the republic to proceed as kingship by other means. The other historical tendency is revolutionary, but requires memory. If our actual condition is the outcome of a swerve away from our potentiality, then we need to retrace our steps in order to move forward.

Milton will not, therefore, respond to his historical present with argument alone; that might have been suitable in the 1640s when it appeared that reason was journeying, and journeying in the right direction. The failure of the revolution requires more than argument; it requires a form of meta-argumentation. How is it, if we are rational, that we fail to actualize our reason? How do we fall? One response is simply to accept our weakness, that we are overpowered, and that the forces to which we were subjected were unfair; this is the Satanic response and relies simply on accepting the outcomes as adequate and complete signs of the origin. If we fell then this is because we were weak. The other response is aesthetic and hermeneutic. If we are presented with two images of life – one that expands, connects, becomes different, proliferates and produces ever more complexity, as opposed to a life that redounds upon itself, repeats, remains the same and refuses relations – then we recognize clearly the difference between paradise and evil. Reason may be led away from its proper potentiality because it confuses these two tendencies; such tendencies *may* be confused precisely because there is no real being or substance that is opposed to life. Evil occurs not with this or that positive thought or act but with the failure to act. Milton will not therefore present good and evil as two choices, for we always *choose* the good. Satan's radical evil of 'Evil be Thou my Good,' is, in effect, a rationalization of not choosing: deciding that he fell because God rendered him weaker and overpowered him by force, Satan refuses to take on the status of a free agent. In accepting that he is always and essentially fallen, and that his good or telos is evil, Satan decides not to decide, not to see himself as a being capable of hope. Eve is seduced by being presented with a liberation from the burden of choice: she will no longer be subject to law but will be a law unto herself. But, as Augustine made clear, this raises the question of why, if the will was in accord with the law and not yet fallen, Adam and Eve transgressed. It is that journey of reason's failure that *Paradise Lost* charts.

Reason and Life

Satan's rebellion occurs when he regards God as a being who impedes his life, who places limits on his power. Satan seduces Eve by arguing that the prohibition, far from giving order and form to her life, precludes her from realizing what she might be. That misreading of one's own power occurs when one regards any force other than oneself as a negation of one's self. *That* style of thinking is a failure of reason, where reason remains only within the self, requiring that everything other than the self must somehow be in accord with the self's own point of view. What reason ought to do – if it is right *reason* and not simply the way in which the self makes sense of the world – is to look beyond its place in life to life in general. This would, for example, have precluded Eve from making the mistake that the majesty of creation exists in order to frame her beauty. Unscientific and irrational thinking interprets what is other than itself in terms of what it already is. Reason, by contrast, examines the world as such, acknowledges a time and order beyond the self, and then allows reason to take its own place in time; 'but to know / That which before us lies in daily life / Is the prime Wisdom' (PL 8.192–4).[148] This means that we are required not to remain within ourselves, and that study of the world is a study of creation. It also requires that there are essential limits on knowing: 'Heav'n is for thee too high / To know what passes there; be lowlie wise: Think onely what concernes thee and thy being' (PL 8.172–4). If knowledge is a genuine journey then this is because we are finite creatures to whom the world is given through relations; only a negation of the world, life and creation would reduce the world to what can be known.

Paradise Lost will therefore place human history and finitude within the frame of a vitalist ethic and aesthetic. We should not see evil as a figure that we might place within life and history, but as the negation of life and history. We should, therefore, see the post-revolutionary position as a historical threshold: either we can interpret the failure of the republic as a sign of what we are and resign ourselves to a government that is imposed, external and conventional, or we could read our current situation as a point of decision. *Paradise Lost* will therefore oppose an evil of inertia, self-devouring, non-becoming and enclosure to a good and rational life of dynamism, actualization, fruition and openness. From that stark aesthetic opposition between the isolated, detached and inward-turning cycle, and the open, developing, productive and diversifying relation, Milton then presents a choice of reason: we can either seek to remember and recall a life beyond the self-present, or we can remain passive, within ourselves.

This allows us finally to return to Milton's revision of Spenser in his scene of Sin and Death, and to the style and syntax of *Paradise Lost* more generally. Reason is the potential to arrive at a self-understanding which no longer accepts 'man' as a simple being; through reason we recognize our finitude, but this recognition gives us a higher life and reason towards which our history may be directed. All the literary and mythic fragments in *Paradise Lost* must be subsumed in such a way that they all become signs of that one rationally-tending universe. One of the ways in which we can understand Milton's relation to his literary past is his appropriation of dichotomies, and their transformation into contraries. Contraries, as we will see in the next chapter, are not in themselves evil; matter, darkness, body, passion are beneficent when coupled with form, light, mind and reason. It is detachment from relation that produces the 'evil angel'. Milton's Christianity is insistently monistic; there is not a God who must battle with evil. Rather there is one living, rational and vital life which may – due to its very dynamism – fail to arrive at its proper potential. That swerve from the actualization of life is evil, not a being in its own right.

Milton has historical and political reasons for this monistic logic; the idea of a positive and simply 'other' force of evil precludes the full rationalization and redemption of the world, and in turn allows for a certain resignation or passivity of reason. Milton will, at all times, insist that evil has no real being and occurs with a failure of reason. This monism is evident at the most fundamental level of Milton's ontology and theology; the 'one first matter' that takes on form is, in itself, neither good nor evil. The progression towards form and essential being is good, while the negation of that trajectory is evil. Good and evil should not be represented as allegorical types, as they are in Spenser, but as contrary modes of being. Evil is the absence of becoming, relations, growth and production. Adam and Eve are not types of the good, but goodness itself; and paradisiacal love is God's divinity in act. God is neither distant nor difficult, and expresses himself directly in created life. There is no need for allegory here. If life itself is divine, rational and fully expressive, then the contrary of life – which Milton depicts in Sin and Death – should not be given as another body or character within life, but as the negation of life.

Milton achieves this axiology stylistically in his use of prosody, where we frequently progress from the absence of order, relation and harmony and move towards relation, balance and quality. In Book Two the journey of the fallen angels in hell – a journey that can have no direction or orientation ('in confused march forlorn') – passes a region so lacking in order that the rhythm breaks down into a series of monosyllables. The rhythm had been proceeding as though the fallen angels were genuinely moving through time, so that the rhythmic line ends with the iamb, 'and found' but this is immediately deflated and halted by the next line's 'No rest'. We see in the very form of the poetry the collapse of propulsive rhythm and the fall into fragmentation. The opening spondaic foot – 'No rest' – anticipates the degeneration into disconnection and atomization – 'Rocks, caves, lakes ...' – with the rhythm only returning when we shift the point of view to the place of that evil disorder within God's design:

> View'd first thir lamentable lot, and found
> No rest: through many a dark and drearie Vaile
> They pass'd, and many a Region dolorous,
> Oe'r many a frozen, many a fierie Alpe,
> *Rocks, Caves, Lakes, Fens, Bogs, Dens, and shades of death,*[149]
> A universe of death, which God by curse
> Created evil, for evil only good,
> Where all life dies, death lives, and Nature breeds,
> Perverse, all monstrous, all prodigious things,
> Abominable, inutterable, and worse
> Than Fables yet have feign'd. (PL 2.617–27, emphasis added)

Milton does not give evil or error an allegorical figure within a historical narrative, but presents a universe of death which is the absence of order and life; evil is also presented as the contrary or negation of expression ('inutterable, and worse / Than fables yet have feign'd'), as though the evil in this world only tends towards that hellish evil beyond all fear and imagination. The difficult phrase, 'Created evil, for evil only good, / Where all life dies, death lives,' directly ties evil to the senseless, paradoxical and almost impossible negation of life. God's 'creation' of evil is explained not by granting evil a distinct existence, but by presenting evil's 'good' as the minimal growth or change which only works in a perverse and monstrous fashion. Like Satan's later 'Evil be thou my good', evil is still in some minimal sense a fragment of a creation that is all good, for there is still movement and change, even if evil is movement perverted and corrupted. Evil will, then, eventually be caught up in the greater and indomitable expression of divine life, and will only be a temporary deviation or swerve from the good: 'the evil soon / Driv'n back redounded as a flood on those / From whom it sprung, impossible to mix / With Blessedness' (7.56–9). Milton will therefore allow those minor disruptions of poetic flow, only to pick up the rhythm again; chaos has no real being.

4

Gender and Contrariety

In a more direct contrast and comparison between Milton and Spenser, we can look at the ways in which the figure of gender operates in the *Faerie Queene* and *Paradise Lost*. Far from being a simple binary within either Spenser or Milton's poetry, gender is used as a figure to present two modes of opposition or difference. The gender binary can either occur as a fruitful relation, in which each term tends to its proper potential, or there can be a collapse of difference and distinction. As I have argued in the preceding chapters, Milton's poetics and politics express a normative image of life, in which spirit and body are in accord, because bodily material life harbours a proper tendency towards rationalization which is actualized through time. The body's proper realization as spirit is also a process of increasing activation: all those aspects of the self which are at present irrational, unthought, compulsive or mechanical ought to become rational and organic, where every part of the body is in accord with the active spirit, and every spirit is in accord with divine expressive life. The privileging of organic life is clear in Milton's poetry and prose, both in his depiction of human bodies as expressive of their glorious maker, and of the commonwealth as 'one huge Christian personage'. While Milton clearly grants feminine bodies a role in this organicism, as properly allowing male reason to recognize itself in just authority, there is a more demonic potentiality of the feminine which we might refer to as a 'body without organs'.[150] Whereas an organized body grants each sensible and mental faculty its proper place in the expression of one vital and animating life, a body without organs is an assemblage of disjointed and divergent powers, or what Milton refers to in *Tenure of Kings and Magistrates* as 'blind affections' (CPW 3.190). If sound becomes the mere noise of Comus's 'barbarous rout' or the bishops' 'lean and flashy songs' in 'Lycidas', if seeing becomes mere semblance or spectacle (as Dalila will present herself in *Samson Agonistes*), if eating is mere consumption without nutrition (Death's devouring of Sin's offspring), and if touch is carnal rather than communicative (in the fallen sex of Adam and Eve), then the body's capacities are detached from an organizing and expressive spirit. That notion of the body uncoupled from its vital and animating potentiality is at once in Milton's poetry a necessary possibility for the progression towards reason, for a *free* body can always fail to realize its proper form; at the same time Milton will associate the tending towards the disorganization and diremption of bodily life with the feminine.

Why, we might ask, is the negation of the good in both Spenser's error and Milton's Sin given female form? One answer lies in the gender inflections of Western ontology,[151] inflections that dominate the Christian literary tradition. Form, ordering, light and bringing merely potential matter into actuality or true substance is associated with masculinity, while the feminine is aligned with the passive or potentiality for existence. This means that there is nothing evil or corrupt about the feminine *per se*, but that the feminine requires the spiritual form-giving act of light to bring it into true being and relation. Gender is not symmetrical: not a binary of two distinct terms, but a contrary where each term has its proper being through the other.[152] This means also that neither term in the contrary can be considered good or evil, for evil only results from an improper coupling. It is not surprising, then, that for both Spenser and Milton evil will be figured as a nightmarish relation (or non-relation) in which the feminine potentiality for material production is uncoupled from the form-giving power of light, truth and reason.

Such an argument regarding the parasitic nature of matter, and the unreality or non-being of a matter devoid of form, unfolds from the traditional understanding of substance, or the privileging of one being that truly is, while all other beings exist only by analogy. Only God exists as pure substance, requiring no other being in order to be. While form, order, boundary, light and act can exist in eternal self-sufficiency, matter can only be known or come into being in its relation with form, or through its illumination. This imagery and ontology pervade *Paradise Lost*, both metaphorically in the invocations which appeal to inspiration as a mode of impregnation, and literally in the scene of God giving bound and definition to the 'one first matter'. Not only is the earth in *Paradise Lost* depicted as bounded, balanced and 'pendant', bordering upon but also delimited from chaos 'the firm opacous Globe, / Of this round World, whose first convex divides / The luminous inferior orbs, enclos'd / from Chaos' (3.418–21) – actual gender relations also reinforce a fundamental ontology which sets form, light, limit, reason and spirit in a dominating or *informing* – but not opposed – relation to matter and body. Thus Eve is not irrational, nor is she equal to Adam; rather, her being is complementary and contrary. She may tend more towards embodiment, passivity, sensuality and visual beauty, but there is nothing evil about this tending *per se*. It is only when that tendency becomes detached from its relation to form and reason, becoming self-sufficient and non-relational, that it is corrupted by evil.

Milton's hierarchical and yet ennobling depiction of Eve can be illuminated with reference to his doctrine of the body. The hierarchical relationship between reason and the body does not seek to pervert or deny the body but to bring it closer to the character of reason. As early as *A Mask presented at Ludlow Castle* Milton introduces the idea of a 'wise appetite,' and in *Christian Doctrine* he claims that the process of resurrection is the attainment of the condition of the soul for all aspects of human being including the body. Just as this doctrine in many ways revalues the body and overcomes dualism, so Milton's attitude toward women and their putative ontological inferiority is at first glance ennobling. In Milton's picture of marriage the wife's due reverence of her husband will mean she is more than a corporeal chattel; she will become a rational and spiritual partner and this will in turn dignify the sexual aspect of marriage. One central argument of Milton's divorce pamphlets is that a law which permits divorce only for adultery or absence of sexual consummation characterizes marriage as a contract between bodies. Milton does not simply want to *add* the issue of spiritual compatibility. He regards the issue of intellectual companionship as more important due to the very character of gender relations.[153]

Milton here, as elsewhere, refuses to place the institution before the ethical reason for its existence. Marriage is correctly a spiritual bond and not a civil contract; its end is the edification of human being. Therefore, while being bound by an institutional and scriptural tradition of the inferiority of women, Milton sees this inferiority not as placing women in an entirely other category of being altogether[154] but as differing in degree (like Adam from the angels). In fact the relationship between woman and man is structurally analogous to that between man and Christ.[155] It is for this reason that woman should not be servile but edified by her relation to a similar yet superior version of herself: 'man is not to hold her as a servant, but receives her into a part of that empire which god proclaims him to, though not equally, yet largely as his own image and glory' (CPW 2.589). Just as God created human beings free so that they could be obedient in a worthy manner, so women must be provided as rational and noble inferiors in order to reflect and exercise the glory of man's image: 'for it is no small glory to him, that a creature so like him, should be made subject to him' (CPW 2.589). Just as the human soul carries the image of a higher transcendence, so woman, if correctly directed towards her proper mode of being, recognizes her image in man: 'the woman is not primarily and immediately the image of God, but in reference to the man' (CPW 2.589). Thus the argument for women's rational inferiority, which is required for men to recognize themselves as rational masters, is part of a broader understanding that sees the life of this world not as heavenly in itself but as all the better and more productive for its gradual historical and rational progression towards goodness.[156]

It is possible to argue that Milton is against a form of misogyny which would reduce women to embodied and irrational beings. Women can and should aspire to become rational. In fact, the entire logic of the divorce pamphlets devolves upon the original state of marriage where hierarchical differences – between the soul and the body and male and female – were properly ordered: 'mariage is a human society, and that all human society must proceed from the mind rather than the body, els it would be by a kind of animal or brutish meeting' (CPW 2.275). The feminine must be like enough to the masculine to reflect male rationality and only inferior in the sense of providing subordinated but not valueless virtues of attractiveness and charming diversion: 'wherin the enlarg'd soul may leave off a while her severe schooling; ... which as she cannot well doe without company so well as where the different sexe in most resembling unlikenes, and most unlike resemblance cannot but please best' (CPW 2.597).

Milton sees marriage as governed by the same laws of hierarchy that operate in the universe as a whole. If a man has married an 'idolatresse' or a woman whose society is such as to bring him into despair and hence atheism he should divorce her for the sake of a higher divine good: 'for there is a certain scale of duties, there is a certain hierarchy of upper and lower commands, which for want of studying in right order, all the world is in confusion' (CPW 2.264).

Not only does Milton invoke a natural hierarchy to govern marital law, he also argues for a transcendental concept of 'divorce' in which the creation of the world is seen to begin with an originary act of division of like from unlike: '[By God's] divorcing command the world first rose out of Chaos, nor can be renew'd again out of confusion but by the separating of unmeet sorts' (CPW 2.273). This argument for divine divorce is extended into a concept of the natural propensity of the universe to produce meetings of similar kinds: 'God's doing is ever to bring the due likenesses and harmonies of his workers together'. Unfit marriages are therefore 'against the fundamental law book of nature' and it is the function of divorce laws to restore that state of nature where like resides with like. Such residing likeness would be the proper and harmonious coupling of contraries. Milton also uses the doctrine of similarity to reject the argument that the Mosaic law's sanctioning of divorce accommodated a sinful people. For Milton, sin and law are 'diagonal contraries' – that is, improperly coupled – and such contraries can have no truck with each other: 'sin can have no tenure by law at all, but is rather an external outlaw, and in hostility with law past all attonement: both *diagonall* contraries, as much allowing one another, as day and night together in one hemisphere' (CPW 2.288).

Just as Milton's arguments on church government claimed that institutions should be based on the validity of inner experience and reason, so his divorce tracts claim that marriage is properly a private and spiritual contract. Excessive attention to the bodily or external aspects of such institutions leads to idolatry, for Milton claims that the divorce laws against which he is arguing make an idol of marriage: 'to injoyn the indissoluble keeping of a mariage found unfit against the good of man both soul and body . . . is to make an Idol of mariage, to advance it above the worship of God and the good of man' (CPW 2.276). What is at issue for Milton in his divorce pamphlets is the spiritual corruption of a soul that becomes chained to the institution. Although Milton argues that both men and women may divorce a heathen or incompatible spouse as a threat to the spiritual solace of the faithful partner, Milton's poetry as well as the examples offered in his prose tend to depict the contamination of partner spirits as a process of 'unmanning' or 'effeminizing'. Thus the divorce laws Milton advocates assert the right of a man to be released from the 'unmanly' subjection to an Idolatresse: 'This law therfore justly and piously provides against such an unmanly task of bondage as this' (CPW 2.626). In *The Doctrine and Discipline of Divorce* Milton claims that being forced to remain in a marriage with a woman who is no meet help threatens both the husband's soul and his manhood: 'to constrain him furder were to unchristian him, to unman him' (CPW 2.353). The effects of women upon men could also extend into the political sphere. In his *History of Britain* Milton denies that women can play any role in the framing of law (CPW 5.32, 74 & 79–80), despite the fact that his reform tracts demanded that all Christian citizens had a duty to oversee right government. In *Eikono-clastes* Milton comments on Charles' letters: 'to sumn up all, they shewed him govern'd by a woman' (CPW 3.538). Again in *Eikonoclastes*, Milton attributed the decline of sound government in his day to a process of effeminization: 'Examples are not far to seek, how great mischeif and dishonour hath befall'n to Nations under the Government of effeminate and Uxorious Magistrates' (CPW 3.421). In *An Apology* Milton declares that 'the Gospell is our man-hood' (CPW 1. 950). The association of the processes of feminization with the fall of nations reveals how deep-seated the ontological associations of gender are in Milton's political theory. Once one remains committed to a form of rational vitalism – that there is an animating life which properly expresses and expands itself through matter – one will always generate a series of dualist hierarchies, insisting that active, forming and immaterial life be always in command of its effected embodied forms. Such an ontology will always be a form of masculinism precisely because the very difference between male and female has always been understood as a difference between two modes of rela-tion: between an ideal, systematizing and informing active spirit, and a recep-tive, informed and material potential. In the divorce tracts Milton uses images of lifelessness ('deadnes of spirit'), formlessness ('sullen masse') and discord to describe the inappropriate wife, with the man becoming 'a living soule bound to a dead corps', while the truly pernicious effects occur with 'contrariety of mind' (CPW 2.147).

It makes sense, then, that both Spenser and Milton will present the relation between good and evil through the image of gender. Neither simply aligns good and evil with a gender dichotomy (women as evil), but both define evil as a mode of male-female relation. Goodness is a productive and complementary coupling, the knight of virtue defending chastity. Evil is the potential for fecundity detached from form and light to operate without any end other than itself: embodiment devoid of reason, desire and consumption released from frui-tion, change divorced from creation – the feminine turned in upon itself. Evil is improper coupling, a 'diagonall contrary' or what Blake would refer to as a negation (as opposed to the fruitful interaction of contraries).[157] If the rational male is coupled with a submissive but responsive female then the contrary yields life and goodness. If that same contrary is not a relation between modes of reason but a mere coupling of bodies, then no genuine creation occurs and life is negated. What must be guarded against is a female potentiality uncoupled from reason and ordered production; what must not occur is mere generation. Milton repeats and revises a literary–philosophical tradition in which the figure of the feminine allows for evil to be presented as the deflection of being from its proper end. Milton is quite clear both in his divorce tracts and in *Paradise Lost* that a simple form of misogyny is symptomatic of our fallenness: Adam's vitu-perative remarks against Eve's bodily form occur after the fall, and Samson's even more disturbing invective attack on Dalila occurs before his moment of vision and renewal. If woman is regarded as mere corrupting viper, then man has already positioned himself not as rational master but as punishing tyrant. Milton will always insist on a reflective and subordinate relation between male and female, because the divine is transcendent and can thereby legitimate a hierarchy in which the less rational (feminine) finds its proper end in the more rational (masculine). If detached from the life of reason the female would be both closer to animality and further away from form and order. Milton thus brings to the fore and gives a more explicit rationale to the imagery of evil as monstrous – destructive of form and order – and feminine, possessing a fecundity that is opposed to the creative expansiveness of life.

In a similar vein Spenser describes error as half-serpent, half-woman, who exists in darkness, breeding uncontrollably. Her offspring bear no determined form ('of sundry shapes'), receive poison rather than sustenance for growth from her breasts, and are so resistant to illumination that they retreat into the maternal body at the approach of light. Spenser offers a powerful image of life coiled in upon itself, resisting form, light, vision and difference. That inward coiling only unfolds with the entrance of the knight and light. The cycle of production and consumption the knight views is without appetite or act; the 'bred' creatures creep back into the dragon's mouth in an image of unwilled ingestion:

> Halfe like a serpent horribly displaide,
> But th'other halfe did womans shape retaine,
> Most lothsom, filthie, foule, and full of vile disdaine.
>
> And as she lay upon the durtie ground,
> Her huge long taile her den all overspread,
> Yet was in knots and many boughtes upwound,
> Pointed with a mortall sting. Of her there bred
> A thousand yong ones, which she dayly fed,
> Sucking upon her poisonous dugs, eachone
> Of sundry shapes, yet all ill favoréd:
> Soone as that uncouth light upon them shone,
> Into her mouth they crept, and suddain all were gone.
>
> Their dam upstart, out of her den effraide,
> And rushéd forth, hurling her hideous taile
> About her curséd head, whose folds displaid
> Were stretcht now forth at length without entraile.
> She lookt about, and seeing one in mayle
> Arméd to point, sought back to turne again;
> For light she hated as the deadly bale,
> Ay wont in desert darknesse to remaine,
> Where plaine none might her see, nor she see any plaine. (1.1.14–16)

Milton repeats this figure of the monstrous feminine but makes a distinction regarding time and being. Spenser's error is a symbol of a principle or threat within this world as we know and live it. Rather than use the form of historical allegory, Milton places Sin and Death outside human history, as a principle, aesthetic or tendency which stands for a certain turning away from time and life.[158] There is not an opposition between good and evil that can then be figured by way of historical narrative. For Milton, good and evil are two modes of history. There is the history presented by Michael to Adam, and produced by Milton in *Paradise Lost,* which looks to the genesis of life and reflects upon how life might have managed to deviate from its proper course. Then there is that other history, given in Satan's forgetting of his origins, in Sin and Death's cyclic non-becoming, and in the image of limbo where those who have directed their life to worldly goals remain suspended without place, direction or *telos.* Spenser's use of allegory means that events within history can stand for an opposition between good and evil, whereas Milton will show history as tending either towards good or towards evil; evil is not a being we encounter within time, but it occurs as a failure or loss of time. Spenser therefore places truth and error as two figures who encounter each other within an allegory, with that allegory then relating in turn to the events of history.

In the scene of holiness and error, the knight slays the dragon who then exudes a spew of 'blind' and inhuman books:

> Therewith she spewd out of her filthy maw
> A floud of poyson horrible and blacke,
> Full of great lumpes of flesh and gobbets raw,
> Which stunck so vildly, that it forst him slacke
> His grasping hold, and from her turne him backe:
> Her vomit full of bookes and papers was,
> With loathly frogs and toades, which eyes did lacke,
> And creeping sought way in the weedy gras:
> Her filthy parbreake all the place defiléd has. (1.1.20)

The narrow allegorical reference is to the Catholic propaganda of Spenser's own time, but there is also a broader reference to the deathly, monstrous literal book opposed to the spirit of the actual word. This marks an opposition between a religion of the letter, circulating as so much repeated but unintended noise, and the protestant spirit of the animated word. Allegory, by its very nature, takes the temporally sequential and creates an extended or schematic overlay. The dragon figure of error is at once a type of error in general, but also a token, containing the specific errors of Spenser's own time. The logic is a binary one, in which history plays out oppositions between good and evil. Milton's scene of Sin and Death, by contrast, is set *against* a genuinely historical becoming: time as empty repetition is opposed to time as becoming. When Milton appropriates Spenser's figure of error he also changes the literary form from an allegory where historical time and mythic time are overlaid, to an analogical time, where moments of the past express something of the truth of life, a truth that will be disclosed in our future. But the stylistic differences between Spenser and Milton also affect the use of tropes.

After the knight's encounter with error, Spenser likens the vomiting dragon or error to the Nile overflowing its bank. The very fecundity that makes the Nile a source of life, can – with an excess that shows no respects for borders – create 'monstrous' shapes. The simile is not merely illustrative – 'x is like y' – but also gives the allegorical scene a natural analogy and justification, so that the moral binary is grounded in life. Nature will also demonstrate the evil of a fecundity that is not tempered, intended or limited; the 'fertile slime' that overflows to leave a breeding mud can only produce shapes without form:

> As when old father Nilus gins to swell
> With timely pride above the Aegyptian vale,
> His fattie waves do fertile slime outwell,
> And overflow each plaine and lowly dale:
> But when his later spring gins to avale,
> Huge heapes of mudd he leaves, wherein there breed
> Ten thousand kindes of creatures, partly male
> And partly female of his fruitfull seed;
> Such ugly monstrous shapes elsewhere man no may reed. (1.1.21)

The trope linking error with natural excess – both of which yield monstrosity – has, however, no temporal structure. The figure of error spewing out vile books and fluid is like a river so swelled as to produce deformed creatures. Spenser can liken his mythic world to phenomena in the natural world, but the relation is itself not reflected upon. Milton's epic similes, however, not only liken one term to another, but draw temporal relations such that a present event is like an earlier, but also *possibly* not quite the same. The historical parallel also exposes the possibility of difference. One of the common ways this is achieved is through the style of subsumption, so that all Milton's likenesses are seen as bearing some likeness to an original, but also not measuring up to the clarity of the origin. Paradise is not quite like all those later imagined scenes of bliss: 'Not that faire field of Enna, . . . nor that sweet Grove / of Daphne . . . nor that Nyseian iile' (4.268–75). Eve is the original against which all our later figures may be compared ('More lovely than Pandora', 4.714); and all these relations have an entirely conditional structure. *If* there is any truth at all to these sequences it can only be by reference to that very original seat of life: 'Hesperian Fables true, / If true here only' (4.250–1).

Even in more direct similes that do not take the structure of explicitly subordinating later reference to the original, Milton still deploys historical resonance. We are always given a sense of time, either the time since that origin of paradise, or the time of the present. Likening the story of Satan's rebellion and his corruption of mankind to the present, Milton opens historical relations to decision. The relations are not allegorical, presenting moments in the present as an image of evil, but analogical. A present moment is not in itself evil, but likened to that original emergence of evil. The distinction is crucial both for style and ethics. It demands that Milton write in such a way as to draw parallels between different temporal moments while also allowing for difference, allowing for the simile to appear as simile and not identity.[159] This occurs, for example, when Satan's shield is compared to the moon, 'whose Orb / Through Optic Glass the Tuscan artist views / At Ev'ning from the top of Fesole, / Or in Valdarno, to descry new Lands, / Rivers or Mountains in her spotty Globe' (PL 1.287–91). That simile likens Satan's shield to a feature of our natural world, but this nature is placed within human time, presented as now observable from a particular geographical and historical point.

I have already commented on Milton's use of 'or': we are given two possibilities, and while we know that divine life must express itself in some way, we may not know which particular image is the actual and proper figure. We must, therefore, consider a number of potential figures, all of which would express that there is divine life, even if we have to suspend just what the being of that life is.[160] In addition to his use of 'or,' Milton's syntax and similes also multiply the possible ways through which the divine is perceived. Perception is not simply passive and receptive; to see something *as* something both discloses the way in which the perceiver relates to the world, and the potential that the world might be seen otherwise. The problem of perception is included within Milton's similes: not just 'x is like y', but *how* x might be likened to y. The simile opens the relation among terms; in the case of Satan's shield and the moon observed by Galileo, we can ask whether the 'Tuscan artist' is likened to Satan (because there is a potentiality for the same turn away from God, with modern science reducing the world to mere matter), *or* whether it is possible that Satan maintains that residual brightness and virtue that could also be realized in genuine discovery, rather than increasing inwardness. The truth of the simile is suspended, for we are given an act of prospective seeing, not its outcome. We are not yet given just how that perception will relate to the world.

Milton's vitalist and rational ontology is directly related to his poetry as an art of perception, and this explains why Satan must occupy such an ambivalent position. He is never fully evil, but always turns away from the world and outward perception, always failing to relate his own life to creation in general. It is always possible that Satan might be drawn away from his principle of identity, where all he can see is what he already is, but even when he approaches Eden and is struck 'stupidly good' (9.465) he turns back into himself. It is just this inability to actualize relations that sets Satan's language of quantitative forces (where the only differences are those of degree) in contrast with Milton's art of simile, where perceptions are both like and unlike, depending upon how we will go on to act.

Here, we might liken Milton's poetics and theology to some of the problems Leibniz was to pursue in his *Monadology*. Every point in the world (or monad) has some apprehension or relation to every other; no aspect of life is outside reason. Every living point of view is relatively clear and distinct: the perceptions with which we are immediately concerned are given clearly, but by virtue of that fact they are tied to our own point of view and so we miss their distinctness (or what they are in themselves). It is clear that there is a God, but by virtue of our point of view the truth and exactness of the divine – which would be utterly distinct and fully rational – can never be given to us. Leibniz's monadology is related directly to his project of theodicy; the local evils we perceive can be understood if we step back from the relations of our own bodies to the world and understand the world as maximizing relations of goodness and harmony. Milton's poetics also plays with the relations of the world: those points that seem devoid of connection have simply failed to move from the simple clarity of what is close and immediate, to the distinct idea that there must also be an infinite divine reason within which each monad is situated. *Paradise Lost* can be read as an essentially poetic theodicy, in accord with Milton's commitment to one vital life which we may or may not perceive in its divinity, and which we may or may not realize as our own. God's justice becomes distinct if we consider the world, not as it is given actually and immediately, but as it is disclosed through relations. Accordingly, Milton's world is analogical: just as Adam's reason does not dominate Eve through force but is rightly recognized as that which will enable Eve to realize her proper potential, so we need to see God not as a force that impedes our reason, but as the very being and life of reason.

In Milton's more complex similes there are, therefore, relations of likeness from one point of view and distinction from another. On the one hand Eve can be likened to all the images of beauty in the literary and mythic tradition; seeing such likeness draws all literary history back to its origin. On the other hand, there is also a difference of kind. Eve is not only *more* beautiful; her beauty is a direct expression of 'the human form divine'. Relating Eve to 'the image of their glorious maker' allows us to read all those other likenesses as also emanating from God. Milton will therefore regard poetry and reading as directly political and directly theological: to see eternity in a grain of sand requires looking beyond what is materially given to the creative life that makes such minute particulars possible. Literalism is not just a failure of the imagination; it is a deadening of life, a refusal to actualize the relations, connections, perceptions and likeness which allow for an image of one divine, divinely complex and productively differentiating life. Milton will also therefore see poetry as prophecy, but this is not the conveyance of vision through poetry, as though poetry were a neutral medium; it is vision *as* poetry. Seeing the world in the complexity of its connections and differences requires both that we recognize the multiple figures through which God expresses himself, and that we see the world itself as poetic: as bearing a clear, if not fully distinct, relation to divinity.

Poiesis is, unlike praxis, a form of activity that creates an object that is different and distinct from the creating subject, and it is this objective character of the poetic object that opens up a fundamental ambivalence. The poem can be seen as an emanation of life, as an expression of its conditions of genesis (and this is how Milton will present his own poetic activity, as bearing an essential relation to the spirit that is its enabling condition). But the poem as object, as that which stands alone and breaks with its conditions of genesis, manifests another sense of *poiesis* as separateness and distinction – essentially divorced from its creative origin. It is that second sense of *poiesis* as detachment that Milton's manifest content seeks to overcome. Milton's style, in its emphasis on relations – not just linking elements, but also emphasizing the creation and mode of connection – will constantly bring the act of poetry to the fore. If there is a likeness or simile, there is also a temporal relation and labour which establishes that simile. Milton's style, therefore, labours to distinguish likeness from identity. It is Satan who will regard all beings as equals in reason and therefore differentiated only by force. For Milton, reading properly and perceiving properly are the same. Both require relating what is given to what is not already given.

In one of the most important moments in the epic – the very point where Satan will not be deterred from destroying a sight of beauty that he is compelled to acknowledge – Milton likens the 'pure now purer air' of paradise to the 'Sabean odours' encountered by sailors. As Satan approaches Eden he encounters 'native perfumes', but it is the temporal structure of the simile that is both typically Miltonic and crucial for Milton's ethics of time:

> As when to them who saile
> Beyond the Cape of Hope, and now are past
> Mozambic, off at Sea North-East windes blow
> Sabean Odours from the spicie shoare
> Of Arabie the blest, with such delay
> Well pleas'd they slack thir course, and many a League
> Chear'd with the grateful smell old Ocean smiles.
> So entertaind those odorous sweets the Fiend
> Who came thir bane, though with them better pleas'd
> Than Asmodeus with the fishie fume,
> That drove him, though enamourd, from the Spouse
> Of Tobits son, and with a vengeance sent
> From Media post to Aegypt, there fast bound. (4.159–71)

First we are given the likeness from the world as we now know it; we begin with the vehicle: 'As when . . .'; something will eventually fill in the term of comparison. If there is a likeness between this phenomenon of our present, and (the subsequently disclosed) approach of Satan to Eden, then we might have to go back and reconsider the ethical status of those 'who sail / Beyond the Cape of Hope'. Perhaps those journeys of trade are like Satan's plundering of Eden, but perhaps not. Just as Milton's text remains poised or suspended on the question of empire, on whether the sailors' delay will be the prelude to transgression, so the pure air of paradise at least offers the potential for pause. Like the earlier prospective gaze of the Tuscan artist, the present image of sailing beyond Mozambique is ethically neutral, *for now*, but the backward likeness of the simile draws attention to the risk or potential fall in the present. The structure of the simile is typically Miltonic in its temporal and intertextual complexity. A present occurrence – a journey through a trade route – is presented as a form of temporal suspension; the 'grateful smell' allows for a delay of enjoyment. That poised present is then likened to a Satanic moment of decision: Satan is about to enter

Eden, but he has been ever so briefly detained before he 'high overleap[s] all bound'. Satan is not held at bay by the air that would 'drive / All sadness but despair'.

Despair, here, like Satan's earlier farewell to hope, closes his perception from the future; neither despair nor hopelessness can envisage transformation. Satan will not be inspired and will refuse recognition of place, path and perspective: 'Due entrance he disdain'd, and in contempt, / At one slight bound high over leap'd all bound' (4.180–1). That leap will later be compared to a wolf preying upon sheep, which in turn is likened to a historical event: 'So since into his church lewd hirelings climbe' (4.193). Before that forward glance is made – the leap being likened to the hirelings' infiltration of the church – the likeness between sailors enjoying the 'Sabean odours' and Satan entertaining the fragrances of the paradise he will destroy, is related to a mythic reference. Satan is presented as better pleased than Asmodeus. Asmodeus is a later apocryphal devil figure, whose jealousy leads him to destroy a series of Sara's potential husbands. Asmodeus is eventually undone by a 'fishy fume' created by Tobias' burning of fish. Asmodeus is repelled by the smoke, flees to Egypt and is then bound. The point at which Satan enters Eden is likened to a fallen present, but also compared to a moment with a different outcome: a devil being bound rather than pleased.

Why, apart from the sheer wordy delight of it all, does Milton form such a complex series of relations? And wasn't it just this mode of connection that allowed T.S. Eliot and the new critics to accuse Milton's poetry of lacking life? For the new critics, poetry was aligned with life because all those words and relations, which operate so efficiently in everyday and scientific language, are released in poetry from their referential function. Reading poetry requires us to bring words into relation again, once more disclosing the way language opens us to the world and experience. Milton, also, will not simply present ethical relations, lining up Satan and the hirelings on one side, paradise and an unfallen new world on the other. The similes include historic and mythic references, but then create complex relations of potential and near likeness. Our present can be likened to Satan's hesitation at the border of Eden: seen as a possible historical threshold depending on how we might act. To give a sense of the other potentialities we can also consider those hidden, apocryphal passages of text where we see other outcomes: a devil repelled and bound.

Regina Schwartz has argued for the ways in which *Paradise Lost* continually insists on such moments of decision and suspension, such that the narrative of the fall is once again brought back to its status of historical event, and not given as the unfolding of an inevitability.[161] This rendering of time as genuinely historical also inflects Milton's style. Delay is perhaps the most important formal and substantive feature of Milton's poetry, and is directly connected with the affirmation of a world in which likeness, rather than identity, is the governing principle. A world without difference and distinction is a world without life. Milton will not only present his own similes and parallels in such a way as to show the reason that lies in drawing relations; he also emphasizes the capacity for history to make a difference. Freedom occurs both if we read history to discover what might have been, and if we look to the future with hope for genuine change and difference, rather than despair. A time of delay, pause and mediation – seeing the world as like this or this – is a time of freedom.

This is one more way in which contraries or the rationale of distinction is set against the horrific coupling of what ought to be distinguished. The 'sweet reluctant amorous delay' that typifies Adam and Eve's relation in paradise distinguishes their marriage from Sin and Death. Delay is freedom. As Henri Bergson noted, a perception that reacts directly to the perceived is devoid of spirit: a material object does not *respond* when it is affected but moves in the way it is compelled to move. Spirit occurs with a 'zone of indetermination', where the relation between received affect and act is not yet decided.[162] Spirit is distinguished from matter in just this delay: spiritual perception establishes a relation, but does not yet respond to that relation. All life is perception: plants responding to light, simple organisms moving immediately in accord with the environment, or minds thinking of the world in terms of memory and anticipation. Only spirit is truly capable of affect: not simply perceiving and responding, but feeling the world before deciding how to act. Freedom is this delay or 'zone of indetermination': a free being does not merely react but decides how it might act.

When Adam and Eve fall, their original relation of delay and reading – seeing each other as an expression of the divine – becomes immediate and actual; they are now nothing more than their bodies, no longer referred or related to a divine life not yet given. That sense of delay also separates the ethical journey of a finite creature who embraces the temporal distance between the given present and future paradise, and Satan who refuses the ready and easy way to paradise. By leaping immediately he also forecloses the possibility of perceiving ethically; he fails to see paradise as a sign that he might be other than he already is, for it is always already so much appropriable property. It is therefore central to Milton's ethics that evil should not be considered as a force within life and time, as though God's creation could include that from which it should be divorced; instead, evil is a loss of distinction, a collapse of contrariety, because of a failure of time. Instead of the suspension that allows for difference, decision and relation, evil remains within itself in a cycle devoid of becoming. The cycle of Sin and Death lacks time and decision, mechanically reiterating the same compulsive reactions. Milton's use of simile and analogy moves from the content – presenting evil as a failure to make a difference – directly to form: reading is the capacity of distinguishing like from unlike, past from present.

Just as Milton casts evil as a figure of static involution, Spenser depicts error as self-devouring, turned in upon itself and devoid of form. Once the knight has beheaded the dragon, her offspring consume her blood with such voracity that they 'with fulnesse burst/ And bowels gushing forth'. In the *Faerie Queene* this figure of error is the very negation of life. Desire and consumption are deflected away from growth and production towards death: 'And sucked up their dying mothers blood, / Making her death their life, and eke her hurt their good' (1.1. 25). That idea of evil as inevitably self-devouring – 'Now needeth him no lenger labour spend, His foes have slaine themselves' – is taken up by Milton, who also insists that evil redounds upon itself. Milton will, however, take that inevitability of self-redounding and present it as a historical problem.[163] If God's divinity is the true and inevitable victor, how do we account for the delay of the present? How do we explain the failure – now – of reasoning subjects to embrace their good and freedom? One way – Spenser's – is to see time as allegorical; human history merely plays out the triumph of good over evil. The other is to grant a more profound temporality to history. Good and evil are modes of time. We can either become worthy of history – think of ourselves as beings who might live in accord with the trajectory of reason – or, like Sin and Death, remain within ourselves. In contrast with Spenser's allegory, which presents a set of virtues which may be conveyed through history as narrative, Milton presents Sin and Death as the failure of history, generated when Satan forgets his own origin, and then perpetuated in a cycle of self-consumption. The opposite of evil will therefore be a time of becoming: but how do we – once fallen – restore reason to its properly historical sense? For Milton that can be achieved only by thinking differently, and this explains both the intrinsic temporal complexity of his style, and the historical trajectory which concludes *Paradise Lost*.

5

History, Becoming and Reason

If *Paradise Lost* is a self-proclaimed theodicy justifying God's ways, then it must also come to terms with the playing out of that justice. For Milton the world is not yet the best of all possible worlds but must come to be so. Even though evil will ultimately be a swerve that intensifies the return to goodness (12.470–4), we nevertheless have to deal – in this world, in the present – with the suspension between the world as it is and the world as it ought to be. For Milton's opponents that difference was a spatial difference between earth and heaven; for Milton the difference between earth and heaven was temporal, for there would be a day when 'the Earth / Shall all be Paradise' (12.463–4). It is worth noting then that the vision of history disclosed by Michael unfolds from three drops of the 'well of life' piercing Adam's 'inmost seat of mental sight' (11.416–18). The vision of history emanates from the coupling of life with inner vision.

Defenders of absolute and unassailable monarchical power regarded human reason as fallen, incapable of ruling the passions. Either we could see monarchy as an extension of divine authority, incapable as we are of becoming divinely rational ourselves; or we submit to an external authority because we have no natural law. Adam, too, when presented with the chaos of history cannot see any hope for rational self-governance. Adam witnesses the tower of Babel, where 'God who oft descends to visit men' sows 'a jangling noise of words unknown,' and thereby throws the hubristic project into chaos:

> O execrable Son so to aspire
> Above his Brethren, to himself assuming
> Authority usurt, from God not giv'n:
> He gave us onely over Beast, Fish, Fowl
> Dominion absolute; that right we hold
> By his donation; but Man over men
> He made not Lord; such title to himself
> Reserving, human left from human free. (12.64–71)

Adam regards the seizing of human power as leading easily to 'encroachment proud' on God's own power. But it is at just this point that Michael introduces a historical subtlety. Correcting Adam, who seems to have forgotten that his reason is now 'obscured', Michael points out that political tyranny occurs only because man has already abandoned his reason. It is not that we need tyranny because we are irrational; it is because we failed to follow our reason that tyranny is possible (but not necessary):

> Justly thou abhorr'st
> That Son, who on the quiet state of men
> Such trouble brought, affecting to subdue
> Rational Libertie; yet know withall,
> Since thy original lapse, true Libertie
> Is lost, which always with right Reason dwells
> Twinn'd, and from her hath no dividual being;
> Reason in man obscur'd, or not obeyd,
> Immediately inordinate desires
> And upstart Passions catch the Government
> From Reason, and to servitude reduce
> Man till then free. Therefore since hee permits
> Within himself unworthie Powers to reign
> Over free Reason, God in Judgment just
> Subjects him from without to violent Lords;
> Who oft as underservedly enthrall
> His outward freedom: Tyrannie must be,
> Though to the tyrant thereby no excuse.
> Yet somtimes Nations will decline so low
> From vertue, which is reason, that no wrong
> But Justice, and some fatal curse annext
> Deprives them of thir outward libertie,
> Thir inward lost. (12.79–101)

What we are seeing, Michael insists, is not a world of chaos and injustice, but the playing out of history in accord with justice. Michael's order of explanation is significant; the loss of reason follows from the original lapse, and this is what precludes humanity now from enjoying a reason that would govern the passions. So much is in accord with God's justice, for God bestows a reason sufficient for human harmony, and it is Adam and Eve who fail to live according to that justice. This then lays humanity open to the threat of tyranny, for only beings who have failed to cultivate their reason could become subject to 'violent lords'. This is to say that the *condition* for political tyranny is a failure of reason, but this does not mean that the tyranny itself is justified. The logical sequence that leads to tyranny is just: in not following reason 'man' disordered the relation between reason and passion. We abandoned reason in that original lapse; but the enthralment of 'outward freedom' is, Michael states, undeserved. It is therefore 'no wrong, / But justice' that yields the present condition, along with what Michael refers to as 'some fatal curse annext'. This suggests that political tyranny is not God's justice itself, for justice only entails that reason is 'obscured', and this because 'they / Gods image did not reverence in themselves' (11.524–5). God's justice leads to the clouding of reason, which followed from Adam and Eve not being their proper selves: 'Therefore so abject is thir punishment, / Disfiguring not Gods likeness, but thir own' (11.520–1). Tyranny follows not from the nature of fallen reason *per se*, but through some 'fatal curse annexed', added on to justice.

That 'fatal curse' which Michael clearly describes as a supplement or accident to divine justice, recalls the language of 'Lycidas,' a poem that is also temporally complex in moving from a cyclic conception of time, where the seeming injustice of early death is compensated by new life, to an apocalyptic time. The language of fate and curse is located in the earlier section of the elegy, while the speaker is still addressing nature in pagan terms, as though the gods were simply vengeful; it is a language of superstition and not of reason, where nature is inscrutable: 'It was that fatal and perfidious bark / Built in the eclipse, and rigged with curses dark, / That sunk so low that sacred head of thine' (100–2). That language of fate and curses which Satan will also employ in his explanations (5.859–63) is, however, broken in 'Lycidas' by the apocalyptic 'pilot of the Galilean lake'. The dread voice, far from accepting the cycle of nature, judges the fallenness of the world to be the consequence of a usurpation of truth by 'Blind mouths'. The image of inward rotting and foul contagion is overcome, not by natural renewal, but by a radical and final break: 'that two-handed engine at the door / Stands ready to smite once and smite *no more*' (130–1). The apocalyptic break with a natural cycle that is not yet rational, just and divine – a world not yet in accord with reason's own law – is strangely announced by the enigmatic 'two-handed engine'. Just as the poem rejects the passive acceptance of inscrutable curses and fates, just as the compensation from natural images is spurned, the poem falls into its own unwitting opacity and noise.[164] It is here that we can begin to read Milton's poetics against its governing images of vital rationalism. At once expressing the inevitable and progressive expansion of reason and lucidity, the poems can do so only by taking on some material vehicle. The possibility that elements of that vehicle may detach themselves from their animating spirit – may be cut off, or clipped by fate – is evidenced by those (many) moments in Milton's poetry that require intense and ultimately insecure exegetical labour. 'Lycidas' is already qualitatively historical, moving from a perception of the world as governed by fate, fates, curses and gods, to a recognition of a break in time that will also be a break in the mode of law: no longer spoken as mere noise – 'their lean and flashy songs / Grate on their scrannel pipes of wretched straw' – for there will be a definitive revelation by a 'dread voice' of judgement. That voice will, however, nevertheless have to adopt an apocalyptic tone, and can never be pure sense at one with its expressive medium.[165] For if it is the very nature of life and time to progress through difference and expression it is also essentially possible that the flowing forth into an expressed form – the taking on of an expressive body that maintains itself through time – will create an insurmountable or discontinuous difference and disjunction.

In Book Twelve of *Paradise Lost* there is also a distinct historical progression, from a world in which reason is obscured and therefore subjected to tyranny because of some 'fatal curse annext,' to an internalization of law. Michael has, at this earliest point in history, acknowledged only that God's justice has entailed man's loss of inward freedom, and that it has been events of history – some fatal curse – which resulted in political servitude. There is, therefore, no disjunction between this world and God's justice. God's justice is not a set of rules imposed upon life, but life itself, as long as we define life – as Milton does – as the progression of each being to its fullest and most rational potential. Because human beings have been created capable of virtue it is perfectly just that they should suffer if they fail to practise virtue. The possibility for overcoming worldly injustice lies in the power of God's implanted conscience to retrieve self-government. Conscience acts as that transcendent power within the human soul to bring reason to a recognition of its self-imposed servitude. As Christ replies to Satan in *Paradise Regain'd*: 'Let his tormentor Conscience find him out / . . . That people victor once, now vile and base, / Deservedly made vassal' (PR 4.130–3). The tradition of relative natural law, which had accounted for worldly injustice by positing a less just world as a consequence of the fall, allows for the presence of tyranny regardless of the character of the persons tyrannized, or their own attitude to reason. Milton's explanation of evil in the world sees tyranny as a consequence of present (but not essential) human self-enslavement: 'For God hath justly giv'n the Nations up / To thy Delusions; justly, since they fell / Idolatrous' (PR 1.442–4). It follows, therefore, that if the disparity between positive law and natural law is perceived through the power of reason, there may be a legitimate rebellion against tyranny in the name of universal justice. If tyranny is attributed not to divine wrath but to the current failure of reason, then a seizure of power must be validated upon the basis of the retrieval of the light of God. As Milton states in *The Tenure of Kings and Magistrates:*

> If men within themselves would be govern'd by reason, and not generally give up their understanding to a double tyrannie, of Custom from without, and blind affections within, they would discerne, what it is to favour and uphold the Tyrant of a Nation. (CPW 3.190)

The world of tyranny viewed by Adam is the consequence of a decline of 'virtue, which is reason'. Living well, living according to the law, is at once in accord with virtue (which Milton in *A Mask* had already defined as a being's excellence or highest potential) and reason. As Milton states in *Eikonoclastes*, practise of the virtues is integral, not contingent, to the well being of a state and its individuals:

> The happiness of a Nation consists in true Religion, Piety, Justice, Prudence, Temperence, Fortitude, and the contempt of Avarice and Ambition. They in whomsoever these vertues dwell eminently, need not Kings to make them happy, but are the architects of their own happiness; and whether to themselves or others are not less then Kings. (CPW 3.542)

Once virtue, or our highest being, is deflected from realizing itself, justice allows for that tyrannical disequilibrium of powers so distressing to Adam. God is not condemning the world to injustice, for it is just that those who follow reason will live a life of order, while those who 'decline so low' as to abandon reason will deprive themselves of law. God's justice had already demanded the expulsion of Satan from heaven and Adam and Eve from paradise – 'die hee or justice must' (3.210) – precisely because the negation or turning away from order could not be admitted into order. The only way in which humanity can be returned to paradise is with a return and revival of reason, but that cannot occur without some historical event that would alter man's very being. It is just – in order – that any man who abandons reason, or who does not live according to his proper being, will be deprived of 'thir outward libertie / Thir inward lost' (12.100–01). No man can have authority over any other as long as we live in accord with reason, but reason and freedom had been decided against when Adam and Eve chose not to act in accord with the law. The moment of fall alters their very humanity, as they choose to act for the sake of their present desires and the sense of themselves as self-sufficient. Reason is no longer the governing mode of their being, and can become so only through a historical process of recognition. Justifying the logic of the fall, Milton's God expresses the expulsion from paradise less as an imposed punishment and more as a necessary consequence of the very harmony of spiritually-infused matter:

> But longer in that Paradise to dwell,
> The Law I gave to Nature him forbids:
> Those pure immortal Elements that know
> No gross, no unharmoneous mixture foule,
> Eject him tainted now, and purge him off
> As a distemper, gross to aire as gross,
> And mortal food, as may dispose him best
> For dissolution wrought by Sin, that first
> Distemper'd all things, and of incorrupt
> Corrupted. (PL 11. 48–57)

Accordingly, the subjection to tyranny that Michael discloses prior to the atonement is not the end of the story, and it is crucial that we see that moment of obscured reason as historical. Only the historical sense can allow us to see the present lack of reason and self-enslavement, not as evidence of human irrationality, but as our failure to realize ourselves historically: to recognize the potential we have for full and right reason.[166] Michael will go on to describe the gift of Mosaic law *not* as a form of law imposed upon a fallen reason, but as an anticipation of a law that will one day be our own, if only we can overcome the fact that 'the voice of God / To mortal eare is dreadful' (12.235–6). While the law informs them 'by types / And shadows' and through a 'Mediator, whose high Office now / Moses in figure beares' (12.240–1), humanity can take on the outward form of reason, but not its full internalization. Michael's history is not just a series of events, but a progression in the status of reason. Fallen reason cannot master itself and is therefore subject to worldly tyranny; with the bestowal of Mosaic law we are given the order of reason, even if the sense of law is not fully transparent.

Mosaic law already provides adequate order for both church and state. Milton will not consign the political world to irrational submission while only the spirit receives grace: God will ordain 'Lawes, part, such as appertaine / To civil Justice, part religious Rites / Of sacrifice, informing them, by types / and shadows' (12.230–3). Not only does the vision of history give Adam a sense of grace – 'O sent from Heav'n, / Enlightner of my darkness, gracious things / Thou has reveald' (12.270–2) – it also discloses the essential temporality of our relation to law. Adam's heart is 'much eased' with that vision of a law which will guide humanity to rational behaviour, but is also troubled by the apparent opacity of law. It is clear that law has been given, but it is no less clear that law is insufficient; indeed, our failure to live in accord with the law evidences the limits of our being. Michael must therefore allow Adam to 'see / His day, in whom all nations shall be blest', while also pointing out the difference between a law given in 'types and shadows' and the eventual 'paradise within'. Adam's question –'how can God with such reside?' – is *the* question of theodicy and politics: if we are rational, if we are made in God's image, how have we so evidently acted in conflict with reason and our own good?:

> . . . now first I finde
> Mine eyes true op'ning, and my heart much eas'd,
> Erewhile perplext with thoughts what would becom
> Of mee and all Mankind; but now I see
> His day, in whom all Nations shall be blest,
> Favour unmerited by me, who sought
> Forbidd'n knowledge by forbidd'n means.
> This yet I apprehend not, why to those
> Among whom God will deigne to dwell on Earth
> So many and so various Laws are giv'n;
> So many Laws argue so many sins
> Among them; how can God with such reside?
> To whom thus Michael. Doubt not but that sin
> Will reign among them, as of thee begot;;
> And therefore was Law given them to evince
> Thir natural pravitie, by stirring up
> Sin against Law to fight; that when they see
> Law can discover sin, but not remove,
> Save by those shadowie expiations weak,
> The bloud of Bulls and Goats, they may conclude
> Some bloud more precious must be paid for Man. (12.276–93)

Michael's answer is not to refer to reason's fallenness and then to promise beatitude in another world; for the very nature of human reason is that it works its way towards divine law, even if it cannot do so on its own. The justification for overriding positive law in *Tenure of Kings and Magistrates* (1649) rests upon the existence of a natural law which is prior to the state. For Milton this natural law is not the law of democracy but the law of 'Justice, which is the Sword of God, superior to all mortal things' (CPW 3.193). In order to challenge the authority of a temporal power there must be some ground for right other than the tradition of law or the will of the people. In the *Tenure* and the pamphlets by other writers involved with the debate, it was argued from scripture that action could be taken against a temporal power in the name of the people even without their consent. This appeal to natural law was neither the divine right of *lex rex* (the natural law of the royalists) nor the democratic *salus populi suprema lex* (the natural law of the Presbyterians); it was God's law of right which transcended human will and temporal powers and revealed itself to the souls of the enlightened:

> For if all human power to execute, not accidentally but intendedly, the wrath of God upon evil doers without exception be of God; then that power, whether ordinary, or if that faile, extraordinary so executing that intent of God, is lawfull, and not to be resisted. (CPW 3.197–8)

What was at issue in determining a law 'not to be resisted' was whether or not the rebelling agent claiming revelation was acting as a private person or for the sake of divine justice. The *Representation* presented by ministers expelled after Pride's Purge stressed the primacy of democracy and denied the validity of any individual's action against such government because the state transcended the collection of 'Private Persons'.

> For the Lawes of God, Nature, and Nations, together with Dictates of Reason, and the common consent of all casuists allow that to those which are intrusted with managing the Supreme Authoritie of a State or Kingdom, which they do not allow to a multitude of Private Persons.[167]

Milton agrees that an individual has no right to act against the government in so far as he acts as a private person, but Milton also constantly sets reason against the 'multitude' and does so because – as the very rhetorical mode of his prose makes clear – reason is that which distinguishes one from the multitude. In the *Tenure* Milton asserts that David did not slay Saul, not because the providence of God had intervened to prevent the destruction of a ruler as the Royalists claimed, but because David was acting as a 'privat person' and would have 'bin his own revenger, not so much the peoples' (CPW 3.216). But Milton also insists (and this is implied in his discussion of David and Saul), against the *Representation* and the Royalists, that an individual may act rebelliously if not acting as a private person. In *Samson Agonistes* this is precisely the position Samson places himself in: 'I was no private but a person rais'd / With strength sufficient and command from Heav'n' (SA 1211–12). The radical individualism of *Samson Agonistes*, which reiterates the concepts of inner light, election and self-redemption ('Making them each his own Deliverer' [SA 1289]), is in no way incompatible with the doctrine that rebellion is only legitimate if carried out for universal rather than personal ends. Samson is 'perswaded inwardly that this was from God' (SA argument); his action is guided by an individual and privileged access to truth. At the same time the truth he acts upon is for the public good and is part of the universal justice informing the world, despite the lack of public support prior to his act. The violence of *Samson Agonistes* is therefore not an act of a personal will but a justifiable part of God's revelation. Milton does not appeal to the private person as a law unto himself, but to a power of reason that is revealed through one's relation to other finite human reasoners but is not reducible to human law. It is in relations with others that the self is taken beyond self-interest and finitude to a recognition of transcendent divine law.

Reason is poised peculiarly, then, between a discursive power that will allow truth to inevitably emerge, and a transcendent power that would allow an outcast individual fallen on evil days to act as a 'person rais'd'. Such a tension in reason, between communicability and radical transcendence, is no accident in Milton's corpus, for it expresses the structure of reading. On the one hand truth must – if it is truth – transcend any of its specific intonations, voices or concrete expressions; on the other hand, in order to be recognized as true, to be acted upon and maintained through time and this world, truth must take on a material and specific form: either the material body of the book, or the acting conscience of the political agent. History must therefore also be a process in which the transcendent brightness of truth is given to privileged agents (not reducible to mere agreement), but also disseminated, recognized and effected as true by a community becoming one giant Christian personage. This negotiation between spirit and letter, between a truth that can never be reduced to mere matter and a matter that gestures beyond itself to what is not given, is sexual. As I have argued throughout, the emphasis on vitalism relies upon a normative image of productive life. This is sexual in two senses. First, as sexual difference: the privileging of spiritualizing, informing and sublime reason over passive, dependent and merely potential matter reinforces a gender binary of male insemination versus female receptivity. Second, as sexual relation: we can either experience a world of relations in which we are directed towards bodies not ourselves (and do so for the sake of a transcendent and expressive life); or we can remain narcissistically enclosed in self-love, abandoning production and fruition. Proper relations are therefore relations of hetero-normativity,[168] and allow for two forms of community. A loving, flourishing and human community refers beyond itself to an ideal of what it ought, rationally, to be; and it does not allow political disputation to be nothing more than the interaction of forces. Hell is pragmatic negotiation of self-interest, the assertion of power, and an occasional grounding of right on one's (supposedly) already given ontology.

As Book Twelve of *Paradise Lost* continues, more and more is made of the relation of love, the relation that was so definitive of paradise. How can love be related so intrinsically to questions of law and reason? The answer lies in the original distinction between two modes of time which organize the aesthetics and form of *Paradise Lost* as a whole. Love as it was depicted in paradise is not the coupling of two beings, but a relation in which each subject becomes in relation to the other: Adam recognizing Eve's beauty as an expression of divine creation, Eve recognizing Adam as one through whom she can bear a relation to divine reason. Love is exposure of the self to what it is not yet, and therefore is definitive of a divine life which never remains within itself but goes forth from itself to be fruitful and multiply. The fall occurs with a reversal of that relation of love, a turn inwards away from becoming and fruition towards self-sameness and stasis. If evil is, as the scene of Sin and Death displays so profoundly, the negation of relations, time, becoming, difference and progression, then the exposure of love towards an other who is not fully known or comprehended in advance, is evil's contrary. This is also how love is connected with law. Paradise occurs when the order that we might regard as imposed and alien is recognized as that towards which we need to journey in order to fulfil our proper being: 'to obey is happiness entire' (6.741). The (Satanic) conception of God as reigning by force and mere difference of degree, can be overcome only through a relation of love in which God grants humanity the grace to regain the reason it had chosen to abandon, and in which humanity recognizes reason and law as a gift, not as a prescription.

Those laws, which to a fallen being appear alien and at odds with our passionate life, ought to appear increasingly as our own. Political freedom will not be possible without an inner reformation. That cannot occur through obscured reason alone, but requires love. Whereas obedience is the submission to an authority recognized as higher, love is offered freely and is neither owed nor expected. If sin and the turn away from reason is a remaining within oneself and a refusal of one's relation to God, love is the counter-principle that, first, allows Christ to sacrifice his own being, and then allows mankind to be redeemed. The logic of love is therefore sacrificial; if evil is a remaining within oneself, then only a free, unrequested and useless giving can be redemptive. The 'shadowy expiations' of Old Testament sacrifice are a sign of that gift, but the true sacrifice can only be achieved when humanity's turning away from divinity is countered by Christ *as man,* for this will restore conscience, which will then act as God's inner light, that very 'upright heart and pure' which composed *Paradise Lost.* Conscience, here, is radically interior, for no ceremony can yield inner peace, and without that inner peace humanity cannot live a moral life. Here, Milton balances the relation between faith and works. Faith is required for righteousness to be imputed by God; only with faith will God then grant conscience, and without that gift of conscience humanity cannot live morally:

> Some bloud more precious must be paid for Man,
> Just for unjust, that in such righteousness
> To them by Faith imputed, they may finde
> Justification towards God, and peace

> Of conscience, which the Law by Ceremonies
> Cannot appease, nor Man the moral part
> Perform, and not performing cannot live.
> So law appears imperfet, and but giv'n
> With purpose to resign them in full time
> Up to a better Cov'nant, disciplin'd
> From shadowie Types to Truth, from Flesh to Spirit,
> From imposition of strict Laws, to free
> Acceptance of large Grace. From servil fear
> To filial, works of Law to works of Faith. (12.293–306)

Acting well does not lead to our redemption, but our redemption through faith allows for the gift of conscience, which will in turn allow us to live morally and act well. Even though the performance of good actions does not *cause* our redemption, it is an expression of a proper relation between faith and conscience. Moral action is not added onto life but is life in its proper form: 'not performing cannot live'. Weakened as we are by having turned away from our better reason, something other than reason, law and justice is required to restore our inward harmony. Time cannot, then, be a sequence but must be marked by an event that will enable us to develop rationally. Our relation to time alters with a certain historical event. Once our reason is redeemed we are capable of determining history for ourselves.

The word that Michael uses – 'disciplined' – allows us to think here about Milton's conception of history in relation to modernity. As Michel Foucault argued in *Discipline and Punish*, modernity occurs not when power acts as an external force on the body but through discipline, and this is achieved through practice. Bodies act in a certain way, and through processes of self-observation, recognize themselves as subjects who possess a soul. The body is the 'prisoner of the soul', rendered docile through the disciplines that produce self-monitoring individuals. One could, then, locate Milton's protestant conception of the inwardness of law, and his rejection of ceremony, as in accord with the modern emergence of the subject and the constitution of capitalist ethic.[169] However, we need to be more careful, both with the way in which we approach Foucault's understanding of modernity and with Milton's seeming endorsement of the modern subject. First, Foucault's general archaeology of the human sciences sought to challenge a certain idea of history as a progressive movement where processes that had once seemed external and arbitrary eventually become recognized as the subject's own. In contrast with Marxism, Foucault rejected the idea of a humanity that goes through time in order to discover that those processes that seemed alien, technical and contingent – such as systems of labour, social division and markets – would ultimately be recognized as grounded in a deeper logic of life.

It is the idea of life, which Foucault marks as specifically modern, that distinguished Marxism from the approach taken in Adam Smith's *Wealth of Nations*.[170] The crucial difference is the difference of time. Smith described wealth, the system of relations among selves and commodities; but Marx worked with the entirely different concept of labour. In the nineteenth-century episteme one does not just describe a system, but accounts for the emergence and logic of the system. The key concept is life, which allows 'man' to be produced as a being who must have a history – not simply go through history, but develop historically. It is because of man's living being – because he must labour to meet his needs – that he subjects himself to systems of technology, which eventually become alien, but which might also then be recognized and internalized as of his own making. Man must turn back and know himself and recognize the conditions from which his reason emerged, conditions which themselves are not fully rational. Smith's concept of wealth described human beings as participants in a system of exchange, while Marx's concept of labour enabled an explanation of the genesis of that system and thereby produced 'man' as an 'empirical–transcendental' double. Man's worldly being, or the way he appears to himself empirically, can be explained by referring back to (transcendental) imperatives of life. It is because of our need to act on the world and produce, in order to sustain our bodily being, that we enter into relations of labour and exchange, and thereby develop historically. Language, like life and labour, is also grasped differently – studied through an entirely different comportment. While the eighteenth-century had known theories of grammar which could allow various languages to be compared, the notion of *language* in the strong sense – that we must speak in order to establish ourselves as knowing beings in relation to the world – emerges in the nineteenth century. For Foucault, those great late nineteenth-century thinkers, Freud, Marx and Darwin, could only think the way they did because man was no longer a being who simply represented the world and gave it order; man's specifically historical being could be explained by transcendental imperatives of life. For Foucault, this is what makes 'man' a historically specific phenomenon. Man as a being who develops through time according to the imperatives of labour – so that in Marxism he will once again be able to recognize himself as a being who produced history through his actions on the world – presupposes a logic of 'life': that time unfolds according to a certain imperative, which we can turn back and recognize as (in part) our own.

Foucault's historicization of the concept of 'man' was felt most directly in literary criticism in the movement of new historicism, where subjects were not deemed to have any intrinsic existence but were seen instead as effected through historical practices. If we were to accept this form of approach we could read Milton's *Paradise Lost*, with its insistent affirmation of the 'upright heart and pure' and the 'paradise within', as a modern shift from external modes of power acting upon the body to internalized modes of discipline, where subjects produce themselves through practices of monitoring and introspection.[171] This would allow us to see *Paradise Lost* as a discursive practice, a way in which subjects are constituted through modes of knowing and reading. What such an approach does not allow us to do is make sense of the fine distinction Milton makes between two modes of introspection and subjectivity. Satan's presentation of himself as nothing more than a rhetorical figure – not as a subject who speaks, but as a force of speaking – is contrasted by Milton with a self that is not transparent to itself. This is the subject of prayer and poetry, in which introspection always encounters that which cannot be rendered fully transparent. Milton's depiction of history (while playing some part in producing and expressing that emergent modern subject of discipline) also reiterates a logic of life which goes well beyond the classical and modern epistemes. The norm of modern discipline is possible only because subjects can come to monitor processes of life which are seen to disclose their own being: eventually our sexuality will be an inner truth we can interpret, study, liberate and articulate. While the modern attention to 'life' that allows for theories such as psychoanalysis and Marxism posits a transcendental process which goes beyond any conscious or divine subject, the force of history for Milton is grounded in a rational life process. According to the modern concept of life, distinct beings *emerge*: there is a general process of change and striving from which individual beings happen to be formed. For Milton life is the process through which forms are expressed. Thus his attention to discipline, practice, introspection and self-monitoring is distinct from the modern notion that the self is its acts. Rather, for Milton, these practices of the self are processes through which forms that transcend the human are discovered: in prayer and poetry one does not (or ought not) find one's inner individual being so much as the light that animates the world in general.

We can, therefore, place Milton's historicism in opposition to modern positive accounts of history. For Milton time unfolds a truth that, while requiring a series of events, has an order and logic beyond time. For modern historicism it is the process of time or life itself that yields history as we know it. In many ways, then, we can begin to see Milton's resistance to a time of mere change and force that would not be oriented to some end as a resistance to the strong historicism that Foucault would mark as definitive of modernity. Milton's response to a time that is nothing more than mechanical, producing relations through chance encounters, is to posit a meaning to time: time is the regaining of paradise, a recognition of our distance and an appreciation of the fall of history and the gift of grace. Foucault's response to modern normalizing time – a time in which man produces himself historically because he is nothing other than self-becoming – was to look at the arts of the self. Far from self-monitoring being a form of self-constitution where the subject springs forth from itself, caring for the self would require negotiation with the body, desires, appetites, relations and moral norms.[172] It is just this sense of the resistance of the body – the self not as mind that masters itself, nor as harmonious network or system – that we can begin to approach in Milton's poetry. First, we can acknowledge the difficult problem of transcendence: Milton constantly acknowledges a force or power that lies beyond the self and its acts. What historicism tries to do is enclose forces within the relations of this world, but in doing so transcendence is always presupposed. As Joan Copjec has argued, to insist that all we have are historical forces in interaction reintroduces some ultimate transcendental logic, for it is now history (not God or man) which provides the logic and foundation for rela-tions.[173] What Copjec has proposed is that we recognize what Lacan referred to as the formulae for sexual difference. We must imagine on the one hand that all beings (men) are subjected to a system of relations and that whatever lies beyond those relations is prohibited or unattainable. This is the formula for man. Nevertheless, we must also imagine what is beyond those relations as some being not subjected to system. This is the formula for woman. Copjec's own claim, following Lacan, is not to remain happily within a historicism that reduces being to its networks of power relations, but to 'imagine there is no woman'.[174] Because we are always in a finite position within a system we ima-gine some ultimate plenitude that would complete our fragmentary and sub-jected lives. To live without that sense of ultimate fulfilment would be to abandon an ethics of dependence.[175] Not surprisingly, Copjec has found further material for this ethic in the work of Alain Badiou. Badiou insists that there is no ultimate One or infinite presence from which our finite being is separated; instead what we experience as existing are just multiplicities – these actual beings we take as existing.[176] Politics occurs as the event of truth when the sub-ject appeals not to actual multiplicities but to a truth not yet given, what is not already counted in the present. Such an act is not representative but creative and enacting, and the subject has no being or substantive existence outside this truth procedure.[177] Such recent arguments as Badiou's allow us to rethink the structure of transcendence in Milton's poetry. Like Milton, Badiou is insistent that evil is not some substantive quality or positive force within the world but a failure of the structures of the ethical subject. If we take truth to be some already given substance within the world – such as 'the German *Volk*' or 'American freedom' – then we allow the procedures of truth to fall back into unthinking enumeration of the already given, simply asserting the rightness and force of some given bodies against others. If Badiou laments an ethics that would allow all bodies, ways of life, differences and cultures to happily co-exist without attending to the powers of human subjects to think of universal truth, then despite all his attempts at a radical break with vitalism and substantialism he nevertheless elevates the *act* of truth and the life of the potential subject over the mere falling back into the given, the passive and the corporeal.

What Badiou's polemic raises, though, is the poverty of historicism. As Milton also recognized, the commitment to the transcendence of truth precludes us from falling back into a merely managerial proceduralism, which would not subject the present to anything other than its already given under-standing of measure. For Milton, though, the transcendence and eternity of truth is not radically distinct from our own understanding and representa-tion but is attainable through the processes of history and retrieval. This brings us to the second problem of transcendence. Not only does Milton posit a truth outside historical conflict as the guide and arbiter of historical deci-sions, he also presents the processes of reading and writing poetry as the means through which the restoration of the transcendental will occur. It is here that Milton's commitment to rationalist vitalism intersects with some of the dominant commitments of contemporary theory and criticism. One of the ways in which the reading of Milton has been sustained is through a process of progressive internalization (retrieving the conditions of the poem's emergence to decide upon its sense) and recognition (where reading Milton matters today because his poetry is constitutive of our present).[178] What is not considered, even though it would be an essential and necessary aspect of any such tradition, is the poetic element that would resist internalization and recognition. Such an element would be evil, circulating without fruition, sense, logic or self-understanding. It is this transcendental evil, or a disturbance that is before moral binaries, that Milton himself implicitly acknowledges in his own historical ethic. If the self and truth must be disclosed in relation – for a purity that remained unto itself would be an 'excremental whiteness' – then the genesis and coming into being of those relations through time must always harbour the potentiality for failure or non-synthesis.

History, in *Paradise Lost,* is the process through which the subject might once more recognize and internalize that law which is now given in figures, texts and types. The subject therefore requires time; reason is placed within a world of texts it is compelled to read, is situated with others with whom it must speak and argue, and is assaulted by passions. Milton is therefore critical of that seemingly modern mode of subjectivity which has detached itself from transcendent norms and recognizes only itself. He sets against the introspection where 'the mind is its own place' a temporal subject that through faith and charity will become its own paradise; the subject must not be overly attached to what it already is. A knowledge of the world will reveal what we cannot be now, and it is this recognition, in knowledge, of what is beyond the subject that provides the basis of a moral life:

> This having learnt, thou hast attain the summe
> Of wisdome; hope no higher, though all the Starrs
> Thou knew'st by name, and all th' ethereal Powers,
> All secrets of the deep, all Natures works,
> Or works of God in Heav'n, Aire, Earth, or Sea,
> And all the riches of this World enjoyd'st,
> And all the rule, one Empire; onely add
> Deeds to thy knowledge answerable, add Faith,
> Add vertue, Patience, Temperance, add Love,
> By name to come call'd Charitie, the soul
> Of all the rest: then wilt thou not be loath
> To leave this Paradise, but shalt possess
> A paradise within thee, happier farr. (12.575–87)

Love, which is also charity or the giving of that which is neither required nor desired, is the very 'soul' of the virtues; and it is the acting out of that virtuous love that will complete the internalization of law. Michael has previously explained to Adam that the 'various laws' given to humanity are 'to evince / Thir natural pravitie' (PL 12.287). Such laws are imperfect until the covenant of the atonement, where law will not be imposed but 'ingraven' on hearts. Only the spirit can discern this inward law. The appropriation of discipline by secular and institutional authorities is therefore a corruption and denial of God's grace. Furthermore, the use of such external laws for the advantage of the powerful causes an atrophy of the individual spirit, which should rightfully be deciding on law; it 'unbuilds' the inner temples. When Milton argues decisively for the disestablishment of the church in his sonnet 'On the Forcers of Conscience under the Long Parlament' he specifically refers to *forcers* of conscience. The presbyters have attributed to themselves the law which is actually discernible in the spirits of all individual believers; the ministers of the established church introduce 'Civill Sword' into the realm of grace and conscience. Not only is there a contamination of the spirit with secular power, but the secular authority also claims to be acting through spiritual jurisdiction: 'feigning still to act / By spiritual'. Like all laws that are used by the powerful, the control of church law by state power can only be a semblance of what it claims to be. By failing to subordinate worldly power to spiritual value, the individual conscience of believers and the true character of the law will be violated. Milton equates liberty not with the rejection of law but with the internalization of law.[179] The rejection of 'outward rites and specious forms' in favour of the spirit of God 'promised alike and given / To all believers' reiterates the concept of the universal attainability of truth and law in *Reason of Church Government*.

Milton therefore criticized the institutionalization of spirit, along with the use of the language of the soul to rationalize worldly powers that were purely temporal and that had no sense of what humanity, through divine reason, might become. In doing so he was at once modern – defending a recognition and internalization of law – and pre-modern: drawing upon the Hellenistic and Augustinian notion that a knowledge of the self would take one beyond the material body and beyond the present. The self was not Cartesian, knowing itself and mastering itself, but virtuous: realizing itself through developing its capacities. Foucault also contrasted two modes of the subject. His controversial history of reason marked a historical shift in which a subject, who had once negotiated its way in the world in relation to the irrational and unknowable, now renders all that is other than himself as calculable and potentially rational. With Descartes' demonstration that even dreams are evidence of the subject's capacity to know itself, reason becomes a purely formal and self-effecting procedure and has no reference beyond itself. Madness then becomes reason's own, a pathology that can be interned, studied and eventually placed within a science that will normalize human beings by referring to their biological life. Prior to that Cartesian turn, Foucault argues that reason had taken a different form. There were *norms* – codes of conduct, ways of proceeding that were or were not acceptable – but these were not *normalized* by being grounded upon some notion of the subject whose unreason would be some type of pathology or social disorder. Indeed, reason had human limits and would always come up against a mysterious 'night' that was not its own but that harboured a more profound truth than any human calculation might proffer.

Foucault's argument that up until the eighteenth century the 'concept of life did not exist'[180] suggests that if there had been a pre-modern form of vitalism, as I have suggested in my reading of Milton, the concept undergoes a radical shift in modernity. Life is no longer the divine spirit bestowed upon the material world that grants each being its proper form, but a transcendental process that accounts for the divergent emergence of distinct beings. Form is no longer trans-cendent, as an idea or ideal towards which life strives; for it is the general move-ment of life that explains distinct forms. We can now explain humanity, language, culture and relations according to a force or energy that is at once their own and alien. Gilles Deleuze, accordingly, has defined modern bourgeois ideology as 'thermodynamic': there is no commitment to an Idea beyond good sense and common sense, and while we may think of a perfectibility that is not given in this world it is merely posited in relation to the subject's own possibility. Deleuze and Guattari challenged the modern ideology of communication, in which life could be understood as a domain of interacting and acting subjects, in favour of a passive vitalism in which forces occur beyond active intentional-ity.[181] Both in his work with Guattari and in his own studies of the history of philosophy, Deleuze constantly identified the ways in which the subject of mod-ernity, who appears as a break with earlier philosophies of God and transcen-dence, nevertheless maintains an ultimate ground of good sense and common sense which precludes us from thinking the more radical and singular powers beyond thought as it already understands itself. Deleuze's passive and inhuman vitalism, which favours a thought that is not committed in advance to commu-nication and production, is set against modern vitalism, which grounds all thinking, living and acting on a good, fruitful and productive will.

For Foucault, this modern normalizing form of vitalism allows at once for a more radical historicism, at the same time as history becomes increasingly pro-blematic. There is no longer a form or principle which governs or unfolds in time; there would be no possibility of history progressing towards some implicit or proper end. Instead, history and change are the effects of 'life', which now has a quite different sense. Any being, in order to live on, to survive, to maintain itself, must take on some form of relative stability but also respond, adapt and change according to its environment. 'Man' as a speaking and labouring being does not express a form that is above and beyond this world. Man comes to speak and labour because he must enter into relations with others. History becomes possible when 'man' recognizes that his being is not timeless but is effected from process of life; man becomes an empirico–transcendental double: at once effected from the flux of life and time, but also – through the language and culture that emerges from life – a being capable of intuiting life and time. What he sees when he looks into time is not some ultimate apocalyptic vision of what he ought to be, but the processes, relations and forces of which he is effect.

Reading Milton today does, therefore, present us with a possibility of self-confrontation. We may allow the text to act as a mirror, at once giving us an image of a pre-modern past (in which God, transcendence and law appears as extra-subjective), while at the same time allowing us to internalize that past.

We would read the poetry and prose as vehicles for historical understanding, allowing us to relive the genesis of modern subjectivity, modern historicism and modern rationalism. Such processes of recognition in reading are inevitable, for the very approach to a text must assume that it harbours a sense that is both not already our own, yet available for retrieval. But the condition for such a circle of recognition is also an inevitable and violent misrecognition: Milton himself acknowledges this in his argument for the free circulation of books in *Areopagitica*. If there were no difference, distinction, disruption or diremption in the world then we would be deprived of trial and becoming, giving us only an 'excremental whiteness'. Now there are two ways (at least) in which we might think of such an originary whiteness before the moral oppositions between good and evil. The first is to imagine an undifferentiated abyss, perhaps something like a chaos or (which would not be the same) a 'one first matter' which is neither good nor evil: neither possessing a tendency towards form, nor negating such form. If we were to think in this manner, which would perhaps be close to Milton's monist ontology,[182] we would have to imagine God as pure act or form that gives being and definition to this original waste devoid of distinction. Reading, writing, thinking and acting would therefore always be set *against* an original indistinction. This would also allow us to contrast two economies: the good original economy that brings order through distinction and difference, allows for a spectrum of colours, a border between good and evil, and would present different terms as differentiations achieved by some inseminating spirit. The evil economy would occur when that original act of formation somehow swerves away from its animating intent. The condition for that swerve or deflection for Milton would be freedom, which in turn is the effect of God having created a being capable of not realizing his proper potentiality. The second possibility, given in the strange figure of 'excremental whiteness' itself, is that difference is not imposed from without, by an act of divine fiat that would determine relations in advance (unless they fail to realize their proper form). Rather, there would be tendencies for difference, relation, disruption and disturbance which would then have to be determined as good (conducive to life and production) or evil (lacking form and direction). Whiteness, in this sense, would be like 'white noise' or 'white light': not one term in a binary or opposition so much as a plane of differences not yet organized into distinct terms. Why think of 'excremental whiteness' in this way, against Milton's poetics that would situate form as the divine ordering of the world working against entropy and chaos? How would we distinguish all Milton's figures of evil – as a system that is mere circulation and repetition without transcendent reference – from the very possibility of freedom itself? Milton labours intensively to distinguish licence (as rebellion from order), from liberty (where a being takes on an order not already their own) and does so because such a recognition of law fulfils their higher potentiality. Freedom is not the absence of order but the potentiality to take on order as one's own, but which therefore requires as its immanent possibility the non-actualization of its higher potential. Good is distinguished from evil by arguing that beings – while not in themselves already fully divine – tend towards the divine. But it is just that grounding of the good on tendencies, proper potential and divine becoming which precludes us from regarding what is other than divine order as mere matter devoid of any quality whatsoever. Recognition of law and all good productive economies must have as their condition a potentiality for difference and becoming which is not yet determined or decided as lawful, as good or evil. And this brings us back to the very condition of reading and history. Without reading, as Milton insists both in his poetry and in *Areopagitica*, the self remains within itself, and relations to what is not the self are determined in advance as mere property.[183] Reading, whether it be the book of nature, the body of an other, scripture or a poem, relates to what is other than the self, not in already given terms but in relation to transcendence. To read is to assume that there is a spirit or sense that subtends the letter or body. Systems of signs must therefore be expressive of the spirit, but not reducible to the spirit. The spirit from which signs emerge is not undifferentiated but that which expresses itself through difference and distinction. The whiteness that would be the condition for trial, reading, becoming and history must be proto-differentiated, neither good nor evil but the condition from which such a binary might be thought.

Conclusion

Excremental Whiteness

How might we read Milton today if we try to think the positivity of evil? One possible path is suggested by plate 11 of William Blake's *The Marriage of Heaven and Hell*, which also offers us a way of thinking about the vitalism that informs contemporary critical practice:

> The ancient Poets animated all sensible objects with Gods or Geniuses, call-ing them by the names and adorning them with the properties of woods, rivers, mountains, lakes, cities, nations, and whatever their enlarged & numerous senses could percieve. And particularly they studied the genius of each city & country, placing it under its mental deity. Till a system was formed, which some took advantage of & enslav'd the vulgar by attempting to realize or abstract the mental deities from their objects; thus began Priest-hood. Choosing forms of worship from poetic tales. And at length they pro-nouncd that the Gods had orderd such things. Thus men forgot that All deities reside in the human breast.

In distinction from the vast proportion of Blake's poetic corpus, this declaration of an originally open, creative and human act that falls into priesthood offers a remarkably clear ethic of literary vitalism. In the beginning is the act. The active poet is not yet the (fallen) Cartesian man of reason who possesses a logic (Blake's Urizen); the poet is a dynamic and energetic body possessing enlarged and numerous senses. There is here at once an image of normative life – crea-tive, expansive, active – and a normative image of the body, operating recep-tively and sensibly rather than efficiently and cognitively. Far from being a retrieval of a radical and 'fettered' energy in Milton's poetry, this (in many ways uncharacteristic) manifesto statement of *The Marriage* reinforces the very values of life and creation that Milton had opposed to Satanic negation. It is perhaps not surprising that Blake will go on to present a more critical image of Satan as an accusing, negating, doubting and punishing being, quite different from his early affirmation of devilish energy and the infernal method of printing with corrosives. Blake will also argue, like Milton, that there is nothing evil about contrariety *per se*, but he will do so while rejecting negations, which are not contraries – not fruitful and interactive opposites – but forces which deny any otherness or relation: 'Contraries are Positives / A Negation is not a Con-trary.'[184] If we follow the Blakean line of reading we tend either to regard the accidental aspects of Milton's text as meaningful and inevitable expressions of a true and proper radicalism, or we correct Romantic Satanism by returning Milton's text to its theology, history, ontology or social context.

What I wish to do in this conclusion is consider another notion of difference from that of either the fruitful contrary or the simple negation. The hint is given in Milton's own tract on reading, *Areopagitica,* which is less an argument for free speech than a reminder that the singleness of truth will inevitably emerge from free and open debate. In that tract Milton makes a number of key rhetorical manoeuvres, including the likening of a book to a living body (where he has earlier in his career declared that the ideal self is a 'true Poem' [CPW 1.890]). A book is more alive than a living body precisely because of its ideality:

> For books are not absolutely dead things, but do contain a potency of life in them to be as active as that soul was whose progeny they are; nay, they do preserve as in a vial the purest efficacy and extraction of that living intellect that bred them. I know they are as lively, and as vigorously productive, as those fabulous dragon's teeth; and being sown up and down, may chance to spring up armed men. And yet, on the other hand, unless wariness be used, as good almost kill a man as kill a good book. Who kills a man kills a reasonable creature, God's image; but he who destroys a good book, kills reason itself, kills the image of God, as it were in the eye. Many a man lives a burden to the earth; but a good book is the precious life-blood of a master spirit, embalmed and treasured up on purpose to a life beyond life. 'Tis true, no age can restore a life, whereof perhaps there is no great loss; and revolutions of ages do not oft recover the loss of a rejected truth, for the want of which whole nations fare the worse. (CPW 2.492–3)

The reasoning and tropology here are thoroughly in accord with Milton's vitalism. The book is an expression of vital life.[185] In being an expression the book also bears the possibility of risk and detachment from its original intellectual aim, and may in turn sow and produce 'armed men'. Just as Milton in his antiprelatical prose works had used the binary between body and soul as a moral ordering principle, so here he uses the book as expression of the soul. But a curious contamination occurs when the man who produces the book is valued as a reasonable creature, or God's image, while the book is reason itself. Milton hints here at a complex theory of ideality: while the intellect and reason may emerge in a material, bodily and human context, such forms once constituted take on a 'life beyond life'. If man is God's image in body and is suffused by reason, that reason can necessarily live on in the absence of the body. Truth is therefore at once transcendent/eternal – not reducible to the material body that articulates its form – and immanent/singular: the loss of a book may kill a truth, may preclude the true and rational sense of life from coming to fruition. What Milton suggests here, with some horror, is precisely what will occur with literary history. The taking on of a body or literary form is essential both for the dissemination of truth and the 'living on' of the spirit who intuited that truth;

but the very condition of giving truth and one's spirit a 'life beyond life' is also a
certain evil. It is precisely because we live in a world where truth is not already
fully present, where truth must be articulated, discerned or differentiated, that
Milton insists upon the production of literary works and the reading and debate
that would ensue. Such an argument is not confined to *Areopagitica* but is articulated also in *Reason of Church Government*:

> The reforming of a Church ... is never brought to effect without the fierce
> encounter of truth and falshood together, if, as it were the splinters and
> shares of so violent a jousting, there fall from between the shock of many
> fond errors and fanatick opinions, which when truth has the upper hand,
> and the reformation shall be perfeted, will easily be rid out of the way, or
> kept so low, as that they shall be only the exercise of our knowledge, bit the
> disturbance, or interruption of our faith. (CPW 1.796)

There must then be a trial of reading, the coming into difference and fragility
of the spirit, which will – in the taking on of a bibliographic body – both enable
an eternal life beyond the body of the author while possessing a textual life that
could be dismembered, distorted and destroyed. A man's ideas or spirit become
immortal through expression in a literary text, but such embodiment also
allows those expressed truths – which until then had remained implicit and vir-
tual – to be susceptible to homicide:

> We should be wary therefore what persecution we raise against the living
> labours of public men, how we spill that seasoned life of man, preserved and
> stored up in books; since we see a kind of homicide may be thus committed,
> sometimes a martyrdom, and if it extend to the whole impression, a kind of
> massacre; whereof the execution ends not in the slaying of an elemental life,
> but strikes at that ethereal and fifth essence, the breath of reason itself, slays
> an immortality rather than a life. (CPW 2.510)

The binary between body and soul, the book and its animating spirit, becomes
here undecidable: the condition for the human spirit's ongoing, eternal and
rational life is the externalization in the body of the book, but it is just that
embodiment which will expose the truth to slaying. Further, if living labour
provides the value that will underpin the life of the book, then we appear no
longer to be able to discern who or what gives life. Is man extended, rendered
immortal and rational through his creation of a book; or is the book enlivened
only by the spirit or soul whose book is described as 'progeny'? This rhetorical
undecidability is not, I would argue, accidental but has to do with the very
structure of evil and difference. An idea, truth or life can only take on form
and go through time if it takes on an external or self-same identity, but once
it does so it is necessarily exposed not only to attack from without but also to
an internal confusion. For how do we discern or differentiate the spirit from
the letter, the body of the book that harbours a once productive soul, or the soul

that is only an image until taking on the intellectual essence of the true book? Milton's own answer to this question – which is the question of the border between life and death, between the animating and the homicidal – is through trial.

Good and evil are not given to us as already divided, for it is the nature of our life in this world as historical and finite beings to labour, write, read and differentiate. Milton will insist that this trial of difference has to do with this world only. There is nothing essentially differential about good and evil, but in this fallen world we only know good through evil (even if – as *Paradise Lost* insists – there was a time when we were not as now):

> Good and evil we know in the field of this world grow up together almost inseparably; and the knowledge of good is so involved and interwoven with the knowledge of evil, and in so many cunning resemblances hardly to be discerned, that those confused seeds which were imposed upon Psyche as an incessant labour to cull out, and sort asunder, were not more intermixed. It was from out the rind of one apple tasted, that the knowledge of good and evil, as two twins cleaving together, leaped forth into the world. And perhaps this is that doom which Adam fell into of knowing good and evil, that is to say of knowing good by evil. As therefore the state of man now is; what wisdom can there be to choose, what continence to forbear without the knowledge of evil? He that can apprehend and consider vice with all her baits and seeming pleasures, and yet abstain, and yet distinguish, and yet prefer that which is truly better, he is the true warfaring Christian. (CPW 2.511)

'As two twins cleaving together': good and evil are at once cleaved (in the sense of being twinned and joined) and cleaved (in the sense of being cut, differentiated through being given an other or double). At the same time as Milton here affirms the classic values of a vitalist ethic – that the proper life takes the form of an active and relational srtriving against non-life – he also acknowledges a certain contamination, even if only at the level of knowledge.

Areopagitica goes on to suggest an even more complex – or evil – understanding of life and difference, where it is not only the case that life must labour and war against corruption and negation. For Milton suggests that a purity without the warring, fragile, temporal and exposing relation to its contaminants would be an excremental whiteness.

> I cannot praise a fugitive and cloistered virtue, unexercised and unbreathed, that never sallies out and sees her adversary but slinks out of the race, where that immortal garland is to be run for, not without dust and heat. Assuredly we bring not innocence into the world, we bring impurity much rather; that which purifies us is trial, and trial is by what is contrary. That virtue therefore which is but a youngling in the contemplation of evil, and knows not the utmost that vice promises to her followers, and rejects it, is but a blank

virtue, not a pure; her whiteness is but an excremental whiteness. Which was the reason why our sage and serious poet Spenser, whom I dare be known to think a better teacher than Scotus or Aquinas, describing true temperance under the person of Guion, brings him in with his palmer through the cave of Mammon, and the bower of earthly bliss, that he might see and know, and yet abstain. Since therefore the knowledge and survey of vice is in this world so necessary to the constituting of human virtue, and the scanning of error to the confirmation of truth, how can we more safely, and with less danger, scout into the regions of sin and falsity than by reading all manner of tractates and hearing all manner of reason? And this is the benefit which may be had of books promiscuously read. (CPW 2.514–16)

A goodness without difference – a pure 'in-itself' of identity – would be unbreathed and unexercised. It is here that Milton betrays the ways in which the axiology of good and evil is tied to the borders of the living body. It is because the body is finite and dependent that it requires breath and act. A body that did not require such relations would be excremental, a purity not of growth and inspiration – not of becoming – but of mere being. Is it any accident that in the criticism of this excremental whiteness Milton privileges the poet Spenser over Scotus or Aquinas? For it was Aquinas who defined God as pure existence, not requiring the determination of essence, while it was Spenser (however inaccurately presented here[186]) who distributed the sense of good and evil in poetic form and trial. Excremental whiteness is a purity so assured it bears no relation or border. It is in this figure, this strange excretion in a text so insistent on the life of books, that we witness the necessity of evil. It is promiscuous reading, a relation to that which cannot be determined in advance, that reassures the body of its proper limits. Milton's theodicy, elsewhere so insistently dichotomous, places evil here not as the negation or contrary of flourishing life, but as the condition for the possibility of distinguishing between life and non-life. If it is the case that life arrives at the proper form of itself through trial, risk, promiscuity, embodiment and relation, then we must at one and the same time both reject a self-contained, indifferent and non-relational whiteness, and acknowledge that we do so – that we journey through difference and relations – only with the promise that beyond this world of knowing good through evil we might arrive at the non-relational after all, at the whiteness and purity of a being that no longer requires becoming, difference or living labour.

Notes

1. The most recent intervention is Terry Eagleton's *The Meaning of Life*, Oxford: Oxford University Press, 2007.
2. T.H. Irwin, *Aristotle's First Principles*. Oxford: Clarendon Press, 1988; Charlotte Witt, *Ways of Being: Potentiality and Actuality in Aristotle's Metaphysics*, Ithaca: Cornell University Press, 2003.
3. Philippa Foot, *Natural Goodness*, Oxford: Clarendon Press, 2001.
4. Nick Lane, *Power, Sex, Suicide: Mitochondria and the Meaning of Life*, Oxford: Oxford University Press, 2005.
5. J.L. Mackie has argued that if God does not exist then evil is not a problem, for the problem of evil only follows from a contradiction between God's goodness and omnipotence and the existence of evil. J.L. Mackie, 'Evil and Omnipotence', *Mind*, New Series, 64.254 (April 1955), 200–12. Despite the theological provenance of the problem of evil the debate remains alive today, primarily because even in a world without God there is still a seeming conflict between humanity's supposedly moral nature and the continued existence of suffering. Theodicy does have a secular pertinence, and in many ways Milton's justification of the ways of God to man is also a justification of the possibility of human morality, so that it is not only God's justice but the rational goodness of humanity which is on trial.
6. John Cottingham, *On the Meaning of Life*, London: Routledge, 2003. Luc Ferry, *Man Made God: The Meaning of Life*, Chicago: University of Chicago Press, 2002.
7. Even more analytic approaches to philosophy have drawn upon Aristotle to argue that the terms of our language can be grounded in the potentialities of nature. See David Charles, *Aristotle on Meaning and Essence*, Oxford: Clarendon Press; New York: Oxford University Press, 2000.
8. Even when readings are not explicitly theological they often bear a theological structure, assuming a spirit which subtends the material letter of the text, a spirit which it is then the task of reading and historical exegesis to unfold. For a critical account of this theology of reading see Louis Althusser and Etienne Balibar, *Reading 'Capital'*, trans. Ben Brewster, London: New Left Books, 1970.
9. Giorgio Agamben, *Potentialities: Collected Essays in Philosophy*, ed. and trans. Daniel Heller-Roazen, Stanford: Stanford University Press, 1999, p. 179.
10. On the importance of the narrative life see Alasdair MacIntyre, *After Virtue: A Study in Moral Theory*, Notre Dame: University of Notre Dame Press, 1981. On the more general claim that human selfhood requires understanding and sense through one's own tradition see Charles Taylor, *Sources of the Self: The Making of the Modern Identity*, Cambridge, MA: Harvard University Press, 1989. On the importance of an ongoing sense of oneself that is defended from the Kantian rather than the Aristotelian tradition, see Christine M. Korsgaard with G. A. Cohen *et al.*, *The Sources of Normativity*, ed. Onora O'Neill, Cambridge: Cambridge University Press, 1996.

11. Aristotle, *The Ethics of Aristotle: The Nicomachean Ethics*, trans. J.A.K. Thomson, 1953, Harmondsworth: Penguin, 1976, 9.4–9; Foot, *Natural Goodness*.

12. This is even so in the case of Immanuel Kant for whom radical evil was a possibility intrinsically tied to human freedom and the capacity of the self to act according to maxims; evil occurs when the self exempts itself from the moral law, even though that very exemption acknowledges the force of law. In the literature on radical evil it is Schelling who refused to see evil as mere accident or failure of potentiality and regarded its actual and not merely potential occurrence as necessary for existence. See Slavoj Žižek, *The Abyss of Freedom*, and F.W.J. von Schelling, *Ages of the World*. Ann Arbor, MI: University of Michigan Press, 1997.

13. Paul Ricoeur, *The Symbolism of Evil*, trans. Emerson Buchanan, New York: Harper and Row, 1967. Using the philosophy of Paul Ricoeur, John S. Tanner has looked at the ways in which 'surplus meanings of symbol and myth' extend beyond the theology of sin in *Paradise Lost*. John S. Tanner, ' "Say First What Cause": Ricoeur and the Etiology of Evil in Paradise Lost', *PMLA* 103.1 (January 1988), 45–56, 46.

14. It is in this sense that Richard Bernstein has criticized the contemporary use of the word evil: as a label or cry that closes off moral debate and understanding. See Richard Bernstein, *The Abuse of Evil: The Corruption of Politics and Religion Since 9/11 (Themes for the 21st Century)*, Cambridge: Polity, 2005. See also Philip Cole, *The Myth of Evil*, Edinburgh: Edinburgh University Press, 2006.

15. Jean-Luc Nancy, *A Finite Thinking*, ed. Simon Sparks, Stanford: Stanford University Press, 2003.

16. Denis Danielson, *Milton's Good God: A Study in Literary Theodicy*, Cambridge: Cambridge University Press, 1982.

17. The most sophisticated and persuasive affirmation of the Romantics' Milton is given by Tilottama Rajan: 'writers like Blake and Shelley were already reading *Paradise Lost* as a transposition when they suggested that Milton was of the devil's party without knowing it. ... The Romantic view that *Paradise Lost* is articulated around a tension between moral and tendency that makes Milton his own rereader focuses on the relationship between Satan and God. More accurately, it focuses on the relation of God as a sign for authority and the *status quo* to Satan as a sign for the Other.' Tilottama Rajan, 'The Other Reading: Transactional Epic in Milton, Blake and Wordsworth', in Lisa Low and Anthony John Harding (eds), *Milton, the Metaphysicals, and Romanticism*, Cambridge: Cambridge University Press, 1994, pp. 20–46, 27. Lucy Newlyn also sees Blake as liberating Milton's proper potential: 'Blake's confrontation with Milton points to some damaging repercussions of the confusion (which I have shown to be habitual) between the author of *Paradise Lost* and his removed, abstracted God'; Lucy Newlyn, *Paradise Lost and the Romantic Reader*, Oxford: Clarendon Press, 1993, p. 262.

18. Arguments that deconstruction is a form of moral relativism or nihilism, which were prevalent in the 1980s, are less common in the contemporary context, both because there is perceived to be an 'end' or demise of theory, and because in the 1990s Jacques Derrida and his commentators worked tirelessly to explicate an ethics of deconstruction. The classic debate regarding the relation between deconstruction and loss of meaning and context takes place between Derrida and John Searle in *Limited Inc.*, Baltimore : Johns Hopkins University Press, 1977.

19. Onora O'Neill, in Korsgaard, Cohen *et al.*

20. Jürgen Habermas, *Theory of Communicative Action*, 2 vols, trans. Thomas McCarthy, Boston: Beacon Press, 1984–7.

21. Jürgen Habermas, *Knowledge and Human Interests*, trans. Jeremy J. Shapiro, Boston, Beacon Press, 1971.

22. Karl-Otto Apel, *From a Transcendental-Semiotic Point of View*, ed. Marianna Papastephanou, Manchester: Manchester University Press, 1998.

23. Jürgen Habermas, *The Philosophical Discourse of Modernity: Twelve Lectures*, trans. Frederick Lawrence, Cambridge, MA: MIT Press, 1987.

24. Alexander García Düttmann, *Between Cultures: Tensions in the Struggle for Recognition*, trans. Kenneth B. Woodgate, London: Verso, 2000.

25. David Reid argues that Milton's 'theological ideas are not at all remarkable or interesting ... They are at best pegs on which he can hang the moral preoccupations of the poem. At worst they supply a rigid structure. ... It is when Milton is doing his job as a poet, representing his characters' actions or thoughts, that his insights are to be found'; David Reid, *The Humanism of Milton's* Paradise Lost, Edinburgh: Edinburgh University Press, 1993, pp. 112–13. Henry Weinfield has also argued, against Stanley Fish's insistence on the poem's ultimate logic, that, 'It is an oversimplification to say, with T.S. Eliot, that '[t]o extract everything possible from *Paradise Lost*, it would seem necessary to read it in two different ways, first solely for the sound, and second for the sense,' but there is certainly tension between the poem's professed doctrine and its poetry. ... What is weakness from the standpoint of theology or metaphysics, however, is converted to a strength as far as poetry is concerned because it means that Milton is able to confront and give voice to his own questions without filtering them beforehand through the systematic channels of theological thought'; Henry Weinfield, 'Skepticism and Poetry in Milton's Infernal Conclave', *SEL* 45.1 (Winter 2005), 191–212, 193, 195. The most questioning reading of Milton in relation both to his historical and philosophical context comes from William Kolbrener: 'Milton may have in *De Doctrina* and *Paradise Lost*, as Fallon argues, offered a "response to an urgent philosophical problem," though Milton's own arguments seem sometimes to frustrate the very *philosophical* terms of that context. It is hard to read Miltonic argument as entailing simply a rhetorical choice or "move" in the Skinnerian sense, for Milton's habit of mind refuses conventional polemical constraints just as he refuses or overgoes other conventions – literary or otherwise'; William Kolbrener, *Milton's Warring Angels: A Study of Critical Engagements*, Cambridge: Cambridge University Press, 1997, 67.

26. Gilles Deleuze, *Difference and Repetition*, trans. Paul Patton, New York: Columbia University Press, 1994, p. 37.

27. *Difference and Repetition*, pp. 244–5.

28. Stanley Fish, *Surprised by Sin: The Reader in Paradise Lost*, Berkeley, University of California Press, 1971. A more explicit theoretical approach, which insists on not allowing Milton's poetry to fall back into the rigidity of a system detached from praxis, is offered by Fred Hoerner, for whom all the images of self-consumption and inertia in *Paradise Lost* should enliven readers to a sense of action: 'a focus on historical action as praxis and not mere "execution" of the rule suggests that the "knuckle-rapping, peremptory prig" invented by Milton scholarship may be the product of the central problem in structuralism, which is, writes Bourdieu, "to slip from the model of reality to the reality of the model." By that prospectivizing slip, Milton might say, scholarly orthodoxy, like papal authority, inclines toward "anthropophagy"'; Fred Hoerner, ' "Fire to Use": A Practice-Theory Approach to Paradise Lost', *Representations* 51 (Summer 1995), 94–117, 97. Refusing both Stanley Fish's insistence on the trial of reading as leading to orthodoxy and

liberal criticism's notions of trial as allowing for self-development, David Mikics has argued that 'Milton's creativity takes the form of trying the reader by confronting him with the possibility of – with our feeling of – a tainted creation, and therefore an imperfect God. Such possibility is a cruelty of our fate, our human circumstances, that far exceeds the comic-strip wickedness of Empson's bad Father, with his adolescent taste for torturing his creatures'; David Mikics, 'Miltonic Marriage and the Challenge to History in *Paradise Lost*', *Texas Studies in Literature and Language* 46.1 (2004), 20–48, 26. Timothy Rosedale, playing *Areopagitica*'s sense of trial against *Paradise Lost* as an allegory of reading, argues that the fall follows from Adam and Eve's confrontation with an enigmatic signifier, while, 'The Law is thus given as a hermeneutic framework by means of which fallen man may accurately read both himself and his relationship to God. It functions as a postlapsarian analogue to the Tree of Knowledge by providing an indication of a proper interpretive perspective; like the Tree, it exists as a pure sign, a symbol of a difference now greater than ever between Almighty God and fallen humanity'; Timothy Rosedale, 'Milton, Hobbes and the Liturgical Subject', *SEL Studies in English Literature 1500–1900*, 44.1 (2004), 161.

29. The classic example of this would be Mary Shelley's *Frankenstein*, in which the roles of benevolent creator, reactive angel and despairing Adam are not attributed to single characters but occur as roles adopted by the same self at different points of the narrative. Victor is at once Milton's God, Milton's Satan, Milton's Adam and Milton's Eve, with the monster also occupying the position of the plaintive Adam, the rebellious angel and the self-captivated Eve.

30. For a defence of Milton's poetry against the accusation of its lack of life, and a critique of those critics who defended its supposed arid formality, see Christopher Ricks, *Milton's Grand Style*, Oxford: Clarendon Press, 1963.

31. Jerome J. McGann, *Social Values and Poetic Acts: The Historical Judgment of Literary Work*, Cambridge, MA: Harvard University Press, 1988.

32. Jerome J. McGann, 'The Text, the Poem, and the Problem of Historical Method', *New Literary History*, 12.2 (Winter, 1981), 269–88.

33. Jerome J. McGann, *The Romantic Ideology: A Critical Investigation*, Chicago: University of Chicago Press, 1983.

34. Walter Benn Michaels attacked what he deemed to be a pernicious (post-De Man) formalism that would preclude considerations of context: 'although some texts are ambiguous, no texts are inherently ambiguous, and although some texts are precise, no texts are inherently precise either … the properties we attribute to texts are functions, instead of situations, of the contexts in which texts are read'; Walter Benn Michaels, 'Against Formalism: The Autonomous Text in Legal and Literary Interpretation', *Poetics Today*, 1.1/2 (Autumn 1979), 23–34, 32. Context, for Michaels, is not some objective ground so much as a shared background, which is also understood through processes of interpretation and evaluation. At the basis of the literary object, and its reading, there is – therefore – an ongoing activity of belief and evaluation. Walter Benn Michaels, 'Saving the Text: Reference and Belief', *MLN*, 93.5 (December 1978), 771–93.

35. The first charge of Milton's lack of sensitivity and feeling in his mastery of poetic form occurs with Samuel Johnson's criticism of 'Lycidas', and continues with T.S. Eliot's criticism of the poetry's lack of sensibility. T.S. Eliot, 'A Note on the Verse of John Milton', *Essays and Studies*, 21 (1936), reprinted as 'Milton 1' in *On Poetry and Poets*, New York: Farrar Strauss, 1957.

36. Bernard Bergonzi, in 'Criticism and the Milton Controversy', quotes Johnson's lament that Milton was governed by 'perverse and pedantick principle' and Keats's letter declaring that 'The Paradise Lost though so fine in itself is a corruption of our Language . . . I have but lately stood on my guard against Milton. Life to him would be death to me.' In *The Living Milton: Essays by Various Hands*, London: Routledge, 1960, pp. 162–80, 162–3.

37. Joseph Wittreich (ed.), *Milton and the Line of Vision*, Wisconsin: University of Wisconsin Press, 1975. Wittreich has recently offered a powerful restatement of the idea of literary history as revivification in his reflections on *Samson Agonistes*: 'What we witness in the juxtaposition of Samson in the Bible, Hebrew and Christian, and the Samson of literary tradition and of Milton's poem, is the development of a legend, its connection to religious life and ethical systems over time, but also, in terms of the English revolution and 9/11, the relationship between ethical systems, the law, and political action. We witness the formation of a critique of culture, all the more remarkable if, begun before and finished after the Restoration, *Samson Agonistes* may be said to illustrate that "the poet writes the poem but major poems sometimes rewrite their authors" '; Joseph Wittreich, 'Joseph Wittreich on Why Milton Matters', *Milton Studies* (2005), 22–39. Newlyn's *Paradise Lost and the Romantic Reader* also argues for the ways in which Milton provided an enabling and expansive context for later poets.

38. Annabel Patterson, *Early Modern Liberalism*, Cambridge: Cambridge University Press, 1997, p. 16.

39. According to Catherine Gallagher and Stephen Greenblatt, 'This ambition to specify the intriguing enigmas of particular times and places distinguishes our analyses from the contemporary pantextualism of the deconstructionists, who have their own version of the proposition that a culture is a text. Stressing the slippages, aporias and communicative failures at the heart of signifying systems, linguistic or otherwise, their cultural textualism has no historicist ancestry. For them, written language is the paradigmatic form in which the problems of making meaning become manifest, and a culture may be said to be 'textual' because its meaningful signs are inherently ambiguous, paradoxical and undecidable. Deconstructionist literary analyses thus continually turn up textuality itself as the source and structure of all enigmas. Although maintaining that there is nothing outside of the text, no place of simple and transparent meaning where the slipperiness of the sign can be escaped, deconstructionists nonetheless tend to draw their examples from the literary canon. While we frequently explore other kinds of texts, they urge that literary language uniquely exposes to scrutiny a textuality that operates everywhere and throughout history. Hence, in addition to skipping the levels of analysis that interest us most – the culturally and historically specific – deconstructionism also seems to reerect the hierarchical privileges of the literary'; Catherine Gallagher and Stephen Greenblatt, *Practicing New Historicism*, Chicago: University of Chicago Press, 2000, p. 14.

40. Stephen Greenblatt, 'Resonance and Wonder', in *Learning to Curse: essays in early modern culture*, New York: Routledge, 2006, p. 170.

41. To give support to this claim I could draw upon anthropology, which has examined the ways in which various cultures must establish taboos on the transgression of bodily integrity. Although inflected differently across cultures, disgust is always prompted by a corruption of the body's borders. (For a philosophical summation of this argument see Martha C. Nussbaum, *Hiding from Humanity: Disgust, Shame, and*

the Law, Princeton: Princeton University Press, 2004.) There has been a long tradition of arguing that norms of purity ultimately refer back to imperatives of cleanliness and order, with the classic study being Mary Douglas's *Purity and Danger: An Analysis of Concepts of Pollution and Taboo*, London, Routledge and Kegan Paul, 1966. This anthropological tradition has recently been reinforced by work in neuroscience and cognitive science which argues that the image of the self as a bounded unity, and the understanding of the world in terms of similar embodied agents, is based on the psycho-physical system of human subjects. See George Lakoff and Mark Johnson, *Philosophy in the Flesh: The Embodied Mind and its Challenge to Western Thought*. New York: Basic Books, 1999. Some work has already been done connecting Milton's poetry with such anthropological and scientific insights. See Beth Bradburn, 'Bodily Metaphor and Moral Agency in a Masque: A Cognitive Approach', *Milton Studies* (2004), 198–260. In this book I will be looking at the ways in which poetry, if read critically, allows us to free ourselves from these images of orderly organicism.

42. Henri Bergson, *Creative Evolution*, trans. Arthur Mitchell, London: Macmillan, 1911.

43. Sigmund Freud, *Beyond the Pleasure Principle*, trans. James Strachey, London: Hogarth Press, 1950.

44. See Humberto R. Maturana and Francisco J. Varela, *The Tree of Knowledge: The Biological Roots of Human Understanding*, Boston: New Science Library, 1987, and Steven Rose, *Lifelines: Life Beyond the Gene*, London: Vintage, 2005.

45. Descriptions of this passage from a once meaningful and hierarchical world of essences to a quantified and meaningless world of quantities vary in their moral tone and valency but include studies as diverse as Basil Willey, *The Seventeenth-Century Background: Studies in the Thought of the Age in Relation to Poetry and Religion*, London: Chatto & Windus, 1934; Arthur O. Lovejoy, *The Great Chain of Being: A Study of the History of an Idea*, Cambridge, MA: Harvard University Press, 1936; Alexandre Koyré, *From the Closed World to the Infinite Universe*, Baltimore: Johns Hopkins University Press, 1957; Hans Blumenberg, *The Genesis of the Copernican World*, trans. Robert M. Wallace, Cambridge, MA: MIT Press, 1987; and Louis Dumont, *Essays on Individualism: Modern Ideology in Anthropological Perspective*, Chicago: University of Chicago Press, 1986.

46. Before technology refers to the systems and machines of contemporary mass-production and mass-communication, *technē* can be considered as the contrary of both *physis* (which grows and expands without the need for a repeatable and systematizable order) and *praxis* (which acts without externalizing its energy into supplemental systems). See Martin Heidegger, *The Question Concerning Technology, and Other Essays*, trans. William Lovitt, New York: Harper and Row, 1977; and Jacques Taminiaux, *Heidegger and the Project of Fundamental Ontology*, trans. Michael Gendre, Albany: State University of New York Press, 1991.

47. Martin Heidegger, *Being and Time*, trans. Joan Stambaugh, Albany: State University of New York Press, 1996.

48. Heidegger, *Question Concerning Technology*.

49. The association of fallen, automatic and technical language with capitalism is most prominent in modernism – and one can think here of Ezra Pound's Hell Cantos and the association between fallen language and usury. But such a notion of the fall of language from animation and vision into system and 'logic' occurs already with Romanticism. In addition to William Blake's argument for the original

animation of the world through the enlarged and numerous sense of the poets, which then falls into system and priesthood, we can also think of Byron's popular Satanism, in which the inspired and energetic will is essentially at odds with the world of propriety.

50. Jean-Pierre Vernant, *Mortals and Immortals: Collected Essays*, ed. Froma I. Zeitlin, Princeton: Princeton University Press, 1991.

51. Henri Bergson, *The Two Sources of Morality and Religion*, trans. R. Ashley Audra and Cloudesley Brereton, New York, H. Holt, 1935.

52. William James, *The Varieties of Religious Experience: A Study in Human Nature*, New York: Longmans, Green, and Co, 1902.

53. William James, *A Pluralistic Universe*, New York, Longmans, Green, and Co., 1909.

54. John Rogers, *The Matter of Revolution: Science, Poetry, and Politics in the Age of Milton*, Ithaca: Cornell University Press, 1996: 'The figure of autonomous material agency peculiar to animist materialism provided fruitful conceptual backing for a range of identifiable groups, including politically minded radicals seeking a liberatory conception of individual political agency, and others, motivated less by political than economic concerns, pursuing a principle of free agency in a hypothetically free market. Vitalist agency, charged with the momentum of revolutionary fervor, could soon be invoked for radical cultural ends, by intellectuals as differently motivated as Milton and Margaret Cavendish, as the "power of matter" ' (p. 9). William Kerrigan also argued that Milton was a vitalist and that it was his commitment to the divinity of matter which led to some of the conflicts of the poem; see William Kerrigan, *The Sacred Complex: On the Psychogenesisof Paradise Lost*, Cambridge, MA: Harvard University Press, 1983, p. 200. Whereas Rogers sees Milton backing away from revolutionary materialism in *Paradise Lost* and moving towards a hierarchical neo-Platonism, Kerrigan argues that it is the sustained belief in the vitality of all life that creates an ambivalence or 'complex' regarding the very nature of life: 'The feeling that mothers give us the balm of life and simultaneously the poisons of disease and death is not uncommon in our mortal species. The art of Milton, which is uncommon, sets in motion the ambivalences surrounding women, food, trust, love, and death in a remarkably direct and undisguised manner, a manner, it should be said, true to the manifest import of the myth he is narrating, then orders these emotions in the lofty structure of a "great Argument" ' (p. 205). Stephen Fallon also regards Milton as a vitalist monist who gave Cartesian and Hobbesian atomist worldviews to his devils. The war in heaven, argues Fallon, is an allegorical 'battle between Milton's vitalist and Hobbes's mechanist monisms'; Stephen M. Fallon, *Milton Among the Philosophers: Poetry and Materialism in Seventeenth-Century England*, Ithaca: Cornell University Press, 1991, p. 7.

55. Henri Bergson, *Matter and Memory*, trans. Nancy Margaret Paul and William Scott Palmer, London: George Allen and Unwin, 1911.

56. Stanley Fish has recently urged a powerful critique of historicism, insisting that Milton's writing matters *as poetry* – or is considered as a good instance of its idiom – not because it can be absorbed in its context but because it operates aesthetically, with aesthetics bearing its own historical mode. Stanley Fish, 'Why Milton Matters; Or, Against Historicism', *Milton Studies* 44 (2005), 1–12.

57. For a reading of Milton that interrogates his use of vitalist metaphors in relation to historical progression see Arthur B. Ferguson, who argues that 'Milton's Truth, then, not only represents the vitality of Scripture and the nourishing power

of the Word, but serves as a figure for history itself, a dynamic process of social transformation characterized by vigorous progression rather than stasis'; Arthur B. Ferguson, *Clio Unbound: Perception of the Social and Cultural Past in Renaissance England*, Durham: Duke University Press, 1979, p. 42.

58. Paul De Man, *Blindness and Insight: Essays in the Rhetoric of Contemporary Criticism*, New York: Oxford University Press, 1971.

59. Jacques Derrida, *Of Spirit: Heidegger and the Question*, trans. Geoffrey Bennington and Rachel Bowlby, Chicago: University of Chicago Press, 1989, p. 134.

60. On the relation between bodily and digestive imagery and Milton's broader ethical commitments, see Michael C. Schoenfeldt, *Bodies and Selves in Early Modern England: Physiology and Inwardness in Spenser, Shakespeare, Herbert, and Milton*, Cambridge: Cambridge University Press, 1999.

61. See Gordon Teske, for whom 'Milton, as a theoretical poet, is concerned with the past and with the future of making. The future of making, or *poiesis*, differs from the past in two respects. First, the future of making is a creation produced entirely by man, constituting what architectural theorists call a "built environment." ... Second, the future of making is not a totality and is therefore not finished but forever emerging, continually cancelling and replacing itself'; Gordon Teske, *Delirious Milton*, Cambridge, MA: Harvard University Press, 2006.

62. More than any other Christian poet of his time, the incarnation was an intensely important issue for Milton, for whom the Son was *essentially* distinct from the Father – and this because Christ 'coalesced in one person with man' (CPW 6.425). On the complexity of this issue see John Rumrich, 'Milton's *Theanthropos*: The Body of Christ in *Paradise Regained*', *Milton Studies*, 42 (2003), 50–67.

63. Gilles Deleuze, *Francis Bacon: The Logic of Sensation*, trans. Daniel W. Smith, Minneapolis: University of Minnesota Press, 2004.

64. Stanley Fish, *How Milton Works*, Cambridge, MA: Belknap Press of Harvard University Press, 2001.

65. On the somewhat fraught relation between love and labour, see Kevin Goodman, ' "Wasted Labor"? Milton's Eve, the Poet's Work, and the Challenge of Sympathy', *ELH*, 64.2 (1997), 415–46.

66. 'The light which we have gain'd, was giv'n us, not to be ever staring on, but by it to discover onward things mor remote from our knowledge' (CPW 2. 549–50).

67. According to Stephen M. Fallon, 'With the God of Descartes or Hobbes, Milton's God maintains an indifference of acting or not acting. ... But with the Cambridge Platonists and against Hobbes and Descartes, Milton acknowledges that God's actions necessarily conform to a priori standard of the good. In attempting to maintain a balance in which neither God's will or wisdom is subordinated, Milton asserts the *tertium quid* between necessity and chance'; Stephen M. Fallon, ' "To Act or Not" Milton's Conception of Divine Freedom', *Journal of the History of Ideas*, 49.3 (July–September 1988), 425–49, 436.

68. According to Herman Rapaport this is a structuring tension of Milton's Christianity, between a rejection of all forms of reified and externalized law, and an acknowledgment of mediation: 'Christianity is a kind of fascism which has not been deritualized. What Michael Fixler calls the "Kingdom of God" is a term which Protestants have used to conceive of a religious transformation in the sense of political revolution, and it is this "Kingdom of God" which conceptually propped up and destabilized at once the social representations of power

and violence, making manifest what Girard sees as a double movement in Christianity: deconstruction-construction, revelation-concealment, antisocial-social, antimetaphysical-metaphysical'; Herman Rapaport, *Milton and the Postmodern*, Lincoln: University of Nebraska Press, 1983, pp. 190–1.

69. Tertullian, *Apology*, Loeb Classical Library, trans. T.R. Glover, London: Heinemann; New York: G.P. Putnam, 1931, p. 151.

70. Eusebius, *In Praise of Constantine: A Historical Study and New Translation of Eusebius' Triennial Orations*, trans. and ed. H.A. Drake, Berkeley: University of California Press, 1976, p. 87.

71. Peter A. Fiore, *Milton and Augustine: Patterns of Augustinian Thought in Milton's Paradise Lost*, University Park: Pennsylvania State University Press, 1981.

72. Augustine of Hippo, *Concerning the City of God: Against the Pagans*, trans. Henry Bettenson, Harmondsworth: Penguin, 1984, p. 228.

73. Ernst Troeltsch, *The Social Teachings of the Christian Churches*, trans. Olive Wyon. 2 vols. London: Allen and Unwin; New York: Macmillan, 1931. See also John T. McNeill, 'Natural Law in the Teaching of the Reformers', *The Journal of Religion*, 26. 3 (July 1946), 168–82.

74. I would therefore contrast Milton's constant references to inwardness (which is a form of inner transcendence) with modern forms of individualism which regard the self as an autonomous thinking substance, devoid of any qualities other than its own self-making or representing capacities. The classic argument aligning Milton with modern rationalism is Andrew Milner's *John Milton and the English Revolution: A Study in the Sociology of Literature*, London: Macmillan, 1981. A more recent statement arguing for Milton's modern notion of the individual in contrast with courtly and aristocratic modes is Matthew Jordan's *Milton and Modernity: Politics, Masculinity and Paradise Lost*, Basingstoke: Palgrave, 2001.

75. C.B. MacPherson, *The Political Theory of Possessive Individualism: Hobbes to Locke*, Oxford: Oxford University Press, 1962.

76. For a recent defence of a polity that would be an expression, rather than a (Hobbesian) imposed limitation, of human individuals, see Michael Hardt and Antonio Negri, *Empire*, Cambridge, MA: Harvard University Press, 2000. Drawing heavily upon Spinoza, Hardt and Negri are opposed to the capitalist reduction of human power to quantifiable labour power and insist on the possibility of an immanent politics, in which humans free themselves from imposed and metaphysical notions of law and realize themselves through sociality. While Milton maintained transcendence in his understanding of a law that would be at one with human flourishing, his transcendence was nevertheless immanent to the human soul: not the recognition of an alien power, but the realization of one's own proper potential.

77. Michael Lieb has also traced the ways in which life and being must grow towards definition and limit, while chaos is the loss of identity. See *The Dialectics of Creation: Patterns of Birth and Regeneration in 'Paradise Lost'*, Amherst: University of Massachusetts Press, 1970.

78. Hegel will argue that a 'bad infinite' is a constantly surpassed limit, a possibility of always adding more; the true understanding of the absolute is of a rational whole which understands itself as self-constituting and defined by its own limitation. G.W.F. Hegel, *Hegel's Logic: Being Part One of the 'Encyclopaedia of the Philosophical sciences'*, trans. William Wallace; fwd J.N. Findlay; 3rd edn, Oxford: Clarendon Press, 1975.

79. On the 'pervasive imagery of the body and monstrous generation' in the political prose of Milton see Barbara K. Lewalski, *The Life of John Milton*, Oxford: Blackwell, 2000, p. 143.

80. As Arthur Barker notes, Milton's attitude to Constantine demonstrates his difference from the Smectymnuans in so far as they referred to the 'admired Constantine, that great promoter and patron of the Christian Church' who demonstrated 'the gracious disposition of princes towards Christian religion.' (*An Answer to ... An Humble Remonstrance*, March 1641, 28, 45, 74) quoted in Arthur Barker, *Milton and the Puritan Dilemma: 1640–1660*, Toronto: University of Toronto Press, 1942, p. 33.

81. Alain Badiou, *Saint Paul: The Foundation of Universalism*, trans. Ray Brassier, Stanford: Stanford University Press, 2003.

82. Pierre Hadot, *Philosophy as a Way of Life: Spiritual Exercises from Socrates to Foucault*, ed. Arnold I. Davidson; trans. Michael Chase, Oxford: Blackwell, 1995.

83. John Milton, *The Poetical Works of John Milton*, ed. Helen Darbishire, London: Oxford University Press, 1958. All quotations from Milton's poetry are taken from this edition; all further references to each work will be abbreviated and incorporated into the text.

84. The clearest expression of such a vitalist doctrine in literary theory would be American New Criticism, where the very essence of poetry is its difference from a language which operates by mere technical and easily functioning tokens; the poetic use of language restores each word to its complex relation to the world, once again enabling the distance between word and life. If it was this value of 'life' in New Criticism which underpinned the sense of the weakness of Milton's too-linguistic poetry, various contemporary celebrations of Milton still urge a vitalist ethics. Milton's poetry matters because it takes our all too coagulated beliefs and complacencies and enables an ethical and rhetorical exercise of the faculties, awakening us from our poetically and theologically dogmatic slumbers. See Fish, 'Why Milton Matters'; and Wittreich, 'Joseph Wittreich on Why Milton Matters'.

85. William Blake, *The Four Zoas*, plate 30, 10–11, *The Complete Poetry and Prose of William Blake*, ed. David V. Erdman, rev. edn, New York: Anchor-Doubleday, 1988, p. 319.

86. Blake, *The Four Zoas*, plate 33, 32–6, p. 322.

87. For Milton liberty is not a capacity of the subject so much as a bestowed power. Liberty 'hath rarify'd and enlighten'd our spirits like the influence of heaven; this is that which hath enfranchis'd, enlarg'd and lifted up our apprehensions degrees above themselves' (CPW 2.559).

88. Helen Vendler has criticized the notion that the life of 'L'Allegro' presents a less worthy existence and poetics than the melancholy of 'Il Penseroso'. While she is no doubt correct to note that Milton does present the legitimate value of the sensuality of his 'Allegro' world, and that the poem is not dismissive, the coupling of the poems does imply the necessary supplement of the divine light of 'Il Penseroso'. Helen Vendler, *Coming of Age as a Poet: Milton, Keats, Eliot, Plath*, Cambridge: Cambridge University Press, 2003.

89. John Rogers in *The Matter of Revolution* has situated seventeenth-century vitalisms, including Milton's, as a reaction against the Cartesian reduction of the world to mere matter with no intrinsic relations other than those of colliding matter. In *Radical Enlightenment* Jonathan Israel has argued that from Cartesianism's very inception there was a counter Spinozist tradition arguing for the expressive, rather than mechanical, nature of the world. Such an approach would preclude reference

to an external law and creator, and to 'man' as a normative thinking subject; Jonathan Israel, *Radical Enlightenment: Philosophy and the Making of Modernity, 1650–1750*, Oxford: Oxford University Press, 2001.

90. Deleuze, *Difference and Repetition*, p. 183.

91. In the twentieth century the 'Cartesian subject' was subject to the same criticisms that Milton directed towards Satan: once the world is disenchanted and seen as mere matter, the subject becomes nothing more than a point from which matter is calculated, mastered and rendered manipulable. Martin Heidegger argued that the idea of Descartes as a philosopher who doubted the world and thereby discovered 'the subject' is nothing more than a 'bad novel'. For Heidegger, Descartes' 'subject' functioned as yet one more way in which the being of the world was granted some logic or order from the basis of a particular and (unquestioned) being (Martin Heidegger, *What is a Thing?* p. 44). For Heidegger the true path to thinking would therefore require an overthrow both of the subject and of all notions of a being that would give order to the world. Heidegger, however, nevertheless insisted that a listening or attending to Being would overcome the fall of thinking into mere logic. It was Jacques Derrida who connected this entire trajectory to a history of evil, for what is always being resisted – in Heidegger and all appeals to a *proper* and originating spirit – is the workings of a 'machine-animal' of pure evil that would not be informed by sense or proper potentiality: 'That which constitutes evil for Heidegger, [is what] haunts spirit in all of its destitution: the certainty of the *cogito* in the position of the *subjectum* and therefore absence of originary questioning, scientific methodologism, leveling, predominance of the quantitative, of extension and of number – so many motifs which are "Cartesian" in type. All of that, which accepts lie and destruction, is evil, the foreigner: foreign to spirit *in* spirit'; Derrida, *Of Spirit*, pp. 62–3.

92. Michel Foucault, *History of Sexuality, Volume One: An Introduction,* trans. Robert Hurley, London: Penguin, 1979.

93. Michel Foucault, 'What is Enlightenment?' in *The Foucault Reader*, ed. Paul Rabinow, Harmondsworth: Penguin, 1986.

94. I would therefore challenge a project such as Joseph Wittreich's *Feminist Milton* that would seek to connect gender-bias in Milton's poetry to the prejudices of his time, arguing for a properly radical and feminist potential which later readers will be able to actualize. Once again we are given the image of reading as restoring or realizing what a text ought to have said, or really meant, despite its contamination in its present system of signification. Joseph Wittreich, *Feminist Milton*, Ithaca: Cornell University Press, 1987. See also Diane McColley, *Milton's Eve*, Urbana: University of Illinois Press, 1983.

95. Jacques Derrida refers to this tropological complex as 'economimesis', where man's representation of nature is not a passive copying but a bringing into active thought and contemplation the proper potentialities of nature as a meaningful and rational whole. Jacques Derrida, 'Economimesis', trans. Renata Klein, *Diacritics*, 11.2 (Summer 1981), 2–25. Denise Gigante's insightful article on eating in *Paradise Lost* also draws from this work of Derrida's. See Denise Gigante, 'Milton's Aesthetics of Eating', *Diacritics*, 30.2 (Summer 2000), 88–112. Stephen Fallon has also noted with respect to *Paradise Lost* that, 'Those who obey are sublimed and rarefied. Those who disobey are purged and excreted. Every significant decision is ontological and metabolic as well as moral'; *Milton Among the Philosophers*, p. 210.

96. It is in just this respect that Martin Heidegger draws attention to the ways in which the Cartesian subject is based on a *subjectum* – the Latin translation of *hypokeimenon*, or that ultimate being which precedes and grounds qualities and relations. Martin Heidegger, *What is a Thing*, trans. W.B. Barton and Vera Deutsch, Lanham: University Press of America, 1985, p. 103. For a feminist critique of the masculinism of this subject as *hypokeimenon* see Luce Irigaray's *Speculum of the Other Woman*, trans. Gillian C. Gill, Ithaca: Cornell University Press. 1985.

97. Augustine, *City of God*, Book 14, p. 273.

98. In *Dialectic of Enlightenment* the progress of reason through history is linked to a process of domination and loss of meaning where the 'multiplicity of forms is reduced to position and arrangement, history to fact, things to matter'. This process of enlightenment, which has its origins in Platonic thought but becomes modern with Bacon's 'scientific attitude', is mathematical in character: 'The same equations dominate bourgeois justice and commodity exchange. [Adorno and Horkheimer then quote from Bacon's *Advancement of Learning*:] "Is not the rule, '*Si inaequalibus aequalia addas, omnia erunt inaequalia*,' an axiom of justice as well as of mathematics? And is there not a true coincidence between commutative and distributive justice, and arithmetical and geometrical proportion?" Bourgeois society is ruled by equivalence. It makes the dissimilar comparable by reducing it to abstract quantities'; Theodor Adorno and Max Horkheimer, *Dialectic of Enlightenment*, trans. John Cumming, London: Verso, 1979, p. 7. The most sophisticated critique of rationalism and rationalization comes from Jürgen Habermas, who acknowledges that once we abandon belief in a metaphysical foundation, such as God or human nature, we should not fall into the nihilism of lacking all values. Instead, we should criticize a world that has become merely functional and instrumental, and we could do this by returning various knowledge practices to the 'lifeworld': the social and communicative domain from which all meanings and values emerge. Jürgen Habermas, *Postmetaphysical Thinking: Philosophical Essays*, trans. William Mark Hohengarten, Cambridge, MA: MIT Press, 1992.

99. According to Stella P. Revard, 'Milton has cast Satan [in *Paradise Regain'd*] in the role of the sceptics of his own time – Hall and Love, Edwards and Baillie, all of whom expressed doubt about or ridiculed the notion of a literal kingdom'; 'Milton and Millenarianism: From the Nativity Ode to *Paradise Regained*', in Juliet Cummins (ed.), *Milton and the Ends of Time*, Cambridge: Cambridge University Press, 2003, pp. 42–81, 69.

100. This logic of nihilism and reactive forces was diagnosed by Friedrich Nietzsche. Once the self despairs of a value beyond life it can only find meaning reactively through ressentiment: it is because there is a posited tyrannical other that the self can take pleasure in its own suffering. What has been lost is all joy of life. Nietzsche, *On the Genealogy of Morality*, ed. Keith Ansell Pearson; trans. Carol Diethe, Cambridge: Cambridge University Press, 2007.

101. On the themes of nourishment in Milton see W.B.C. Watkins, *An Anatomy of Milton's Verse*, Baton Rouge: Louisiana State University Press, 1955.

102. On good and evil modes of self-relation and consumption see Jacques Derrida, *Of Spirit*, p. 80, and ' "Eating Well," or the Calculation of the Subject: An Interview with Jacques Derrida', in *Who Comes After the Subject*, ed. Eduardo Cadava, Peter Connor and Jean-Luc Nancy; trans. Peter Connor and Avital Ronnell, London: Routledge, 1991, p. 112.

103. Augustine, *Sermons on Selected Lessons of the New Testament*, vol.2, Oxford, 1845 (*Sermon* 166.4), p. 845.

104. Heidegger, *What is a Thing*, p. 105.

105. Immanuel Kant, *Critique of Pure Reason*, trans. and ed. Paul Guyer and Allen W. Wood, Cambridge: Cambridge University Press, 1998.

106. Ludwig Wittgenstein, *Philosophical Investigations*, trans. G.E.M. Anscombe, Oxford, Basil Blackwell, 1968, p. 93.

107. William J. Grace, 'Milton, Salmasius, and the Natural Law', *Journal of the History of Ideas*, 24.3 (July–September 1963), 323–36.

108. Clay Daniel has argued that we should be wary of identifying Raphael's neo-Platonism too readily with Milton's own views about redemption. Instead we should see the dialogue between Raphael and Adam as a diagnostic presentation of Adam's neo-Platonizing response to Raphael: 'The angel cites the *scala naturae* – the Great Chain/Ladder of Being. Adam invokes the ladder of contemplation. Adam's interpretation is suspect, as these ladders were not identical. . . . Certainly Raphael says nothing about anyone becoming God in the way often envisioned by Neo-Platonists and apparently by Adam. Adam all too readily conflates Raphael's "Heav'nly Paradises" (5.500) – plural, significantly – with Heaven'; Clay Daniel, 'Milton's Neo-Platonic Angel?', *SEL Studies in English Literature 1500–1900*, 44.1 (2004), 173–88, 177.

109. Stephen Fallon, in *Milton Among the Philosophers*, has also identified the process of 'downward ontological movement' with evil.

110. Shoshana Felman, *Jacques Lacan and the Adventure of Insight*, Cambridge, MA: Harvard University Press, 1987.

111. Milton therefore follows Augustine in insisting that the fall is that of a relation between reason and the will, and not a corruption of reason *per se*. Originally the will is not in opposition to reason: 'The injunction . . . was so easy to observe, so brief to remember; above all, it was given at a time when desire was not yet in opposition to the will . . . Therefore the unrighteousness of violating the prohibition was so much greater, in proportion to the ease with which it could have been observed and fulfilled'; Augustine, *City of God*, Book 14, ch.13, p. 571.

112. Harold Bloom, *A Map of Misreading*, New York: Oxford University Press, 1975.

113. Jacques Derrida, *Edmund Husserl's Origin of Geometry: An Introduction*, trans. John P. Leavey, Lincoln: University of Nebraska Press, 1989.

114. Edmund Husserl, *The Crisis of the European Sciences and Transcendental Phenomenology: An Introduction to Phenomenological Philosophy*, trans. David Carr, Evanston: Northwestern University Press, 1970.

115. This was how Hannah Arendt described the singular logic of totalitarianism in *The Origins of Totalitarianism*, San Diego: Harcourt, 1968. Whereas earlier forms of despotism and tyranny had exercised power in order to achieve the despot's or group's interests, totalitarianism unleashes a destructive will to system that is not subordinated to any end or measure (p. 456). Arendt sees the threat of this peculiarly modern form of evil as dependent upon the increasingly disenchanted nature of a modern world that no longer has any sense of a polity in common towards which all individuals are directed in dialogue (p. 336): 'The very fact that the "original sin" of "original accumulation of capital" would need additional sin to keep the system going was far more effective in persuading the bourgeoisie to shake of the restraints of Western tradition than either its philosopher or its underworld' (p. 156).

116. A world in which the good is freely recognized is a better created world than one in which order is produced by compulsion: such an argument was launched as early as Irenaeus of Lyon (ad 130–200) in *Against Heretics*, IV: xxvii–xix, in *The Ante-Nicene Christian Library, Volume 9*, ed. Revd Alexander Robertson and James Donaldson, Edinburgh: Clark, 1869.

117. Regina Schwartz, *Remembering and Repeating: On Milton's Theology and Poetics*, Chicago: University of Chicago Press, 1993, 74.

118. In 'On Authorship, Sexuality and the Psychology of Privation in Milton's *Paradise Lost*', *ELH*, 67.4 (2000), 905–24, Katherine O. Acheson has examined the ways in which the distinction between good and bad sexuality (which reinforces other oppositions) is threatened with dissolution precisely through its rehearsed presentation in *Paradise Lost*: 'If the display and demarcation of the difference between good sexuality and bad sexuality establishes the identity and authority of the divine poet, we are placed, in the temptation scene, at the moment of his origin as the scene generates the urgent necessity for such discernments, as the combination of chiastic and oxymoronic relationships between good and evil, and their embodiments within Eve and Satan, are what give the scene its compelling power and its ability to make the temptation and the conflict our own' (915).

119. Linda Gregerson argues that the self's relationality, through the drama of its constitution throughout *Paradise Lost*, is riven with conflict: 'precisely because Milton so conspicuously rejects the sequestering of the erotic object from intellectual aspiration, because of his rich insistence on conjugal conversation in the divorce tracts and *Paradise Lost*, he is encumbered with an embarrassing anomaly ... Petrarchism and Platonism had strenuously to negotiate the relationship between erotic desire and longing for the transcendent, but Milton in his peculiar blend of radicalism and orthodoxy has done away with a critical margin for negotiation: Adam's desire in earthly marriage can only move downward on the scale of creation'; Linda Gregerson, *The Reformation of the Subject: Spenser, Milton and the English Protestant Epic*, Cambridge: Cambridge University Press, 1995, p. 176.

120. Koyré, *From the Closed World*; Hans Blumenberg, *The Genesis of the Copernican World*, Cambridge, MA: MIT Press, 1987; Louis Dumont, *From Mandeville to Marx: The Genesis and Triumph of Economic Ideology*, Chicago: Chicago University Press, 1977.

121. Linda Gregerson argues that 'According to the Augustinian of Milton's allegory, Satan's failure in obedience is also a failure in reading, since turning from God to prefer God's handiwork or image (the self is both) is an act of idolatry'; Gregerson, *The Reformation of the Subject*, pp. 207–8.

122. Augustine described these two modes of relation, parsing them as good and evil, through the distinction between charity and cupidity: 'I call "charity" the motion of the soul toward the enjoyment of God for His own sake, and the enjoyment of one's self and of one's neighbour for the sake of God; but "cupidity" is a motion of the soul toward the enjoyment of one's self, one's neighbour, or any corporal thing for the sake of something other than God'; Augustine, *On Christian Doctrine*, trans D.W. Robertson Jr, New York: Liberal Arts Press, 1958, 3.10.16.

123. C.A. Patrides, *Milton and the Christian Tradition*, Oxford: Clarendon Press, 1966.

124. Thomas Corns argues that Milton, in his Christology, 'reverses' Aristotle's metaphysics in which matter is devoid of form. According to Corns, when Christ takes on a human body at the incarnation he must also become, in some part, human and this is because matter has a 'singular form'. In general we can say, then, that Milton refuses the idea of matter as devoid of all form, so that the form it takes on is

appropriate for the matter concerned. Thomas N. Corns, '"With Unaltered Brow"': Milton and the Son of God', *Milton Studies*, 42 (2003), 106–21. Convincing readings of Aristotle have made just this point: there is no form that exists free of matter, but there is no matter that does not have a tendency towards form.

125. Immanuel Kant, *Religion within the Boundaries of Mere Reason*, trans. Allen W. Wood and George di Giovanni, Cambridge: Cambridge University Press, 1996, pp. 64–5. Since Kant, another seemingly opposed account of radical evil has been put forward by Hannah Arendt. For Kant evil can only be a function of the human will, for nature in itself is neither good nor evil; evil is located in maxims and decisions and not in natural life. For Arendt 'radical evil' refers to an evil beyond thought, decision and justification. Her description of the 'banality' of evil is not of a radical will, or a tendency of the self to make an exception of itself from the moral law, but of a certain non-thinking or failure of thinking. Despite their differences, in both cases 'radical evil' is entwined with human rationality's potential for thinking and right reason. In the case of Kant the will uses that reasoning power to make an exception of itself, and is therefore in principle already entwined with thinking and the law (if only implicitly), while for Arendt 'evil' is the non-activation of thinking and reasoning. See Henry E. Allison, 'Reflections on the Banality of (Radical) Evil: A Kantian Analysis', in Maria Pia Lara (ed.), *Rethinking Evil: Contemporary Perspectives*, Berkeley: University of California Press, 2001, pp. 86–100.

126. Juliet Cummins offers an insightful reading of *Paradise Lost* and the evil of ontological decay by placing Milton's poetics in the context of alchemical notions of purification, whereby matter itself may take on more being and goodness by becoming refined, or fall back into non-being. In Cummins' reading a modern notion of goodness as material is combined with a spiritual process of purification: 'The corruption of the incorrupt self through the unnatural decision to sin reverses the process of purification ordained by God, and substitutes a contrary process of ontological decay'; 'Matter and Apocalyptic Tranformations in *Paradise Lost*', in Juliet Cummins (ed.), *Milton and the Ends of Time*, Cambridge: Cambridge University Press, 2003, pp. 169–83, 176.

127. Or, as John Rumrich notes in relation to *Paradise Regain'd*: 'the Son incrementally negates the Fall, which was a sudden and total negation'; Rumrich, 'Milton's Theanthropos', 64.

128. Paul de Man, 'Pascal's Allegory of Persuasion', in Andrzej Warminski (ed.), *Aesthetic Ideology*, Minneapolis: University of Minnesota Press, 1996, pp. 51–69.

129. The most insistent defence of *Paradise Lost* as an allegory is Kenneth Borris's *Allegory and Epic in English Renaissance Literature: Heroic Form in Sidney, Spenser and Milton*, Cambridge: Cambridge University Press, 2000. In addition to the allegory of Sin and Death Borris argues for a more general level and mode of allegory that would present the entire cosmos of the poem as both expressed in the body of Christ and in the type of the hero (p. 85). Catherine Gimelli Martin argues that while Milton presents Cartesian clarity as Satanic he also manages to salvage some aspects of allegorical presentation but that these are neither dualistic nor clear: 'whereas allegory's traditional role is to point toward eternal stasis, baroque allegory embraces linguistic modulation as the only mediation consistent with the uncertainties of temporal revelation'; Catherine Gimelli Martin, *The Ruins of Allegory: Paradise Lost and the Metamorphosis of Epic Convention*, Durham: Duke University Press, 1998, p. 24.

130. Borris will go so far as to argue that Adam and Eve are allegories for the relation between male and female faculties: 'The poem's allegorical portrayal of Satan's character unfolds through his interaction with personifications of Sin, Death, and other progeny that originate in his mental involvements with evil. Likewise, the relationship of Adam and Eve is partly an allegorical means of portraying the "union of mind, or in both one soul," constituted of diverse faculties within, so as to explore the inner proceses of good, evil, and the fall itself' (*Allegory and Epic*, p. 185). Arguing for Adam and Eve as allegorical figures diminishes the sense in which Milton wanted to present paradise as an actual scene not so different from the married bourgeois life we might imagine and regain today. It might be more appealing today to read *Paradise Lost* as an allegory, for that would mean detaching the poem's moral message from its commitment to a specific and authoritative story of origins. But Milton's insistence throughout the poem is that literary history only offers types and images of the one true Christian story.

131. That subjectivity is intrinsically accountable is an idea that is made explicit by Kant. It is precisely because we are beings who represent the world to ourselves that we have no direct relation to an ultimate foundation. For that reason – in the absence of being determined – we must give a law to ourselves; we are therefore not free to not be moral. Twentieth-century reiterations of this essential tie between subjectivity and subjection have been less sanguine, but no less insistent. The very fact that I speak and recognize myself as an 'I' is only possible because I situate myself in a symbolic order that is radically distinct from any supposedly self-present nature that might allow me to simply be at one with my bodily or passionate being. See Judith Butler, *The Psychic Life of Power: Theories in Subjection*, Stanford: Stanford University Press, 1997.

132. The idea that tyranny is not so much an exercise of one's own power but an enslavement to compulsion became a prominent theme of the Enlightenment, articulated most persuasively by Mary Wollstonecraft, who argued that as long as men exercised mere force over women they could not fully exercise their reason. Mary Wollstonecraft, *A Vindication of the Rights of Woman*, Oxford: Oxford University Press, 1994.

133. According to Mary C. Fenton, 'For Satan, hope is a form of power rather than a form of spirituality, and thus he materializes hope, basing hopes to regain power on the acquisition of land'; 'Hope, Land Ownership, and Milton's "Paradise Within"', *SEL Studies in English Literature 1500–1900*, 43.1 (2003), 151–80, 151.

134. Gerard H. Cox has outlined the theological background of the sin of despair in relation to Marlowe's *Doctor Faustus* and its Scholastic and Augustinian sources. See Gerard H. Cox, 'Marlowe's "Doctor Faustus" and "Sin against the Holy Ghost"', *The Huntington Library Quarterly*, 36.2 (February 1973), 119–37.

135. Immanuel Kant, *Critique of Judgment*, trans. James Creed Meredith, Oxford: Oxford University Press, 1952.

136. Wittreich, *Milton and the Line of Vision*.

137. Teske, *Delirious Milton*, p. 78.

138. Stephen Greenblatt, *Renaissance Self-Fashioning: From More to Shakespeare*, Chicago: University of Chicago Press, 1980.

139. Alexander Nehamas presents both Foucault and Nietzsche as writers who present the active creation of a self, rather than the expression of truths, as the role of

philosophy. Alexander Nehamas, *The Art of Living: Socratic Reflections from Plato to Foucault*, Berkeley: University of California Press, 1998.

140. Matthew Jordan has convincingly argued that Milton's conception of self might be contrasted with the self of social performance: 'The worth of the self is supposed not to depend on the estimation of others but to consist in the self's independent consciousness of its own truth'; Jordan, *Milton and Modernity*, p. 2.

141. Rogers, *The Matter of Revolution*. Twentieth-century vitalisms, most notable Henri Bergson's, were also critical of a world that might be construed according to a single model of quantitative force. Instead, for Bergson life expresses itself in the creation of differences, with the world of uniform quantities being merely the way in which the intellect manages and manipulates durations that are not its own; Bergson, *Creative Evolution*.

142. Fredric Jameson claims that Satan is not a modern revolutionary but a 'great feudal baron' whose rebellion is 'a reminiscence of the distant feudal past'; Fredric Jameson, 'Religion and Ideology: a Political Reading of *Paradise Lost*', in Francis Barker, Peter Hulme, Margaret Iversen and Diana Loxley (eds), *Literature, Politics and Theory: Papers from the Essex Conference 1976–84*, London: Methuen, 1986, pp. 35–56. Gordon Braden and William Kerrigan have argued that Satan is closer to the model of the Renaissance man, concerned with esteem, prestige and distinguishing (rather than affirming) relationships with others. Gordon Braden and William Kerrigan, *The Idea of the Renaissance*, Baltimore: Johns Hopkins University Press, 1989.

143. Peter Herman will argue that Milton's 'or' presents an undecidable universe at odds with his more certain theological claims. Peter C. Herman, 'Paradise Lost, the Miltonic "Or," and the Poetics of Incertitude', *SEL Studies in English Literature 1500–1900*, 43.1 (Winter 2003), 181–211.

144. Aristotle, *Metaphysics*, 1006b 12–13, in Jonathan Barnes (ed.), *The Complete Works of Aristotle*, Princeton: Princeton University Press, 1984.

145. On the discovery and formation of new modes of time in philosophy and literature see Susan Snyder, *Pastoral Process: Spenser, Marvell, Milton*, Stanford: Stanford University Press, 1998.

146. Gilles Deleuze marks this formal and important distinction between Platonic reminiscence, in which thought opens to a time not its own, and Cartesian innateness, in which the self finds only its empirical capacities for representation. See *Difference and Repetition*, p. 183.

147. According to Catherine Gimelli Martin, 'Raphael has been encouraging a proto-scientific attitude concerning the gradual, cumulative nature of the empirical enterprise, in contrast to the instantaneous, mystical penetration of divine secrets that Satan will sophistically offer Eve'; Catherine Gimelli Martin, ' "What If the Sun Be Centre to the World?": Milton's Epistemology, Cosmology, and Paradise of Fools Reconsidered', *Modern Philology*, 99.2 (November 2001), 231–65, 239. Karen Edwards has also argued for a pro-scientific attitude in this speech of Raphael's: 'As the book of the world is always in the process of being written, so too it must always be in the process of being read. The necessary incompleteness of the task is the most striking – and historically the most crucial – feature of Raphael's lesson on how to read the book of the world. It implies that no final, nor even single, interpretation of the densely rich text of Creation is available for readers, and that therefore interpretation must be ongoing and continual';

Karen L. Edwards, *Milton and the Natural World: Science and Poetry in Paradise Lost*, Cambridge: Cambridge University Press, 1999, p. 42.

148. A similar break in propulsion occurs as the narrator presents the fallen angel's argument becoming bogged down in theological discourse: 'Fixt Fate, Free will, Foreknowledge absolute' (2.259).

149. This term was originally used by Antonin Artaud but was taken up by Gilles Deleuze and Félix Guattari. Although the term has a number of uses and deployments in their corpus, its general sense enables a distinction between two modes of vitalism and two approaches to aesthetics. A cerebral and active vitalism folds sensation around a body that masters and represents the world; a passive and 'nervous' vitalism begins from sensibility which is not yet recognized by conceptual categories. See Gilles Deleuze and Félix Guattari, *What is Philosophy?*, trans Hugh Tomlinson and Graham Burchell, New York: Columbia University Press, 1994, p. 213.

150. Pierre Bourdieu, *Masculine Domination*, trans. Richard Nice, Cambridge: Polity, 2001. On the ways in which Aristotelian potentiality is associated with the masculine see Charlotte Witt, who argues that despite Aristotle's argument tying male potency with the bringing of matter into form, such an association is historical and not essential to his metaphysics; Witt, *Ways of Being*.

151. On the premodern scientific background to this idea of the 'one sex' model, see Thomas Laqueur, *Making Sex: Body and Gender from the Greeks to Freud*, Cambridge, MA: Harvard University Press, 1990.

152. The relationship between marriage and the polity is reciprocal. As a number of writers have observed, not only does the demand for liberty requires a rational private sphere; a private sphere grounded on harmonious passions is the basis for the good polity. According to Victoria Kahn, 'for the natural order to be a moral order, it − or our response to it − must be mutable, though not too mutable. The discourse of passion is one locus of this divided imperative: it both naturalizes and moralizes, and thus legitimates, the relationship of husband and wife, sovereign and subject'; Victoria Kahn, ' "The Duty to Love": Passion and Obligation in Early Modern Political Theory', *Representations*, 68 (Autumn 1999), 84–107, 88. For John Rumrich, Miltonic marriage 'not only indicates the harmony in which God's glory finally consists, but also helps constitute that harmony'; John Rumrich, *Matter of Glory: A New Preface to Paradise Lost*, Pittsburgh: University of Pittsburgh Press, 1987, p. 108.

153. Here I would disagree with Sandra Gilbert, who claims that Milton maintains the representation of women as 'other': 'The story that Milton, "the first of the masculinists," most notably tells is of course of women's secondness, her otherness, and how that otherness leads inexorably to her demonic anger, her sin, her fall, and her exclusion from that garden of the gods which is also, for her, the garden of poetry.' See Sandra Gilbert, 'Patriarchal Poetry and Women Readers: Reflection's on Milton's Bogey', *PMLA*, 93 (1978), 368–82, 370. I would argue that the problem with Milton's texts for a feminist reading lies in the fact that he sees women not so much as 'other' and excluded but as the same in kind while failing in degree.

154. According to Christine Froula such hierarchical relations reinforce a process of authority which robs self-evidence of its validity and confers truth only upon transcendent sources: 'Eve's relation to Adam as mirror and shadow is the paradigmatic relation which canonical authority institutes between itself and its believers in converting them from the authority of their own experience to a

"higher" authority'; Christine Froula, 'When Eve Reads Milton: Undoing the Canonical Economy', *Critical Inquiry*, 10 (1983–4), 321–47, 328–9. On this point see also Kathleen M. Swaim, ' "Hee for God Only, Shee for God in Him": Structural Parallelism in Paradise Lost', *Milton Studies*, 9 (1976), 121–50.

155. Such an argument is not unique to Milton and characterizes modern forms of theodicy. The most significant instance of such an argument is articulated by John Hick, who regards the world's and the individual's progression to rational and moral perfectibility as necessary for God's goodness: 'the world is not intended to be paradise, but rather the scene of a history in which human personality may be formed towards the pattern of Christ'; John Hick, *Evil and the God of Love*, rev. edn, New York: Harper and Row, 1978, p. 257.

156. 'There is a Negation, & there is a Contrary /The Negation must be destroyd to redeem the Contraries', William Blake, *Milton*, plate 40, 32–3.

157. In *History of Madness* Foucault comments on the ways in which evil was, prior to the seventeenth and eighteenth centuries, represented as a figure; in modernity this figure loses its specific form and becomes a threat of 'unreason' in general. There is, accordingly, a shift from a tragic experience in which reason must make its way in the world always threatened by excesses and limits it can never master, to an experience of unreason as an ethical decision or a failure to live freely and rationally. Anything that is not rational and comprehended is not positively other and radically different, but merely a failure of the proper form of true reason to be actualized. Michel Foucault, *History of Madness*, ed. Jean Khalfa; trans. Jonathan Murphy and Jean Khalfa, London: Routledge, 2006. In *Paradise Lost* Milton will present evil as a figure or monstrous form, while at the same time presenting that figure not as beyond all reason and comprehension but as the very power of rational, productive and harmonious life in its negative, unproductive and failed mainfestation.

158. Geoffrey Hartman discusses this simile and draws attention to Milton's use of time and point of view – or the 'observer *ab extra*' – in *Paradise Lost*. See Geoffrey Hartman, 'Milton's Counterplot', in *Beyond Formalism: Literary Essays 1958–1970*, New Haven: Yale University Press, 1970, pp. 113–23.

159. This principle might be likened to that of contemporary intuitionist logic where it is not the case that we can necessarily appeal to the law of excluded middle: either 'a' or 'not-a'. Thus in *Christian Doctrine* Milton will not insist on deciding the very nature of what will count as apocalypse as 'abolition of the world's substance, or only a change in its qualities' (CPW 6.619–27).

160. Schwartz, *Remembering and Repeating*.

161. Bergson, *Matter and Memory*.

162. Catherine Gimelli Martin has argued for a contrast between two concepts of temporality in Marvell and Milton, with the former requiring some radical disjunction to yield redemption, while Milton's monism or 'cosmic continuum' allows him to believe in the progressive and certain journey towards truth. Catherine Gimelli Martin, 'The Enclosed Garden and the Apocalypse: Immanent versus Transcendent Time in Milton and Marvell', in Juliet Cummings (ed.), *Milton and the Ends of Time*, Cambridge: Cambridge University Press, 2003, pp. 144–68.

163. For a recent explanation of 'perhaps the most famous crux in English literature', see David Sansone, 'How Milton Reads', *Modern Philology*, 103 (2006), 332–58.

164. See Jacques Derrida's commentary on reason's necessary but impossible resistance to the adoption of an apocalyptic tone, in Peter Fenves (ed.), *Raising the*

Tone of Philosophy: Late Essays by Immanuel Kant, Transformative Critique by Jacques Derrida, Baltimore: Johns Hopkins University Press, 1993.

165. John Rogers has challenged the identification of Michael (and his providential view of history) with Milton (who was a material monist); instead, Rogers sees a conflict between expulsion as the process of material forces and the fall and redemption as an outcome of divine intention: 'The expulsion is a matter either of logical or juridical consequence: either the first sin results naturally – in accordance with autonomous physical laws – in the spontaneous evacuation of the couple from paradise, or the fact of sin requires a transcendent punitive God to intercede in the realm of nature and forcibly eject the first parents from their home'; John Rogers, 'Milton and the Mysterious Terms of History', *ELH*, 57.2 (Summer 1990), 281–305, 288.

166. 'A Serious and Faithfull Representation of the Judgements of Ministers of the Gospel within the Province of London' (1649); quoted in introduction, CPW 3.53.

167. Michael Warner, 'Introduction: Fear of a Queer Planet', *Social Text*, 1991; 9 (4 [29]), 3–17.

168. Andrew Milner, *John Milton and the English Revolution: A Study in the Sociology of Literature*, London: Macmillan, 1981.

169. Michel Foucault, *The Order of Things: An Archaeology of the Human Sciences*. New York: Vintage, 1994, p. 128.

170. Jordan, *Milton and Modernity*.

171. Michel Foucault, *History of Sexuality, Volume Three: The Care of the Self*, trans. Robert Hurley, Harmondsworth: Penguin, 1990.

172. Joan Copjec, *Read my Desire: Lacan Against the Historicists*, Cambridge, MA: MIT Press, 1994.

173. Joan Copjec, *Imagine There's No Woman: Ethics and Sublimation*, Cambridge, MA: MIT Press, 2002.

174. Jacques Lacan, *The Ethics of Psychoanalysis, 1959–1960: The Seminar of Jacques Lacan*, ed. Jacques-Alain Miller, trans. Dennis Porter, London: Routledge, 1992.

175. Alain Badiou, *Being and Event*, trans. Oliver Feltham, London: Continuum, 2005.

176. Alain Badiou, *Ethics: An Essay on the Understanding of Evil*, trans. Peter Hallward, London: Verso, 2001.

177. Thus Joseph Wittreich considers his own questioning of Milton's (already questioning) poetics as a continuation of Romantic empowerment: 'If they did not invent the question, "Why Milton?" the Romantics lent fashion to it, empowering Milton by making him whole again and, simultaneously, giving force to his poetry by reading it as if it were a true history; but also by reading it in the future tense so that poems emerging from one moment of crisis could reflect upon, and explain, another crisis in history when, once again, tyranny and terror ruled'; Wittreich, 'Why Milton Matters', 22.

178. According to Richard Helgerson, *Paradise Lost* provides 'an example to the English nation of an inner freedom from which political freedom can arise – not, to be sure, an anarchic freedom but freedom found in obedience to a thoroughly rational and God-centered state'; Richard Helgerson, *Forms of Nationhood: The Elizabethan Writing of England*, Chicago: University of Chicago Press, 1992, p. 61.

179. Foucault, *The Order of Things*, p. 128.

180. 'Vitalism has always had two possible interpretations: that of an idea that acts, but is not – that acts therefore only from the point of view of an external cerebral

knowledge . . . ; or that of a force that is but does not act − that is therefore a pure internal awareness. . . . If the second interpretation seems to us to be imperative it is because the contraction that preserves is always in a state of detachment in relation to action or even to movement and appears as a pure contemplation without knowledge'; Deleuze and Guattari, *What is Philosophy?*, p. 213.

181. 'The original matter was not an evil thing, nor to be thought of as worthless: it was good, and it contained the seeds of all subsequent good. It was a substance and could only have been derived from the source of all substance. It was in a confused and disordered state at first, but afterwards God made it ordered and beautiful' (CPW 6.308).

182. This is the key insight of Regina Schwartz when she argues that 'With full awareness that we inhabit a realm of representation, that the true and the good must be interpreted, not discovered, Milton took up a task not unlike our own: to forge an ethics to ground his politics, his life, and his work, one not received but hammered out personally with great labor and considerable pain. He devotes his chief epic, not to the event of the fall of mankind (whose narration he accords only a stark half-line: "she pluck'd, she eat," IX. 781), but to the questions of how do we discern good from evil, how do we know truth when we hear it, how do we express such truth when language is fraught with error, how do we interpret the divine will when it is offered, how do we steer a course that is creative rather than destructive, that is, how do we distinguish life from death?' Schwartz, *Remembering and Repeating*, xi.

183. William Blake, *Milton*, plate 30, line 4–5.

184. In arguing that 'the personification of books is not a metaphor but a metonymy' John D. Schaeffer suggests that the book would then be a part or *extension* of the self, taken for the whole. ('Metonymies We Read By: Rhetoric, Truth and the Eucharist in Milton's *Areopagitica*', *Milton Quarterly* 34.3 (2000), 84–92, 84.) Such an argument for writing as an exteriorization at one with the self is at odds with the very structure of the text, which bears as its defining possibility its capacity to be repeated and to live on, independent of its authoring body. In distinction from Milton's otherwise Monist logic Schaeffer argues that *Areopagitica*'s logic is Eucharistic: 'Books are Eucharistic for Milton not just because they are consumed but because their spiritual contents, human reason as image of divinity, enter the mind of the reader through the body by means of their materiality, paper, print, etc.' (6). The problem, of course, with such a notion of reading as a form of eating and transubstantiation is that the materiality of the text is intensive and spiritual, rather than extensive and actual. Whereas food is a finite resource, and does not remain after its consumption, a text can be shared and circulated without a diminution of its being. The sacrament of the Eucharist also claims to share a body (Christ's) through eating (matter) while not exhausting the body consumed. This evidences the extent to which Eucharistic logic must posit a spirit that is given consumable and divisible form through matter, but is not itself reducible to that matter.

185. Ernest Sirluck points out that Palmer did not accompany Guyon to Mammon's cave. CPW 2.516.

Works Cited

Acheson, Katherine O. 2000. 'On Authorship, Sexuality and the Psychology of Privation in Milton's *Paradise Lost*', *ELH*, 67.4 (2000), 905–24.

Adorno, Theodor and Max Horkheimer. 1979. *Dialectic of Enlightenment*, trans. John Cumming, London: Verso.

Agamben, Giorgio. 1999. *Potentialities: Collected Essays in Philosophy*, ed. and trans. Daniel Heller-Roazen, Stanford: Stanford University Press.

Allison, Henry E. 2001. 'Reflections on the Banality of (Radical) Evil: A Kantian Analysis', in Maria Pia Lara (ed.), *Rethinking Evil: Contemporary Perspectives*, Berkeley: University of California Press, pp. 86–100.

Althusser, Louis and Etienne Balibar. 1970. *Reading 'Capital'*, trans. Ben Brewster, London: New Left Books.

Apel, Karl-Otto. 1998. *From a Transcendental-Semiotic Point of View*, ed. Marianna Papastephanou, Manchester: Manchester University Press.

Arendt, Hannah. 1968. *The Origins of Totalitarianism*, San Diego: Harcourt.

Aristotle. 1953. *The Ethics of Aristotle: The Nicomachean Ethics*, trans. J.A.K. Thomson, Harmondsworth: Penguin.

—— 1984. *Metaphysics*, in Jonathan Barnes (ed.), *The Complete Works of Aristotle*.

Augustine of Hippo, St. 1845. *Sermons on Selected Lessons of the New Testament*, vol. 2, Oxford.

—— 1958. *On Christian Doctrine*, trans D.W. Robertson Jr, New York: Liberal Arts Press.

—— 1984. *Concerning the City of God: Against the Pagans*, trans. Henry Bettenson, Harmondsworth: Penguin.

Badiou, Alain. 2001. *Ethics: An Essay on the Understanding of Evil*, trans. Peter Hallward, London: Verso.

—— 2003. *Saint Paul: The Foundation of Universalism*, trans. Ray Brassier, Stanford: Stanford University Press.

—— 2005. *Being and Event*, trans. Oliver Feltham, London: Continuum.

Barker, Arthur. 1942. *Milton and the Puritan Dilemma: 1640–1660*, Toronto: University of Toronto Press.

Bergonzi, Bernard. 1960. 'Criticism and the Milton Controversy', in *The Living Milton: Essays by Various Hands*, London: Routledge, pp. 162–80.

Bergson, Henri. 1911. *Creative Evolution*, trans. Arthur Mitchell, London: Macmillan.

—— 1911. *Matter and Memory*, trans. Nancy Margaret Paul and W. Scott Palmer, London: George Allen.

—— 1935. *The Two Sources of Morality and Religion*, trans. R. Ashley Audra and Cloudesley Brereton, New York: H. Holt.

Bernstein, Richard. 2005. *The Abuse of Evil: The Corruption of Politics and Religion Since 9/11 (Themes for the 21st Century)*, Cambridge: Polity.

Blake, William. 1988. *The Complete Poetry and Prose of William Blake*, ed. David V. Erdman, rev. edn, New York: Anchor-Doubleday.

Bloom, Harold. 1975. *A Map of Misreading*, New York: Oxford University Press.

Blumenberg, Hans. 1987. *The Genesis of the Copernican World*, trans. Robert M. Wallace, Cambridge, MA: MIT Press.

Borris, Kenneth. 2000. *Allegory and Epic in English Renaissance Literature: Heroic Form in Sidney, Spenser and Milton*, Cambridge: Cambridge University Press.

Bourdieu, Pierre. 2001. *Masculine Domination*, trans. Richard Nice, Cambridge: Polity.

Bradburn, Beth. 2004. 'Bodily Metaphor and Moral Agency in a Masque: A Cognitive Approach', *Milton Studies*, 43 (2004), 198–260.

Braden, Gordon and William Kerrigan. 1989. *The Idea of the Renaissance*, Baltimore: Johns Hopkins University Press.

Butler, Judith. 1997. *The Psychic Life of Power: Theories in Subjection*, Stanford: Stanford University Press.

Charles, David. 2000. *Aristotle on Meaning and Essence*. Oxford: Clarendon Press; New York: Oxford University Press.

Cole, Philip. 2006. *The Myth of Evil*, Edinburgh: Edinburgh University Press.

Copjec, Joan. 1994. *Read my Desire: Lacan Against the Historicists*, Cambridge, MA: MIT Press.

—— 2002. *Imagine There's No Woman: Ethics and Sublimation*, Cambridge, MA: MIT Press.

Corns, Thomas N. 2003. ' "With Unaltered Brow": Milton and the Son of God', *Milton Studies*, 42 (2003), 106–21.

Cottingham, John. 2003. *On the Meaning of Life*, London: Routledge.

Cox, Gerard H. 1973. 'Marlowe's "Doctor Faustus" and "Sin against the Holy Ghost" ', *The Huntington Library Quarterly*, 36.2 (February 1973), 119–37.

Cummins, Juliet. 2003. 'Matter and Apocalyptic Transformations in *Paradise Lost*', in Juliet Cummins (ed.), *Milton and the Ends of Time*, Cambridge: Cambridge University Press.

Daniel, Clay. 2004. 'Milton's Neo-Platonic Angel?', *SEL Studies in English Literature 1500–1900*, 44.1 (2004), 173–88.

Danielson, Denis. 1982. *Milton's Good God: A Study in Literary Theodicy*, Cambridge: Cambridge University Press.

Deleuze, Gilles. 1994. *Difference and Repetition*, trans. Paul Patton, New York: Columbia University Press.

—— 2004. *Francis Bacon: The Logic of Sensation*, trans. Daniel W. Smith, Minneapolis: University of Minnesota Press.

Deleuze, Gilles and Félix Guattari. 1994. *What is Philosophy?*, trans. Hugh Tomlinson and Graham Burchell, New York: Columbia University Press.

de Man, Paul. 1971. *Blindness and Insight: Essays in the Rhetoric of Contemporary Criticism*, New York: Oxford University Press.

—— 1996. 'Pascal's Allegory of Persuasion', in Andrzej Warminski (ed.), *Aesthetic Ideology*, Minneapolis: University of Minnesota Press, pp. 51–69.

Derrida, Jacques. 1981. 'Economimesis', trans. Renata Klein, *Diacritics*, 11.2 (Summer 1981), 2–25.

—— 1989. *Edmund Husserl's Origin of Geometry: An Introduction*, trans. John P. Leavey, Lincoln: University of Nebraska Press.

—— 1989. *Of Spirit: Heidegger and the Question*, trans. Geoffrey Bennington and Rachel Bowlby, Chicago: University of Chicago Press.

—— 1991. '"Eating Well," or the Calculation of the Subject: An Interview with Jacques Derrida', in Eduardo Cadava, Peter Connor, Jean-Luc Nancy, Trans. Peter Connor and Avital Ronnell (eds), *Who Comes After the Subject*, London: Routledge.

Derrida, Jacques and John Searle. 1977. *Limited Inc.*, Baltimore: Johns Hopkins University Press.

Douglas, Mary. 1966. *Purity and Danger: An Analysis of Concepts of Pollution and Taboo*, London: Routledge and Kegan Paul.

Dumont, Louis. 1977. *From Mandeville to Marx: The Genesis and Triumph of Economic Ideology*, Chicago: Chicago University Press.

—— 1986. *Essays on Individualism: Modern Ideology in Anthropological Perspective*, Chicago: University of Chicago Press.

Düttmann, Alexander García. 2000. *Between Cultures: Tensions in the Struggle for Recognition*, trans. Kenneth B. Woodgate, London: Verso.

Eagleton, Terry. 2007. *The Meaning of Life*, Oxford: Oxford University Press.

Edwards, Karen L. 1999. *Milton and the Natural World: Science and Poetry in* Paradise Lost, Cambridge: Cambridge University Press.

Eliot, T.S. 1936. 'A Note on the Verse of John Milton', *Essays and Studies* 21 (1936), reprinted as 'Milton 1' in *On Poetry and Poets*, New York: Farrar Strauss, 1957.

Eusebius. 1976. *In Praise of Constantine: A Historical Study and New Translation of Eusebius' Triennial Orations*, trans. and ed. H.A. Drake, Berkeley: University of California Press.

Fallon, Stephen M. 1988. ' "To Act or Not" Milton's Conception of Divine Freedom', *Journal of the History of Ideas*, 49.3 (July–September 1988), 425–9.

—— 1991. *Milton Among the Philosophers: Poetry and Materialism in Seventeenth-Century England*, Ithaca: Cornell University Press.

Felman, Shoshana. 1987. *Jacques Lacan and the Adventure of Insight*, Cambridge, MA: Harvard University Press.

Fenton, Mary C. 2003. 'Hope, Land Ownership, and Milton's "Paradise Within" ', *SEL Studies in English Literature 1500–1900*, 43.1 (2003), 151–80.

Fenves, Peter (ed.). 1993. *Raising the Tone of Philosophy: Late Essays by Immanuel Kant, Transformative Critique by Jacques Derrida*, Baltimore: Johns Hopkins University Press.

Ferguson, Arthur B. 1979. *Clio Unbound: Perception of the Social and Cultural Past in Renaissance England*, Durham: Duke University Press.

Ferry, Luc. 2002. *Man Made God: The Meaning of Life*, Chicago: University of Chicago Press.

Fiore, Peter A. 1981. *Milton and Augustine: Patterns of Augustinian Thought in Milton's* Paradise Lost, University Park: Pennsylvania State University Press.

Fish, Stanley. 1971. *Surprised by Sin: The Reader in Paradise Lost*, Berkeley, University of California Press.

—— 2001. *How Milton Works*, Cambridge, MA: Belknap Press of Harvard University Press.

—— 2005. 'Why Milton Matters; Or, Against Historicism', *Milton Studies*, 44 (2005), 1–12.

Foot, Philippa. 2001. *Natural Goodness*, Oxford: Clarendon Press.

Foucault, Michel. 1979. *History of Sexuality, Volume One: An Introduction*, trans. Robert Hurley, Harmondsworth: Penguin.

—— 1986. 'What is Enlightenment?' in Paul Rabinow (ed.), *The Foucault Reader*, Harmondsworth: Penguin.

—— 1990. *History of Sexuality, Volume Three: The Care of the Self*, trans. Robert Hurley, Harmondsworth: Penguin.

—— 1994. *The Order of Things: An Archaeology of the Human Sciences*, New York: Vintage.

—— 2006. *History of Madness*, ed. Jean Khalfa; trans. Jonathan Murphy and Jean Khalfa, London: Routledge.

Freud, Sigmund. 1950. *Beyond the Pleasure Principle*, trans. James Strachey, London: Hogarth Press.

Froula, Christine. 1983–4. 'When Eve Reads Milton: Undoing the Canonical Economy', *Critical Inquiry*, 10 (1983–4), 321–47.

Gallagher, Catherine and Stephen Greenblatt. 2000. *Practicing New Historicism*, Chicago: University of Chicago Press.

Gigante, Denise. 2000. 'Milton's Aesthetics of Eating', *Diacritics*, 30.2 (Summer 2000), 88–112.

Gilbert, Sandra. 1978. 'Patriarchal Poetry and Women Readers: Reflections on Milton's Bogey', *PMLA*, 93 (1978), 368–82.

Gilson, Etienne. 1957. *The Christian Philosophy of St. Thomas Aquinas*, London: Victor Gollancz.

Goodman, Kevin. 1997. ' "Wasted Labor"? Milton's Eve, the Poet's Work, and the Challenge of Sympathy', *ELH*, 64.2 (1997), 415–46.

Grace, William J. 1963. 'Milton, Salmasius, and the Natural Law', *Journal of the History of Ideas*, 24.3 (July–September 1963), 323–36.

Greenblatt, Stephen. 1980. *Renaissance Self-Fashioning: From More to Shakespeare*, Chicago: University of Chicago Press.

—— 2006. 'Resonance and Wonder', in *Learning to Curse: essays in early modern culture*, New York: Routledge.

Gregerson, Linda. 1995. *The Reformation of the Subject: Spenser, Milton and the English Protestant Epic*, Cambridge: Cambridge University Press.

Habermas, Jürgen. 1971. *Knowledge and Human Interests*, trans. Jeremy J. Shapiro, Boston: Beacon Press.

—— 1984–7. *Theory of Communicative Action*, 2 vols, trans. Thomas McCarthy, Boston: Beacon Press.

—— 1987. *The Philosophical Discourse of Modernity: Twelve Lectures*, trans. Frederick Lawrence, Cambridge, MA: MIT Press.

—— 1992. *Postmetaphysical Thinking: Philosophical Essays*, trans. William Mark Hohengarten, Cambridge, MA: MIT Press.

Hadot, Pierre. 1995. *Philosophy as a Way of Life: Spiritual Exercises from Socrates to Foucault*, ed. Arnold I. Davidson, trans. Michael Chase, Oxford: Blackwell.

Hardt, Michael and Antonio Negri. 2000. *Empire*, Cambridge, MA: Harvard University Press.

Hartman, Geoffrey H. 1970. 'Milton's Counterplot', in *Beyond Formalism: Literary Essays 1958–1970*, New Haven: Yale University Press, pp. 113–23.

Hegel, G.W.F. 1975. *Hegel's Logic: Being Part One of the 'Encyclopaedia of the Philosophical Sciences'*, trans. William Wallace; foreword by J.N. Findlay, 3rd edn, Oxford: Clarendon Press.

Heidegger, Martin. 1977. *The Question Concerning Technology, and Other Essays*, trans. William Lovitt, New York: Harper and Row.

—— 1985. *What is a Thing*, trans. W.B. Barton and Vera Deutsch, Lanham: University Press of America.

—— 1996. *Being and Time*, trans. Joan Stambaugh, Albany: State University of New York Press.

Helgerson, Richard. 1992. *Forms of Nationhood: The Elizabethan Writing of England*, Chicago: University of Chicago Press.

Herman, Peter C. 2003. 'Paradise Lost, the Miltonic "Or," and the Poetics of Incertitude', *SEL Studies in English Literature 1500–1900*, 43.1 (Winter 2003), 181–211.

Hick, John. 1978. *Evil and the God of Love* (rev. edn), New York: Harper and Row.

Hoerner, Fred. 1995. ' "Fire to Use": A Practice-Theory Approach to Paradise Lost', *Representations*, 51 (Summer 1995), 94–117.

Husserl, Edmund. 1970. *The Crisis of the European Sciences and Transcendental Phenomenology: An Introduction to Phenomenological Philosophy*, trans.David Carr, Evanston: Northwestern University Press.

Irenaeus of Lyon. 1869. *Against Heretics*, IV: xxvii-xix, in Revd Alexander Robertson and James Donaldson (eds), *The Ante-Nicene Christian Library, Volume 9*, Edinburgh: Clark.

Irigaray, Luce. 1985. *Speculum of the Other Woman*, trans. Gillian C. Gill, Ithaca: Cornell University Press.

Irwin, T.H. 1988. *Aristotle's First Principles*, Oxford: Clarendon Press.

Israel, Jonathan. 2001. *Radical Enlightenment: Philosophy and the Making of Modernity, 1650–1750*, Oxford: Oxford University Press.

James, William. 1902. *The Varieties of Religious Experience: A Study in Human Nature*, New York: Longmans, Green, and Co.

—— 1909. *A Pluralistic Universe*, New York: Longmans, Green, and Co.

Jameson, Fredric. 1986. 'Religion and Ideology: a Political Reading of *Paradise Lost*', in Francis Barker, Peter Hulme, Margaret Iversen and Diana Loxley (eds), *Literature, Politics and Theory: Papers from the Essex Conference 1976–84*, London: Methuen, pp. 35–56.

Jordan, Matthew. 2001. *Milton and Modernity: Politics, Masculinity and Paradise Lost*, Basingstoke: Palgrave.

Kahn, Victoria. 1999. ' "The Duty to Love": Passion and Obligation in Early Modern Political Theory', *Representations*, 68 (Autumn 1999), 84–107.

Kant, Immanuel. 1952. *Critique of Judgment*, trans. James Creed Meredith, Oxford: Oxford University Press.

—— 1996. *Religion within the Boundaries of Mere Reason*, trans. Allen W. Wood and George di Giovanni, Cambridge: Cambridge University Press.

—— 1998. *Critique of Pure Reason*, trans. and ed. Paul Guyer and Allen W. Wood, Cambridge: Cambridge University Press.

Kerrigan, William. 1983. *The Sacred Complex: On the Psychogenesis of Paradise Lost*, Cambridge, MA: Harvard University Press.

Kolbrener, William. 1997. *Milton's Warring Angels: A Study of Critical Engagements*, Cambridge: Cambridge University Press.

Korsgaard, Christine M. with G. A. Cohen *et al.* 1996. *The Sources of Normativity*, ed. Onora O'Neill, Cambridge: Cambridge University Press.

Koyré, Alexandre. 1957. *From the Closed World to the Infinite Universe*, Baltimore: Johns Hopkins University Press.

Lacan, Jacques. 1992. *The Ethics of Psychoanalysis, 1959–1960: The Seminar of Jacques Lacan*, ed. Jacques-Alain Miller, trans. Dennis Porter, London: Routledge.

Lakoff, George and Mark Johnson. 1999. *Philosophy in the Flesh: The Embodied Mind and its Challenge to Western Thought*, New York: Basic Books.

Lane, Nick. 2005. *Power, Sex, Suicide: Mitochondria and the Meaning of Life*, Oxford: Oxford University Press.

Laqueur, Thomas. 1990. *Making Sex: Body and Gender from the Greeks to Freud*, Cambridge, MA: Harvard University Press.

Lewalski, Barbara K. 2000. *The Life of John Milton*, Oxford: Blackwell.

Lieb, Michael. 1970. *The Dialectics of Creation: Patterns of Birth and Regeneration in 'Paradise Lost'*, Amherst: University of Massachusetts Press.

Lovejoy, Arthur O. 1936. *The Great Chain of Being: A Study of the History of an Idea*, Cambridge, MA: Harvard University Press.

MacIntyre, Alasdair. 1984. *After Virtue: A Study in Moral Theory*, 2nd edn, Notre Dame: University of Notre Dame Press.

Mackie, J.L. 1955. 'Evil and Omnipotence', *Mind*, New Series, 64.254 (April 1955), 200–12.

MacPherson, C.B. 1962. *The Political Theory of Possessive Individualism: Hobbes to Locke*, Oxford: Oxford University Press.

Martin, Catherine Gimelli. 1998. *The Ruins of Allegory: Paradise Lost and the Metamorphosis of Epic Convention*, Durham: Duke University Press.

—— 2001. '"What If the Sun Be Centre to the World?": Milton's Epistemology, Cosmology, and Paradise of Fools Reconsidered', *Modern Philology*, 99.2 (November 2001), 231–65.

—— 2003. 'The Enclosed Garden and the Apocalypse: Immanent versus Transcendent Time in Milton and Marvell', in Juliet Cummings (ed.), *Milton and the Ends of Time*, Cambridge: Cambridge University Press, pp. 144–68.

Maturana, Humberto R. and Francisco J. Varela. 1987. *The Tree of Knowledge: The Biological Roots of Human Understanding*, Boston: New Science Library.

McColley, Diane Kelsey. 1983. *Milton's Eve*, Urbana: University of Illinois Press.

McGann, Jerome J. 1981. 'The Text, the Poem, and the Problem of Historical Method', *New Literary History*, 12.2 (Winter 1981), 269–88.

—— 1983. *The Romantic Ideology: A Critical Investigation*, Chicago: University of Chicago Press.

—— 1988. *Social Values and Poetic Acts: The Historical Judgment of Literary Work*, Cambridge, MA: Harvard University Press.

—— 2002. *Byron and Romanticism*, ed. James Soderholm, Cambridge: Cambridge University Press.

McNeill, John T. 1946. 'Natural Law in the Teaching of the Reformers', *The Journal of Religion*, 26.3 (July 1946), 168–82.

Michaels, Walter Benn. 1978. 'Saving the Text: Reference and Belief', *MLN*, 93.5 (December 1978), 771–93.

—— 1979. 'Against Formalism: The Autonomous Text in Legal and Literary Interpretation', *Poetics Today*, 1.1/2 (Autumn 1979), 23–34.

Mikics, David. 2004. 'Miltonic Marriage and the Challenge to History in *Paradise Lost*', *Texas Studies in Literature and Language*, 46.1 (2004), 20–48.

Milner, Andrew. 1981. *John Milton and the English Revolution: A Study in the Sociology of Literature*, London: Macmillan.

Milton, John. 1953–1982. *Complete Prose Works*, ed. Don M. Wolfe *et al.*, New Haven: Yale University Press.

—— 1958. *The Poetical Works of John Milton*, ed. Helen Darbishire, London: Oxford University Press.

Nancy, Jean-Luc. 2003. *A Finite Thinking*, ed. Simon Sparks, Stanford: Stanford University Press.

Nehamas, Alexander. 1998. *The Art of Living: Socratic Reflections from Plato to Foucault*, Berkeley: University of California Press.

Newlyn, Lucy. 1993. *Paradise Lost and the Romantic Reader*, Oxford: Clarendon Press.

Nietzsche, Friedrich. 2007. *On the Genealogy of Morality*, ed. Keith Ansell Pearson; trans. Carol Diethe, Cambridge: Cambridge University Press.

Nussbaum, Martha C. 2004. *Hiding from Humanity: Disgust, Shame, and the Law*, Princeton, Princeton: Princeton University Press, 1984.

Patrides, C.A. 1966. *Milton and the Christian Tradition*, Oxford: Clarendon Press.

Patterson, Annabel. 1997. *Early Modern Liberalism*, Cambridge: Cambridge University Press.

Rajan, Tilottama. 1994. 'The Other Reading: Transactional Epic in Milton, Blake and Wordsworth', in Lisa Low and Anthony John Harding (eds), *Milton, the Metaphysicals, and Romanticism*, Cambridge: Cambridge University Press, pp. 20–46.

Rapaport, Herman. 1983. *Milton and the Postmodern*, Lincoln: University of Nebraska Press.

Reid, David. 1993. *The Humanism of Milton's* Paradise Lost, Edinburgh: Edinburgh University Press.

Revard, Stella P. 2003. 'Milton and Millenarianism: From the Nativity Ode to *Paradise Regained*', in Juliet Cummins (ed.), *Milton and the Ends of Time*, Cambridge: Cambridge University Press, pp. 42–81.

Ricks, Christopher. 1963. *Milton's Grand Style*, Oxford: Clarendon Press.

Ricoeur, Paul. 1967. *The Symbolism of Evil*, trans. Emerson Buchanan, New York: Harper and Row.

Rogers, John. 1990. 'Milton and the Mysterious Terms of History', *ELH*, 57.2 (Summer 1990), 281–305.

—— 1996. *The Matter of Revolution: Science, Poetry, and Politics in the Age of Milton*, Ithaca: Cornell University Press.

Rose, Steven. 2005. *Lifelines: Life Beyond the Gene*, London: Vintage.

Rosedale, Timothy. 2004. 'Milton, Hobbes and the Liturgical Subject', *SEL Studies in English Literature 1500–1900*, 44.1 (2004), 149–72.

Rumrich, John. 1987. *Matter of Glory: A New Preface to Paradise Lost*, Pittsburgh: University of Pittsburgh Press.

—— 2003. 'Milton's *Theanthropos*: The Body of Christ in *Paradise Regained*', *Milton Studies*, 42 (2003), 50–67.

Sansone, David. 2003. 'How Milton Reads', *Modern Philology*, 103 (2006), 332–358.

Schaeffer, John D. 2000. 'Metonymies We Read By: Rhetoric, Truth and the Eucharist in Milton's *Areopagitica*', *Milton Quarterly*, 34.3 (2000), 84–92.

Schoenfeldt, Michael C. 1999. *Bodies and Selves in Early Modern England: Physiology and Inwardness in Spenser, Shakespeare, Herbert, and Milton*, Cambridge: Cambridge University Press.

Schwartz, Regina. 1993. *Remembering and Repeating: On Milton's Theology and Poetics*, Chicago: University of Chicago Press.

Snyder, Susan. 1998. *Pastoral Process: Spenser, Marvell, Milton*, Stanford: Stanford University Press.

Swaim, Kathleen M. 1976. ' "Hee for God Only, Shee for God in Him": Structural Parallelism in *Paradise Lost*', *Milton Studies*, 9 (1976), 121–50.

Taminiaux, Jacques. 1991. *Heidegger and the Project of Fundamental Ontology*, trans. Michael Gendre, Albany: State University of New York Press.

Tanner, John S. 1988. '"Say First What Cause": Ricoeur and the Etiology of Evil in Paradise Lost', *PMLA*, 103.1 (January 1988), 45–56.

Taylor, Charles. 1989. *Sources of the Self: The Making of the Modern Identity*, Cambridge, MA: Harvard University Press.

Tertullian. 1931. *Apology*, Loeb Classical Library, trans. T.R. Glover, London: Heinemann; New York: G.P. Putnam.

Teske, Gordon. 2006. *Delirious Milton*, Cambridge, MA: Harvard University Press.

Troeltsch, Ernst. 1931. *The Social Teaching of the Christian Churches*, trans. Olive Wyon, 2 vols, London: Allen and Unwin; New York: Macmillan.

Vendler, Helen. 2003. *Coming of Age as a Poet: Milton, Keats, Eliot, Plath*, Cambridge: Cambridge University Press.

Vernant, Jean-Pierre. 1991. *Mortals and Immortals: Collected Essays*, ed. Froma I. Zeitlin, Princeton, NJ: Princeton University Press.

Warner, Michael. 1991. 'Introduction: Fear of a Queer Planet', *Social Text*, 1991; 9 (4 [29]), 3–17.

Watkins, W.B.C. 1955. *An Anatomy of Milton's Verse*, Baton Rouge: Louisiana State University Press.

Weinfield, Henry. 2005. 'Skepticism and Poetry in Milton's Infernal Conclave', *SEL*, 45.1 (Winter 2005), 191–212.

Willey, Basil. 1934. *The Seventeenth-Century Background: Studies in the Thought of the Age in Relation to Poetry and Religion*, London, Chatto and Windus.

Witt, Charlotte. 2003. *Ways of Being: Potentiality and Actuality in Aristotle's Metaphysics*, Ithaca: Cornell University Press.

Wittgenstein, Ludwig. 1968. *Philosophical Investigations*, trans. G.E.M. Anscombe, Oxford, Basil Blackwell.

Wittreich, J.A. (ed.). 1975. *Milton and the Line of Vision*, Wisconsin: University of Wisconsin Press.

—— 1987. *Feminist Milton*, Ithaca: Cornell University Press.

—— 2005. 'Joseph Wittreich on Why Milton Matters', *Milton Studies*, 44 (2005), 22–39.

Wollstonecraft, Mary. 1994. *A Vindication of the Rights of Woman*, Oxford : Oxford University Press.

Žižek, Slavoj. 1997. *The Abyss of Freedom*, and F.W.J. von Schelling, *Ages of the World*, Ann Arbor, MI: University of Michigan Press.

Index